Lovecidal

Lovecidal

Walking with the Disappeared

Trinh T. Minh-ha

Fordham University Press
New York 2016

All art works are by Jean-Paul Bourdier (www.jeanpaulbourdier.com)

Fordham University Press also publishes its books in a variety of electronic formats. Some content that appears in print may not be available in electronic books.

Visit us online at www.fordhampress.com.

Library of Congress Control Number: 2016938823

Printed in the United States of America
18 17 16   5 4 3 2 1
First edition

In loving memory of

Trịnh Đình Phi
(1928–2014)

whose gentle silent walk in life
through times of war, exile, and isolation
taught us to remember
kindness
shining our light
when feeling the darkness

Contents

Lovecidal

Somewhere in the process the flowers wither and the whole world smells of open wounds. The peculiar odor of fire powder, dust and dirt, concrete and steel; the very odor of blood, carbolic acid, decaying insides and burnt carnality has been trapped for sometime in the air, but only the child in me—a child of the war—notices it. The wounded adult-me weeps at the sight of the wreckage, loudly deplores the tragedies, vocally condemns the abuses, then visually gets inoculated with the constant replay on screen of serialized destruction. And, when the shock has faded, finds it quasi natural to move about band-aided with an invisible muffler. The dis-ease goes on unacknowledged. The toxic spill effect, felt but largely unseen, is slowly laying waste in the overexposed cities—these immense man-made wildernesses where its inhabitants caught in between walls of metal, zinc, or concrete have little access to the light innerscape of blood flowers.

Again, the heart meanders for no one knows why. Sudan, Tibet, Iraq, Afghanistan, Palestine, Rwanda, Congo, Burma, and . . . and . . . and, with the recurring specters of Bosnia, Kosovo, South Africa, Cambodia, Vietnam. What is it that makes both talks and silences stained with shame? Everyone readily comes up with an answer and everyone is eager to fill in the blanks. But once raised, the question never fails to fold back, returning to just where one thinks one last knows. Rising like the murmurs of an underground river, it persists in infinite whisperings, striking randomly when it is least expected. Could it be the sound? The places in sight? The lie, the fear, the excess, or, *that shadow of a frail body in flight*? Sometimes the mind freezes and the heart goes on fasting: name, nation, identity, citizenship disappear. *Once I was a human.*

Blind Energy

When thought picks up again, it cruises along blindly, inquiring: Who's fleeing and where to? Through defiance and loss, from wasteland to wasteland, into the transborders zone of the denizens whose earthwalk is characterized by an indefinite state of being-in-expulsion: exiled, expatriated, segregated, deported, displaced, discarded, repudiated, estranged, disappeared, unsettled and unsettling. Countless shadows of terrified bodies in flight, moving alone en masse, searching in vain for the lost ones, faring in a no-man's-land as a no-nation people. The higher the risk taken, the greater the danger at play: the flows of out-of-bounds humans across frontiers and outside men's law have politically threatened and undermined every modern state power founded on citizen's right, free will, and social contracts. Wandering in a no-man's-no-land stateless state. Neither citizen nor simply a living being, the one who leaves, the phantom-turned-refugee, hurtles along with loads of other empty bodies, driven by the sheer movements of waves of humanity in distress. Sometimes the hope to get out at all costs makes one walk on illegally, irredeemably; leaving all behind, including the rights of longing and belonging. From one side of the wire to the other, one wonders where to, when going a-way likely entails being dis-charged (from "settled" nations) with no return ticket? Today, by the magnitude of the tides of displacement, this shadowy figure relegated to the outer margins of society has become a central figure of political history, one whose mere existence challenges the modern nation-state in its very foundation.

One upon another, small wounds, large wounds, continue to be inflicted upon oneself—by oneself. Like a weed, the mind game flourishes whichever way, while quiet, the true flower wilts and withers. Nearby, someone's choking weird. Perhaps the child again, and this time, yelling her head off as the stink hits hard. Startled, the adult-me learns to feel the world anew, realizing as if for the first time what human cruelty keeps on doing to us all. Too many interactions amid the sea of enraged bloods, and the stomach convulses, releasing ever-stranger cries of the wound. Cast adrift, the numbed move in the desert of interpreted and encoded realities, carrying out spooky actions from the distance, doing violence to everything in their passage and, often impulsively, to themselves.

After all, isn't cruelty a word standing in for the manifested state of utter fear—fear of fear itself and of death? Being the first, the best, the most, the more, the only one . . . all, so as to conquer that terror inducing D-word in its innumerable faces. Consciousness fills itself with social noises, but the heart in shock (*and in awe*) knows neither north south nor east west, as all recognizable emotions seem to be wiped out at once. To receive straight in the eye the unspeakable is also to take in what one continues to offer of oneself to oneself as spectacle. It is said that in the profound crisis of our civilization—a crisis far more dangerous and frightening than the nuke nightmare itself—*man forgets to be man*. Like the blind walking by an abyss, one finds oneself living by one's shadow, hiding and drifting dazed as one witnesses one's own participation in the darkest side of humanity's inhumanity.

A warning from the fourteenth Dalai Lama, a refugee who lost his country at the age of twenty-four, cuts right to the core of emptiness: "The urgent problem of humanity is that of the heart." The word at once sets our cynics going. For, as with every final word at the core of being, it is both evident and elusive. Despite its die-hard connotation of romantic sentimentality in the modern mind, its power in survival remains intact. To have a heart is a necessity. Depending on who's saying it, the voice from the seat of love is likely to be dismissed. Daily media's bleeding heart is often a female organ; and every effort is made carefully to silence and remove the heart from our existence—even and especially when its moral and transcendental virtues are extolled.

Hardheaded and hard-hearted go hand in hand. Some call our times "the age of strange diseases," and, as an oncologist puts it, modern illnesses are characteristically "cooling, hardening, and chronic." Cancer, arteriosclerosis, multiple sclerosis, recurring pain, and fatigue syndrome. Although the healing power of love is widely recognized as necessary to breaking the vicious cycle of hardening and cooling, to have a warm heart, unlike having brainpower, continues to connote unpaid shadow work earmarked for the "weaker," prone-to-emotions gender—what society degrades, which also remains refractory to modern economy's sophisticated measurements. And yet, as a resonance event, the heart links the here, the overthere, and the elsewhere, creating new possibilities not yet, not quite known. Profound dis-ease lies in the inability both to hear all that is there within earshot and to stop hearing what is not there to be heard. To the sound of "Who's speaking?" that of "Who's listening?" echoes back. Moving out into the winds of time, it resonates anew in every course of inquiry. When? Where? How? In what tongue and skin, and from which riverbank?

Words, turning strange, taking room, as if heard for the first time.

No one has the final answer and everyone seems to have forgotten why the dreadful stench, the fumes, the smoke, the sensations of burning and drowning linger on. Why, whenever the wounded adult-me comes across the named Justice, it immediately morphs into Injustice. From fear to fury, fury to grief, the shame arises and regresses as mute energy. In forgetful spasms, the heart re-members. How the wound has come to open wide in the dark, red on the world map, sending women across nations into white and *black widow*–ship. And yet, there at the body's gate, caught raw in the madness of the day,

still it throbs

While everyone seems certain, no one truly knows. Why the loud wind keeps on striking near and far, uprooting and scathing everything it finds in its way, turning safe haven into circles of hell. Why people die at dawn and are born into dusk, mourning their own doings, condemning the waste they help to spread, being irremediably wedded to the turbulent times, to destruction by fires, devastation by flood, storm, earthquake, and drought, and each of them in their own ways, to the abyss of freedom.

how to write an ending?

> The end of every game is a gain or a loss: but of what? What were the real stakes? At checkmate, beneath the foot of the king, knocked aside by the winner's hand, nothingness remains: a black square or a white one.
>
> Italo Calvino, *Invisible Cities*

Wartime: the time of hazy definitions of victory. From V to V, language errs, unable to keep still, always awaiting translation and making of silence a way of speaking. All around, on the immense screen of life, every event speaks, every blade of grass whispers; somewhere, a body's tuning in again; and endlessly, each single form waves to inscribe anew. Having no memory, writing begins somewhere in the middle, following its own course from silence, swallowing up order, producing while identity fluctuates between the all-too-formed, the barely- and yet-to-be-formed. Excess, unbound to the logical mind, traces the movement of a writer's waning self. Some thinkers seek coherence in weaving a story, others demand precision in classification and purport to spin a theory in analysis. But each word is a hyperword—a multiplicity whose field of interfertile references spreads, implodes, or dwindles over time, hybridizing and bypassing its own rules of survival. Old resonances fade and empty out. The transient, the ephemeral, the fragmentary, and all that threaten to disappear are the very forms and forces that drive writing as manifesting. In the passage from life to language and back, clarity often fares without central rational light. And rather than yearning constantly for the whole, the creative fragment contains it, dissolving as it goes, the stability of a totality (such as the book system), and dilating itself through a constant movement of spacing, overlapping, delaying and relayering, disconnecting, recombining—and rewiring.

Despite the constant urge to elucidate and illuminate, what unfolds itself in writing with the wounds of our time is, necessarily, the work of *resonance*—the way different events, both natural and man-made, vibrate across times and places, tune in to one another, and deeply affect our life processes. Telling inflects what is being told; the two are joined in a single practice and social space. As complex systems of harmonic frequencies, body and word remain powerful channels for conducting and mediating resonance. When language meets its own edge, pain, at its worst, even and especially when it can't be silenced, is first and foremost a word. So is blood, for example, whose idiom power is often fond of speaking. Thus, language unfurling at quasi-zero degrees further calls for a work of *exteriority* freed not only from any single claim to *interior*'s essences but also from any tendency to abide by the *ex-* versus *in-* divide.

In unplanned delays and detours, writing returns via its bodily origins to unknown sources. Writing with a nose, with fingers and toes in motion, for example. The text as a layering of scented threads, a weaving of unexpected accords, attuned to the olfactory regions of events—there where words fail, despite the precision of what is experienced. Or else, the text as a sound score, whose creation solicits a dragon ear, at once hybrid and empty, so as to listen to the diversifying texture, rhythm, and resonance of people's voices in random consent and utter dissent—the one-*with*-many voices spreading across the national map and emerging from the countless crevasses of a culture of abundance. Rather than offering the unequivocal joy of triumph over the enemy, the war story discloses, instead, profoundly unsettling nooks and corners in the netherworld of consciousness. From V to V, Victory restlessly morphs into Void as it travels across cyber maps and sites, in defiance of the very social and cultural boundaries it is made to reify. Arising endlessly at each turn of the road are not questions like Who wins? or What kind of victory is it? but rather,

Through what Night does victory make its way?

Liquid Denouement

Pause. Time to withdraw and redraw. As the threat of irreversible downward slide associated with the waning influence of the globe's hyperpower continues to haunt broadcast writing, headlines of critical analyses in the media repeatedly pronounce: "The American Century Is Ending," "The American Century Is Over." Pessimists depicted America as a civilization in decline, and to follow up, optimists announced "The Tide of War Is Receding." With the wave of popular uprisings rolling across the Arab world and the literal liquidation of Osama bin Laden, the press has been quick to declare the passing of an era and the emerging of a "Post-bin Laden World." For a man whose name has come to designate one of history's most notorious fugitives, his secretive burial in the Arabian Sea appears both inappropriate and befitting—at once a curse and a blessing. Aside from having initially set off a round of speculation about whether he was truly dead, or how long ago the al-Qaeda's leader might have been dead, the rapid disposal of his remains has kept the myth eerily walking on for many miles over . . . .

The long-bearded mortal, elevated into a pop-culture heavyweight and a world-defiant figure with the very help of his foe, has emerged as *undead* in numerous debates across the Internet. "This is not an ending, this does not satisfy justice," said a poster on Free Republic; "WTF with this burial at sea before the body is cold . . . . Something about this smells," said another. Angry concerns were voiced both as to how such an epilogue was too respectful ("for a terrorist") and too disrespectful ("for an Islamist" or "for such a major figure"). Had he died of kidney failure, the myth would have perished with the man. But clandestinely submerged in this liquid wrap-up, his death marks neither the end of *our* effort nor that of *his* (to paraphrase President Obama in his speech). "Now, Kill His Dream" cried the cover page's headline of the *Economist* (May 7–13, 2011). There has been no clear *sight* of the body that disappeared without trace, and one could easily *image* bin Laden laughing away from the lower depths of his watery grave, weepily ecstatic at his fabled power even in death. What he seemed to have always excelled in doing—in absentia—had been to take over Washington's deepest fears and thirsts and turn them to his own ends.

Bin Laden's demise felt surreal to many, including those who lost loved ones in the fall of the Twin Towers. Such an operation of immersion (or of *emmerement* [en-sea-ment], as the French press called it) done under cover of dark was likely to leave disbelievers with no satisfying closure. Still bound by a need for visible "conclusive" proof, some badly wanted to *see with their own eyes*, whose doubts were fuelled not only by the use of darkness and speed as essential weapons in this bloody end and burial at sea but, moreover, by President Obama's ethical and political decision not to release the postmortem images. "There are going to be some folks who deny it," said the president in an interview, but "*the fact of the matter* is, you will *not see* bin Laden *walking* on this earth again."[1] Thus, all the while skeptics asserted, "I will not believe until I see a picture of his dead body," a doctored photo of bin Laden's perceived bloodied head surfaced on Pakistan's Geo TV and circulated widely on the Internet, including several British newspapers' websites and YouTube. The hoax may have succeeded, as CBS News reported, to dupe a few senators who claimed to have seen the actual postmortem photos (one of whom later admitted he was fooled by one such Photoshopped image).[2] But ultimately, it spoke volumes for the reactive urge among many of us, "folks," to see and to prove his demise at the same time as it deftly undermines (whether intentionally or inadvertently) the very validation of visible "proofs."

No matter how stern, dignified, carefully nontriumphant and noninflammatory the president's announcement of bin Laden's death managed to be while vindicating the military operations of the past decade, his choice not to indulge in gory photos and not "to trot out this stuff as trophies" has brought about a range of thought-provoking reactions from the public at home. In the office of a manufacturing steel company in El Cerrito, California, for example, hangs another doctored photo, showing the Statue of Liberty in its full glory, holding up in place of the torch the severed trophy head of bin Laden with blood splashed and dripping underneath. Thanks to new technology and to the nimble imaginations of "some folks," headhunting as ritual violence and as display of manhood in the mortification of the enemy seems to have had a new lease of life. No wonder that the term "barbaric gloating," as related to the assassination, surfaced in more than one press. The photomontage's joke seems remarkably talkative in its connotations: take off the Light, or Lady Liberty's flame lighting the world, and replace it with . . . the red of blood shed from a rival's *decapitation*. Let darkness reign. The image thus speaks volumes for the explicit triumph of revenge and, more important, for what freedom in the Western world (as symbolized by the statue) means to "some folks."

> We didn't learn a dang thing from the attack, except to be stupidly surprised that some of our innocent citizens got what we've been steadily dishing out to others.
>
> A posting on NationofChange

Democracy's double standard, which is supposed to be found merely among the bad guys on the top, is here shown to permeate the social body, determining the way many of us think, act, and consume in our everyday. Behind Lady Liberty's bloodied image, *who's the headsman*? (The executors, the commanders, the producers-and-Photoshop-artists, the exhibitors, or the workers-and-clients-consumers?)[3] Much has been said about the violence inherent in celebrating an assassination and the wave of patriotism it evokes—as displayed in certain manifestations of unbridled euphoria across the country and of triumph among jubilant youths draping the American flag while chanting "U-S-A! U-S-A!" in front of the White House. Bin Laden's death has inevitably given rise to abundant claims of victory in the major media, claims that largely replay the hubristic tune of how, defeated long ago, the worst of the Bad-Weak-Snakehead-and-Extremist failed to change Us, the Good-Strong-Humane-and-Tolerant. Former president George W. Bush, for example, hailed bin Laden's death as "a victory for America," and similarly, Republican Peter King heralded it as a "magnificent victory for the United States and a devastating defeat for al-Qaeda and international terrorism." A voice in the *Christian Science Monitor* went even further to affirm it to be "A Victory—for the 21st Century," while another voice, at *Time*, asked "How to mark V_OBL day?" The *Economist*, trying with scorn to limit the importance given to the "waning star's" death, despite it being splashed over the front pages of newspapers across the Middle East, insisted that "the thrill of seeing the American lion's tail violently yanked proved short-lived."[4]

Alongside the triumphant cheering, other voices from the media fringe reminded readers and netizens from around the world of the Other Victory gained in the very treadmill of reciprocal violence. A voice from the blogosphere exclaimed: "It was as if the lynchers are convincing themselves of getting rid of their own by-product." Another voice, writing in *Salon*, remarked how such unbridled celebrations "inadvertently" gave bin Laden his "most enduring victory—a victory that will unfortunately last far beyond his passing . . . . This is bin Laden's lamentable victory: he has changed America's psyche from one that saw violence as a regrettable-if-sometimes-necessary act into one that finds orgasmic euphoria in news of bloodshed. In other words, he's helped drag us down into his sick nihilism by making us like too many other bellicose societies in history—the ones that aggressively cheer on killing, as long as it is the Bad Guy that is being killed."[5] Living, for the last decade, in a climate of *enhanced* fear and a culture of *enhanced* suspicion, one often finds oneself gaping at the disproportionate price one pays for the loss of balance between national security and human rights. Americans are repeatedly said to have fundamentally altered who they are. Critics commenting on the pathetic inadequacies and counterproductive techniques of *enhanced* security measures inflicted upon people have pointedly objected to many Bush-era policies that continue to plague the present administration and are "taken to the next step"—giving the government incommensurate powers of surveillance and secrecy, detention and interrogation, both at home and abroad.

A recent revelation that seems to have stunned the American public concerns precisely the way the Patriot Act (section 215) has been interpreted and "taken to the next step" by the Obama administration. Already, a month after the Boston bombing (April 15, 2013), a long due *Time* article on "Homeland Insecurity" reported how the FBI's preemptively aggressive "terrorist-hunting" powers have been quietly expanded by the Justice Department since 2011.[6] The article's deceptive question, "How far should we go?," pointed to the results of a new Time/CNN/ORC international poll that asked whether citizens should let their government "sniff through their communications" and showed nearly twice as many Americans concerned about protecting liberty as are eager to gain false security. Worried about excessive antiterrorist policies, the former remain particularly opposed to government monitoring of their private cellphone, e-mail interactions, and other online activities. And yet, by the way things often turn out, it seems more adequate to acknowledge, instead, such no-answer-question as "What do They care, really?" For, even when violating the Constitution, They/the administration would always make sure the law is made to serve Them or, to quote a voice interceptor at the Georgia National Security Agency facility, "use any excuse to justify a waiver to spy on Americans anyway." Barely another month after the publication of these mainstream statistics, thanks to the release of significant secret documents by an ex-CIA employee and principled NSA whistleblower (Edward Snowden, compelled indefinitely to become a "Man without a Country," with "No Place to Hide"), the public shockingly learned that under the Obama administration, the government has been massively spying on all Americans and the NSA is covertly collecting the private communication records of millions of US citizens, examining internet traffic, eavesdropping on phone calls, and inspecting e-mail—in bulk, not only targeting "foreign enemy" communications as officially claimed.

Size always seems to matter to superpowers, and it is hardly surprising to learn that "for the good of the nation," for storage in yottabytes of the humongous volume of information, in other words, for wiretapping and data mining without warrant, the United States has built the world's biggest spy center: a million-square-foot data storehouse, a.k.a. the Intelligence Community Comprehensive National Cybersecurity Initiative Data Center in Utah, with ever-faster supercomputing programs and the largest capacity for storing, searching, monitoring, and reporting on intercepted global Internet traffic. Over a year before Snowden's revelations, a *Wired* article had, indeed, already detailed with alarming precision—also courtesy of yet another former NSA operative (William Binney) in charge of automating the agency's worldwide eavesdropping network—how for the first time since Watergate, the NSA had secretly turned its gigantic espionage apparatus on the United States and its citizens.[7] Although warned then of the dangers of a "turnkey totalitarian state," it took the leak of flagrant proofs of the government being given unlimited domestic spying powers under a top-secret court order to spark public outrage—both at Washington's double standard and at those who, for their urge to expose the government's secret workings, have come to represent a new type of dissident: "the twenty-first century mole" or "The Geeks Who Leak."[8]

The disclosure of this global electronic spying campaign deployed at an unprecedented scale has not only shown how American core civil liberties and constitutionally protected rights have been secretly and comprehensively trampled on, setting off a national debate about the NSA's expanding powers to spy at home and abroad. It has also, through the extent of the data breached in the public interest, catapulted questions about security and freedom into the international spotlight and prompted an avalanche effect among riled US allies. Compelled to reassure their citizens about the legality of their own spying activities when given access to information collected by Washington, they are also left in deep quandary about American global power politics in what Germany's liberal *Süddeutsche Zeitung* considers "the worst imaginable nuclear accident for legality and Atlanticism."[9]

The dream for "total information awareness" and "perfect security" or, rather, the craving for total control and endlessly expansive surveillance, which allows Uncle Sam to indulge in policing thought on a global basis while eavesdropping even on people's privy whispers, seems to be one of the conceits new technology is made to yield to when it serves to bolster government abuses of power. The level of intrusion into the privacy of citizenry knows no limit, and such a comprehensive, ubiquitous centralization of information ultimately gives the databases' controllers totalitarian power over who can speak, who can be heard, and what can be said. Think twice, watch what you write and say, even what you confide in private. Bite your tongue, move it seven times in your mouth as the French proverb advises. When your thoughts and lips start moving, beware! Your life, your acts are no longer yours to discuss. Your whispers could be criminalized. In essence, You are being watched! But don't You pride yourself on this, for dissenters are not the only ones being snooped on.

In this new global security world, "taken to the next step" means everyone with communication is a target. Everything anyone does gets charted on a graph, and the line drawn by the agency to define who is "a potential adversary" and who is not admits no rule of law. The challenge of collecting in ever-more colossal sizes dwarfs in relation to that of (mis)reading, (over)interpreting, (mis)arranging, and (mis)using the accumulative data. Says a voice on Truthout, "The only change [Obama] has made in the Bush surveillance policy is to increase it to dragnet-like proportions" (Marjorie Cohn).[10] Says another voice, in NationofChange, "We are living in an era of unprecedented Washington BS. The odor at this point is beyond what it was when Tricky Dick Nixon was president . . . . If the place stunk like an uncleaned stable back then, today it stinks like a Nebraska cattle feedlot, and trust me, you don't even want to visit one of them without a gas mask" (Dave Lindorff).[11]

In the name of "national security," objections to the undermining of civil liberties have been overridden, debates muffled, dissidence silenced. And as bloggers have repeatedly expressed, such abuses of power, with punitive energy focused on every Insider's potential threat, remain "fundamentally un-American and deeply undemocratic." "When there is an elephant in the room, introduce them," so the proverbial saying goes. Yet, rather than addressing the problems exposed and investigating the misuse of power, the messengers are attacked, reviled, and persecuted. For having dared to reveal the inner workings of the national security complex and its totalitarian control practices to the people it deceitfully claims to protect, the (NSA) whistleblower has been made the subject of an implacable international manhunt. Dead set on getting the fugitive's head, the biggest spy on the planet is, ironically enough, seeking revenge and prosecuting the fugitive for . . . "spying." The rogue superpower has been turning itself into a global spectacle by pressuring numerous foreign governments and heavy-handedly elbowing its way.

The situation is such that it triggers the following remark from a voice in NationofChange: "In 2013, Planet Earth isn't big enough to protect the American version of 'dissidents.' Instead, it looks ever more like a giant prison with a single implacable policeman, judge, jury, and jailer" (Tom Engelhardt).[12] Says another voice, in the *Atlantic*: "Democracy requires an informed citizenry in order to function properly, and transparency and accountability are essential parts of that. That means knowing what our government is doing to us, in our name. That means knowing that the government is operating within the constraints of the law. Otherwise, we're living in a police state . . . . Our government is putting its own self-interest ahead of the interests of the country" (Bruce Schneier).[13] In the end, notes a voice from the *Guardian*, "Washington has handed Osama bin Laden his last and greatest triumph. The Prism files revealed in *The Guardian* indicate how far his bid to undermine Western values has succeeded in the 12 years since 9/11. He has achieved state intrusion into the private lives and communications of every American citizen. He has shown the self-proclaimed home of individual freedom as so paranoid in the face of his 'terror' as to infiltrate the entire internet, sucking up mobile phone calls, emails, texts and, we may assume, GPS movements" (Simon Jenkins).[14]

Although the man is dead, there is, strangely enough, *no end* to bin Laden's "lamentable victory."

Enhanced Security: "He Won"

> Fear is the product being sold for the sole purpose of maintaining power and control by those who themselves fear the power of the people.
>
> John Cory

Extra-ordinary rendition, racial profiling, arbitrary detention and prosecution, warrantless raids and confiscations, overuse of paramilitary forces, illegal spying and eavesdropping, "soft target" inspections at random times and places . . . so it goes for the impressively long list of damages done and the profound change wrought in the United States. "How Have We Come to This?" "Is This Victory or Humiliation?" "Now What?" and "What's Next?" are some of the critical questions repeatedly surfacing in the media. Further enabled rather than reversed in post–bin Laden times, Patriot Act policies and the Homeland Security apparatus with its wretched bureaucracy seem to spread on like an incurable cancer. It suffices to take a look at airport security enforcement practices to note how the hassle of flying in, to, and from America keeps getting worse for both US and foreign citizens over the last decade and why numerous have felt that this is where, sadly, "Osama had won." Federal and airport officials often try to downplay the humiliating and abusive nature of the security ritual imposed, whose dubious effectiveness in making flying any safer often goes unquestioned. There doesn't seem to be an end to first-hand tales about the Transportation Security Administration (TSA) security state going berserk in the United States, and even some of the security agents readily joke about the uselessness of their agency's policies. The outcry provoked by the invasions of privacy and assaults on dignity has been hastily dismissed as "a drop in the ocean" by TSA and Department of Homeland Security (DHS) executives, whose disregard for America's constitution and people has become notorious to anyone concerned in the subject.

Complaints of TSA *extra-ordinary* abuses and crimes transpire every day among travelers of all ages. Accusations of rampant theft and corruption abound, but these are more expected news. Some of the outrages that got media attention involve, for example, children of young age and toddlers being subjected to aggressive pat downs; a cancer survivor and flight attendant forced to show her prosthetic breast; or a ninety-five-year-old cancer patient in a wheelchair hassled for her adult diaper during the security check; and, last but not least, transgender passengers subjected to mistreatments that speak volumes for the dysfunctional, dehumanized, and ill-devised policies of *enhanced* security. Despite the intimidation and the indignity, a growing number of American citizens have vigorously fought back, sometimes in rather unusual ways. Such was, for example, the case of the young man at the Richmond International Airport who, in protest against current security airport procedures, stripped down to his shorts, displaying on his chest the text of the Fourth Amendment of the Constitution. Humiliated in direct retaliation for his act, handcuffed and arrested, the twenty-one-year-old filed a lawsuit.[15] The refrain routinely trotted out in support of these highly intrusive and punitive measures plainly speaks of the vicious cycle of bureaucracy's mindset: the TSA agents were said to have "acted appropriately," they were "just doing their jobs," and their superiors were "just following federal laws." A no-brainer response to which those in support of the young man's protest answered by waiving placards outside the courthouse that read: "Don't TSA Me, Bro." Commenting on the case online, a poster wrote: "The TSA is now screening for tumors, gallstones, general overall health, bombs, knives and other weapons, in order to solve the health care crisis *and* airport security. It's called the peTScAn."[16]

TSA slowdowns often look more like TSA showdowns. What comes around goes around, and the mirth at seeing a power so intrusive being challenged lies at the core of many people's responses to innocent passengers' interventions. In another case at Phoenix's Sky Harbor International Airport, a sixty-one-year-old woman reciprocated as she was subjected to the invasive pat down. Instinctually reversing the role and returning the treatment inflicted (without her approval), she was accused of groping, squeezing, and twisting the TSA agent's left breast "without the victim's permission," thus having to face the government's felony charges of sexual abuse (which a judge reportedly declined to entertain, leaving the case to local prosecutors). With the TSA being given "a taste of its own medicine," as the *New York Post* put it, the two women's reversible victimization placed them both at the mercy of patriarchal health care enforcement.[17] Be thankful, it's all for your own good, girl, or "Don't fly if you don't like it" are the standard responses, which, when "taken to the next level," mean: shut (yourself) up, don't fly, don't ride, don't go anywhere. Reactions to this case of role reversal were black and white as with others, but there has been an outpouring of support for the passenger's temerity, for the inevitable laughter her story raised, and for the "delicious 'turnabout is fair play' ring to it," as another reporter remarked. A Facebook page created in support of her acquittance had nine hundred backers three days after the news was released and nearly five thousand backers less than a month later (each with their own story of TSA abuses), one of whom called her "a modern day Rosa Parks, standing up to Authority." Thus, an American woman writing in Britain's *Guardian* did not hesitate to use suitable terms to expose "The TSA's State-Mandated Molestation," its "perverted violations of liberty," and its creepy pat downs policy now extended to all forms of mass transit—as an Orwellian assault on American freedom.[18]

Who would have thought that *free* citizens traveling nowadays must routinely endure *enhanced* frisking-cum-biopolitical-tattooing (a.k.a. biometrics—the subjecting of travelers to photographing and fingerprinting) or undergo *heightened* screenings—denounced by the American Civil Liberties Union as the "virtual strip search"—that require full-body backscatter scanners used for years in prison to detect weapons? By what irony of fate did prison measures end up becoming extra-prison measures? Writing in the context of planetary financial crisis and the dire US economy, a founder and managing director of the China Market Research Group (a strategic market intelligence firm) contributed a different, if not materially more convincing, angle of "Bin Laden's Victory" (his terms) when he focused on the additional time a traveler must spend in the airport to make it through security. Based on calculations he made of the 615 million airline passengers per year in the United States in 2009, he estimated the current inefficient security situation to have cost the United States $250 million in lost time and productivity over the last decade.[19] Thus in addition to the *extraordinary* costs of airport security technology, as well as the stream of hidden mounting fees sneaked into bills for plane tickets, the country and its people also pay dearly for the *heightened* loss of time, of productivity, and of creativity. In response to American law playing out in our *enhanced*-security every day, an exasperated poster commented online:

"Bin Laden won . . . . The stupid Americans spent billions on defense, thousands of young soldiers killed, and American public outraged . . . . Troops leaving without any gain. America more unsafe as ever."[20]

Every time the authorities slipped up and failed to catch a new attempted attack, they punished the public for their oversight by adding yet another costly security measure. This is how delusions are fed so as to keep "the security theater" running (a term widely used among experts on the subject). A theater indicative of the perceived transition to a police state, and a theater no longer confined to airports, which threatens to spill out to wherever the government deems it appropriate to subject its citizens to random pat downs. Taking the TSA "to the next level" may soon mean that there will be no location safe from the infamous groping of the TSA and its Visible Intermodal Prevention and Response (VIPR) task forces, with mass transit immigrant-, foreign-, or queer-looking passengers being particularly vulnerable targets. As stop-and-frisk searches hit record highs in New York City, for example (with over four million, mostly men of color, being patted down since 2004), accusations of racial profiling by the New York Civil Liberties Union also mount, as certain people are "swept" for little more than their appearance ("We all look like criminals to them"). At the June 17, 2012, march endorsed by 299 organizations to protest the New York Police Department's stop-and-frisk policies, several thousand demonstrators silently walked down Fifth Avenue holding signs that read: "Skin Color Is Not Reasonable Suspicion" and "Stop & Frisk: The New Jim Crow." With 684,330 stops recorded in 2011, ordinary Black and brown New Yorkers have been made to feel like suspects just by walking down the streets in their city. Said a voice from the National Association for the Advancement of Colored People (Benjamin Todd Jealous, president of the NAACP): "In this city of so much hustle and bustle and clamor, sometimes the loudest thing you can do is move together in silence."[21]

More recently, abusive discriminatory policing of people of color, culminating in the nonindictment of the white officers who killed Michael Brown in Ferguson and Eric Garner in New York, has galvanized the nation and the world in protest. *Americide* is the term used to characterize the treatment of African Americans in the United States, as America is said to undergo unrelenting self-destruction. Always lurking is the question: Who are those the police routinely perceive as *a threat* to security (even when they have no weapon or are physically subdued on the ground or in a chokehold, for example)? *We all look like criminals to them.* A cursory look at the list of other late victims of police violence—Walter Scott in North Charleston, South Carolina, Jessie Hernandez in Denver, Colorado; Ezell Ford in Los Angeles; Akai Gurley in New York; Tamir Rice, Tanisha Anderson, John Crawford in Ohio—reveals how systemic terror together with racial profiling, rampant sexism, and lack of accountability often underlie police brutality across the country. The 2014 Millions March brought together people from all walks of life to protest the rise of the American police state and the dire conditions of those whose lives it deems worth ending—"the shot and the choked . . . the American citizens *who can't breathe* in their own communities" (Reverend Al Sharpton). The dynamic leadership of Black women on the front lines in Ferguson and beyond is not only committed to ending state violence against Black bodies by stating the evident while marking the exclusion, emphasizing how certain lives, disproportionately targeted for demise, remain lesser lives and how differently affected we are by injustice ("nobody's free until everybody's free"). Such a leadership is also characterized, through assertion of Black life, by deep life-affirming practices toward systemic change in the wake of collective pain.

Thanks to the initial work of a new generation of queer, Black, women activists (Alicia Garza, Patrisse Cullors, Opal Tometi, Johnetta Elzie, Brittany Ferrell, Umaara Elliott, Synead Nichols, Erica Garner to mention just a few), the hashtag #BlackLivesMatter joined by #icantbreathe moved from social media to the streets, while the Millions March in New York (December 13, 2014) gathered over fifty thousand participants, unexpectedly outnumbering the estimated thirty-five thousand NYPD officers. In the light of global violence and state racism, the rallying cry "Black Lives Matter" speaks not only to the disproportionate amount of authority state policing has over our lives but also to the differential treatment it has for those deemed disposable because they do not fit the norms of "good" white society—namely, all Black lives: queer, trans, disabled, undocumented, women, intersex, genderfluid, as well as cis men. The cry also helps to build and sustain a movement that has been reviving a hibernating national conversation about race, justice, and state terrorism. It was in the wave of Black Lives Matter protests that the NAACP kicked off a 120-mile, seven-day march (Ferguson to Jefferson City, November 29 to December 5, 2014), entitled "Journey for Justice." Ferguson has become emblematic of how, when local law enforcement agencies carry on their own version of the military, a developing chasm between the police and the people could dangerously lead to massive societal eruption and the spread of anarchical violence across America. As Garner's daughter Erica remarked, "This is not a black-and-white issue. This is a national crisis."[22]

What happens nationally applies internationally—as widely reflected in US foreign policy. The movement has extended its impact in major cities both across and beyond the United States. "People are realizing just how far its reach actually is," said Synead (Cid) Nichols. "It doesn't just affect Black people here in America. It affects people in the Philippines . . . there's an NYPD headquarters in Manila . . . . The systemic racial destabilization of all these bodies is a worldview."[23] The way America treats its marginalized citizens at home is mirrored in the way it treats both its foreigners of color within and its others abroad. (As reminded by protesters' signs, "We Will Not Forget," the memory of the forty-one gunshots fired in 1999 by four white New York City police officers at the unarmed Guinean immigrant, Amadou Diallo, has also not faded in cyberpublic opinion.) The America we live and believe in has become, as noted in NationofChange, "an Orwellian nightmare, a soft fascism that could become hard overnight at the flick of a switch. In effect, we have all become exiles in need of asylum."[24] The militarization of the police goes hand in hand with the rise of the police state and what it sees de facto as a looming threat to security. Through fear, the previous Bush leadership was repeatedly said to have let itself be goaded "into violating US core standards of morality," and the harm inflicted on America continues today to extend well beyond the lives lost on September 11. No wonder, in a piece titled "He Won," a voice writing on the Agitator blog discusses how bin Laden fulfilled his vow, succeeding to draw the United States and the West into a prolonged war, both on a local (Afghanistan) and a global (Islam) scale: "He achieved all he set out to achieve, and a hell of a lot more. He forever changed who we are as a country, and for the worse. Mostly because we let him. That isn't something a special ops team can fix."[25]

> I'm so glad I was able to meet them before they were killed.
>
> Hopi elder Leonard Selestewa, on the Twin Towers

When asked how they felt about the news of bin Laden's death, most survivors of September 11 responded with neither joy nor triumph. A man who made it down the stairs of the north tower with third-degree burns was quoted as having said after a long silence: "I just can't find it in me to be glad one more person is dead, even if it is Osama bin Laden . . . the dead are still dead. So in that sense, there is no such thing as closure."[26] Another man, who lost his sister on that fated day, wrote: "I suppose people who ask us about our reactions are often uncertain how to react themselves—how much to celebrate or still fear. . . . There are lessons we have not yet learned . . . . American imperialism, corporate avarice, abuses of our power abroad and our historical support of corrupt dictators like Hosni Mubarak have created an abhorrence of us that, unfortunately, persists. We need to recognize how the rest of the world sees us, and figure out how to change that. Until we do that, more Osama bin Ladens will arise, and more innocent people like my sister will die."[27]

Everyone is eager to turn the page on a dark chapter in American history. But, in this generational war, questions arise as to what the next face of Evil will look like? *Who's facing me? Under cover of dark, who's carrying her corpse as she shadow walks?* With the undermining of the nation's basic freedoms and the pandemic effects of the scandals around the NSA's spying program, the United States's world reputation has again fallen to an all-time low. After all, if feelings of uncertainty remain with bin Laden's death, these may well speak to the *enhanced* circumstances of his disappearance. In its dual impact, the man's aquatic ending has allowed him to fare on further both as a haunting myth and as an all-pervasive force that has been turning planetary patriots into nomads and exiles. On the one hand, a spirit condemned to wander the sunken waterways where the specter of his threats continues its rippled-out course, keeping the American "security theater" dancing to the tune of every terrorist attempt. On the other hand, a watery creature of our watery planet, who died, as he predicted, not captured but "a free man"—buried at sea and, hence, returned to the very heart of all life's processes. Was it a hazard that the dead man's body was reportedly hosted by and disposed from the deck of the "Gold Eagle," the nickname of "America's favorite aircraft carrier" whose motto reads "*Vis Per Mare*" or "Strength from the Sea"?

With bin Laden gone, the initial justification for deploying troops in the region also went down sinking. Questions widely raised in the media read: "If This Is Victory, Shouldn't US Forces Go Home? Why Are We Still in Afghanistan?" Now that we've got him, "It's Time for the US to End the Wars." The wear and tear keeps showing as defections from the coalition ranks continue, while more and more soldiers in Afghanistan reportedly attempt to commit suicide. Arising from all walks of life in the United States are people's voices that demand closure and question the involvement of a deeply indebted nation in three costly open-ended wars. Says a poster online: "Pay attention to war-makers when they try to defend their current war . . . if they move their lips they're lying." All the top actors involved agreed that withdrawal has and will happen. But the sticky question remains, How? And with it, What (which forces) and When (what time frame)? What gets trotted out as new often proves to be abysmally old. Most soporific to the ear are, for example, the repetitive resonances between the current planned drawdown in Afghanistan and the previous withdrawal of US "combat forces" in Iraq.

"We are starting this drawdown from a position of strength," said President Obama. The tune sounds familiar even in its solemn, laconic tone. Over and over, something of the near past resounded with what happened in the further past and is happening now, laying the seed for a yet-to-come happening. However, resonance also has its dark side. When taken to an extreme, it can cause things to break in a most unexpected, shocking way. In the rapid building up of oscillations, an entity, an object, a bridge, a system can tear itself apart, collapse, and end in disaster. Frighteningly, in the field of vibration modes, resonances between America's wars abound and multiply perilously, and unless damping occurs, one wonders where their swirling course of rehashed, repetitive vibrations could end up leading. As the media agrees, neither war nor occupation has really ended with some soldiers coming home. In newspeak, "troop withdrawal" is known to stand for non-public war or war by other means—less publicized and more covert. With the wind of the West dying and the wind of the East rising, the specter of Vietnam keeps looming, and although many have convincingly affirmed that "A'stan is not 'Nam,'" the tune of that earworm of bygone days is still lurking in our collective memory: again and again the critical press expands on how "we win the battle, but lose the war."

In fact, the true battle often begins after victory is declared, and the new normal is *a state of pending ending*. America finds itself caught in the cycle of fighting long-lost wars and dragging on inconclusively. "There's a lack of clear endgame." "The Way Out?" Again and again the people voiced their anxiety, well before the "true nature" of a failing occupation was exposed to the public worldwide via Wikileaks's massive release of secret war logs. Which war, indeed? For, in this nadir of war rhetoric, what was said about Iraq is being said again, memory-less, about Afghanistan. Déjà vu rhetorical moments reappeared in bold headlines in the presses: "When Wars Turn Sour," "Why the US Won't Leave Afghanistan," or "Losing Afghanistan: The War after McChrystal." Although President Obama asserted the Wikileaks reports have not revealed "any issues that haven't already informed our public debate on Afghanistan," how badly the "Afghan job" has gone was confirmed in its continuous gruesome everyday practices. No, there was no big revelation, only the small detail in its proliferation, which bore witness to the ceaseless bloodletting, the arrogance of high-tech warfare, and the comprehensive way the military-security-industrial complex gorged itself on war. As with the one in Vietnam, America is said to be irreversibly bled by small cuts. Again and again, bobbing up in media waters is the old image of America as a dog suffering from having too much to defend and not enough to fight his fight—for, it is quasi impossible to come to grips with an enemy at once too small and too pervasive. With the building of a permanent state of wartime at home, the V-word in its multiply dark side has not only returned but also persisted among war analysts.

Exiting: "The Dark Night Policy"

The wars were said to be basically over. Time to move on, so it has been persistently implied in American mainstream news media. The formal ending of the nine-year war in Iraq was officially declared more than once. Announced with extensive press coverage, the withdrawal was, so to say, completed on December 18, 2011, with the last US convoy leaving and cheering over America's closing of the gates on Iraq at the Kuwait border. Ironically, with President Obama affirming the United States was leaving behind a "sovereign, stable, and self-reliant" Iraq, the drawdown took place under cover of darkness, and the last five hundred soldiers were said to have slipped out of their base in secrecy in the dead of night, without telling their Iraqi partners that they were heading out.

Today, with deepening rather than receding US military involvement in the Middle East, and with the merging of the conflicts in Syria and Iraq, the question "Who lost Iraq?" bitterly reappears in the news. In their march across northern and eastern Iraq, where over half a million people were displaced, the Islamic State (IS) militants have quickly captured not only broad areas of territory but also a large amount of

US-supplied military equipment. Memory recalls with much cynicism how not so long ago the cover title of the March 8, 2010, *Newsweek* shouted in wide assertive letters: "Victory at Last." While a glance at the periodical's featured articles—busily claiming the rebirth of a nation, the emergence of a democratic Iraq, and the officially taunted success of the surge in Afghanistan—might have induced the reader to expect something like "a watershed event" in the global democratic conversion, a closer reading of their very reports revealed such triumphal assumptions to be largely ungrounded, if not downright deceptive. Set against the familiar background of Washington's "cautious optimism," they mentioned a dramatic turnaround with the March 7 elections in Iraq, only to say further that nothing could be affirmed as to the sustainability of the Iraqis' political experience. The talk was all about Iraqis' passion for democratic processes and how the rhetoric of sectarianism had given way to a sense of solidarity among survivors of the country's recent history. Yet, all too fearful to give the event the long expected D name, and all too willing to take the general (David Petraeus) at his word, they called it "Iraqcracy."

Baghdad Now and Then . . . The pictures and comments released at the time of the official withdrawal dwelled convincingly on the binary set up between past and present, and the return to normalcy in daily life was hailed as the happy result of US intervention in the history of a region deemed, by the light of Our all-seeing power, to be "massively undemocratic" (at least until the shock wave set in motion by the Arab popular uprisings since Spring 2011 yielded a far more complex political picture). "A free Iraq at the heart of the Middle East," so it was already announced by George W. Bush in his speech of November 2003, while American forces were caught in the midst of a growing insurgency and a spiral of violence that spread in proportion with the length of US occupation. Since then, at the slightest sign of "something that looks an awful lot like democracy" (voices of *Newsweek*), the dominants hasten to lay claim to first-authorship and copyrights. Praising and vilifying the Other—here the men they have put in charge of the country—as they see fit, they make sure the credit goes back to . . . those most in need of a save-face closure to a long, trumped-up "mission accomplished." What has, indeed, been accomplished? Asking for the new so that no significant new could really happen, and more of the old would continue under the guise of the "almost there," seems thus to have defined the path for America's "dark victory."

As soon as the war in Iraq was announced as having come to "an end," one realizes another phase of war has just begun. The occupation continues in a different guise. As expected, there is a significant gap between official public assertions and the reality surrounding the United States's departure from Iraq. For a while, the daily news from corporate media wanted us to believe that the clock was really ticking on America's presence in Iraq. June 30, 2009, was once the deadline for US forces to withdraw from all of Iraq's cities. But then, as the US Secretary of Defense testified on June 9, 2009, an average of at least a hundred thousand troops would remain in Iraq through 2010, with half of them staying on further until the end of 2011. Rather than decrease, the number of military contractors (132,610) also increased as these were then busily building newly added or expanded bases in rural Iraq. In the process of deciding which bases within the host nation's city limits should be moved and which should be kept in operation, city limits were redrawn, apparently to the convenience of the US military. Such relocation into the edge of the city or into the countryside, such tactical reclassification of bases and renaming of occupation by other means, were again strategically deployed in the drawn down of the AfPak surge. It unavoidably brought to mind examples of other "free" and "independent" nations with large US armed forces stationed for an indefinite time on their territories. Always recurring as a key concern among the occupied is the unlikeliness that the United States would withdraw entirely from any country it had conquered and occupied. When urging Iraq's parliament to reject a security pact with the United States, for example, the Shiite cleric Muqtada al-Sadr warned: "The occupier will retain its bases." More recently, a voice from *Asia Times* and *Al Jazeera* raised anew the Pentagon's full spectrum dominance doctrine (which implies a global network of military bases, more particularly the one stretching from the Mediterranean to the Persian Gulf and South and Central Asia) as the key reason for the United States remaining in Afghanistan forever.

The focus of the American war on terrorism has moved twice back and forth between Afghanistan and Iraq, with Pakistan and Syria looming large in media consciousness as the central front. After the withdrawal, every time killings in Iraq were reported in the news they were mentioned as an occasional event, a surge of violence, "a nerve-racking spasm," in other words, an unfortunate state of exception rather than a continuing state of war. "The country is mostly at peace," and while the death toll on the American side was repeatedly said to slide "mercifully downward," the Iraqi civilian toll in these violent events has been admittedly "harder to count." Until the advent of the Islamic State, the situation in Iraq might not have quite dropped out of popular consciousness, but the media largely lost interest in reporting the country's continuing challenges under the war's dark impact. The same seems to apply to the fine print of President Obama's plan in Iraq and Afghanistan that has gone largely undisputed. As Obama acknowledged and promised, the difficulty of his task was that of inheriting an American ship of state functioning more like a supertanker than a speedboat: "You've got to slowly move it and then eventually you end up in a very different place."[28] But, despite the president's making good on his promise that the United States would keep no bases in Iraq in his much-heralded address to the Muslim world at Egypt's Cairo University (June 4, 2009), the new American posture in Iraq and Afghanistan has been viewed as a subtler form of colonialism: an administrative push for political reconciliation through a "dark night policy"[29] that allowed the United States to withdraw without totally withdrawing and to control key decisions without being seen to do so. This so as to make sure both countries would remain, in official jargon, "a long-term partner with the United States in the Middle East."

Wartime: the time of evanescent, asymmetrical victory. "The situation with Iraqis is as if one eye is crying and one eye is laughing," said a Shiite leader in Baghdad (Sayid Hashem al-Shamaa), after US victory was declared on May 1, 2003. The triumph was short lived, for what was predicted to be "a fast war" (*Economist*, April 5, 2003) turned out to be a prolonged, disastrous one. Over a decade after the invasion of Iraq—years of interminable onslaught of the mightiest military machine and the most sophisticated weapons in the world—our political leaders were still struggling to write the ending chapter of the Iraqi saga. Despite all the talk around its incompetence, intensive corruption, and uncertain fate in Western media, the Iraqi government reasserted its authority in key decisions and had all along been pressing on for a firm American withdrawal. Optimists, rising above the unwelcome twists and turns of this saga, conveniently saw in such resolution an American victory snatched from the jaws of defeat. But, despite the Iraqis' urge to sling the Americans out and the latter's reluctant agreement to pull back (President Obama's decision to fully pull out two weeks ahead of the date scheduled at the end of 2011 was reportedly due to the Iraqis' assertion of their sovereignty and refusal to give legal immunity to US troops), the formal withdrawal left many questions unanswered, including those of immediate concern as to the nature of such departure, *how* it was carried out, and *what was and still is going on in the deep of night* when most can't see or aren't looking?

Conflicts over details of the withdrawal marked the evolving relationship between the United States and Iraq. "Withdrawal" (of combat forces) may have ultimately meant "surge" (of "advisors" and "private contractors") with intensified covert military influence—a familiar replay, as the tune of the drawdown process in Afghanistan, with its promise of "a possible residual assistance force of unspecified size thereafter," also tells. But on June 30, 2010, the date of the previously much-touted American military withdrawal from their cities, Iraqis were shortly seen on television celebrating their "Sovereignty Day" with cheers, dance, fireworks, and even a military parade—ironically, in the fortified Green Zone rather than in the streets of Baghdad. Prime Minister Nouri al-Maliki had declared "victory" for Iraq and proclaimed it a national holiday. The step toward limiting the occupation might be small in actuality, but it is hugely significant symbolically.

Ending the occupation as quickly as possible was the platform shared by all those elected in the provisional council, and although there was not much cause for celebration, even "a withdrawal in name only" would suffice to trigger an overblown reclamation of sovereignty and a burst of festivities akin to those following a hard-fought victory. More recently, two weeks after the last convoys of US troops crossed into Kuwait, the Iraqis celebrated again the long-waited-for day of American complete withdrawal as the "Iraq Day" or "Day of Defeating the Occupier" on Baghdad TV. The crowd outside a Sunni mosque reportedly chanted "American cowards." As it has been reported in the *New York Times*, the basic operations (of dismantling, removing, and transferring) surrounding the US troops' pullout were all intentionally carried out during the dark of night, when sleep dominates and normal sight is radically limited. In other words, when it was difficult for most Iraqis and the world to see that the American withdrawal is not really what it has been vaunted to be.

Every diurnal gesture has a nocturnal side to it. Day works at its empire, while night constantly threatens to disappear in the bright artificial light of broadcasted acts. To maximize its leverage on key leaders in occupied territories, the dominant would have to see when others cannot see, to see more than what a normal situation requires, to see through surfaces, and to see even in the absence of light. If advances in adaptive camouflage, concealment, and deception with a high-tech twist continue to revolutionize the age-old art of warfare, night vision technology's development was central to what the US military regarded as the pre-eminent technological advantage they had over their enemies since the first Gulf War. Infrared protection devices were developed that allow American soldiers to *disappear*—so as to be *heard but not seen* in their night operations; a tactic whose effect on the enemy can be most intimidating. As these new techniques in visual detection and protection show, the occupiers have gone through great expenses not only to spot without being caught watching but also to maintain their privilege to see from high above, to see through darkness, and to "see whatever man made."

Such a stance of stretching and distending sight—literally, at all costs—further expands to seeing in absentia: unmanned airplanes are being used in the drone war in Pakistan, and elsewhere, and these flights with no pilot on board have become, according to a CIA official, "the only game in town." The advent of drones is changing our very concept of war, erasing the notions of frontier, battlefield, or "legal killing" locations, and establishing a risk-free ethics of killing that may well render the mobilization of citizens' support for war irrelevant in political decision making. Analysts at the New America Foundation elaborate on the "Revenge of the Drones," while in zones under target, the "wasp" attacks—a name given by the local inhabitants to the flying robots—have inevitably stirred up the fire of resentment among Pakistani people. Predator technology is aiming for ever smaller "cybug spies" or unmanned aerial robots patterned after insects that could fly undetected into places where no human could sneak in to snoop on the enemy. As miniature robots have proven a challenge so far, tests are being carried out (at the Pentagon's Defense Advanced Research Projects Agency, DARPA) on a range of insects whose manipulation via embedded devices would allow them to be recruited in great numbers in order to participate in humankind's unending wars. "Eventually a swarm of cybugs could converge on targets by land, sea, and air," so it is reported.[30]

The dream of imbuing insects or man-made objects with the superpower of Iron Man resonates well in Day's work. Both aimer and target are dehumanized, and the inhumanly human, dirty work of fighting the enemy at close range would thus be dispensed with. (This in spite of all the tactical inefficiencies, the blind spots, and the history of accidents created with these night-drone-Predator technologies—including, for example, the legalizing of a new form of clandestine voyeurism; or the highly disputed "collateral damages," or "friendly fires," whose numbers always need "corrections" by administrative officials.) We are thus made to believe that exterminating via remote control, without direct risk to American life, is a natural privilege of our high-tech posthuman age. The president's emphasis on drones has been expanding and "taken to the next step." Not only has it paved the way for drone warfare in the world and normalized their use in the military, but it also opens the door to a guilt-free and risk-free ethics of killing. Now sold by the hundred thousands during holiday seasons, small, unmanned, aerial vehicles have infiltrated the entertainment as well as the surveillance domain. Soon, drones could easily fill the skies over America, as they become ubiquitous tools of law enforcement agencies, gaming industries, and numerous other business entities.

What comes around goes around, and with the privilege comes the worry. What if our favorite weapon is turned against us? Or what if the advantage of the robotics revolution shifts hands? So it has been asked among anxious technology analysts. Inevitably, this has already happened, as past historical events have shown. On the one hand, citizens across the country warned against official abuses and the dangers of surveillance drones in the hands of the police force. As a voice from Berkeley, California, puts it, the nation is becoming "the greatest surveillance state the world has ever known" (Peter Warfield). On the other hand, the threat of this new wave of technology has been mostly yielding rather indulgent reactions, such as that of downplaying (or trumping up) the possibility of "terrorists" acquiring a Predator to deliver explosives, or of assuming that its use is an exclusive prerogative of the all powerful. Whenever the others use it, it is simply said to have fallen into "the wrong hands." Things continue as if the main solution lies in giving oneself the license to determine who should have access to "such dangerous technologies." The illusion of omni-seeing thrives on selective blind spots that allow the mind to go on claiming, for example, its rights as first-mover, both in war and in technology. If only Our weapons could distinguish between "right" and "wrong hands"...

Today, it is reported that at least forty other countries around the world (including Iran, China, India, Pakistan, and Russia) have begun to build or buy and deploy unmanned aerial vehicles (UAVs). What would it be like for the Sky-Ruler to live under the constant fear of unmanned biological air attacks and the paranoia of having perpetually to beef up its air defenses? The diurnal side of every technological triumph . . . 150 million US dollars in the president's war supplemental to increase the number and technology of drones, to multiply killing machines that allow one to kill well, remotely, and to kill without direct risks. With boundaries between geographical spaces rendered inefficient in drone warfare, every place becomes a potential site of violence and of targeted assassination. When drones attack, civilians die—all neatly, via remote control.

The withdrawal in Iraq was said to be quite an "illusion" and a mere "moving of chess pieces" (James Denselow, *Guardian*[31]; Janet Weil, CODEPINK[32]). It was under darkness's cover that the boundaries between inside and outside—what is interior and exterior to a city, for example—were modified so as to exempt certain operations from scrutiny. *Overnight*, "combat" would become noncombat, and in Secretary of Defense Robert Gates's own terms, forces previously called "brigades combats" would, for the *outside* world, be called "advisory and assistance brigades," while *inside* the army, they would be known as "Brigades Enhanced for Stability Operations" (BESO). These would be part of a US command in Iraq to be redesignated as a "transition force headquarters" after August 2010.[33] American plans for Iraq seem to be characterized in its nature by a peculiar "acting in the dark of night," as an analyst of the war (Michael Schwartz) put it. The administration's sleight of hand in the "withdrawal" is viewed as yet another lie, typical of colonialism in the twenty-first century.[34] But to scrutinize these plans is to find not so much what contradicts as what unrelentingly stalk (their) Day's publicized gestures. Daylight's presence is here ubiquitous, and the (man-made) derivative night that follows and precedes it is, in fact, always lurking, barely concealed under the banner of Democracy's protection. In this culture without night, perhaps for D's sake, night-vision technology should be turned around, made so as to allow us to see not only *at* night but also Day's hidden vision—or Day's night. As a voice intent on mulling over the logic of withdrawal from Iraq, insists: "The empire has not folded up its tent, and neither should we" (Anthony Arnove).[35]

specter of vietnam

The Smell of Victory

Just leave. It was a lost cause from the start, so it has been repeatedly voiced. Scoffing at what the United States could achieve in its renewed intervention in Iraq in 2014, critics have been exhorting the government to do what it did in Vietnam in 1975—"just leave." Past questions around the ever-pending ending in Iraq resonate anew as they return to haunt the present with a vengeance. *Exiting Iraq: How?* Again, a "Victory in Defeat" as some would insist and compare in trying to rewrite the Vietnam syndrome. With a departure enforced, the presses spoke about the troops' pullback in 2011 in terms of a "humiliation of defeat," and a "colossal blow to American prestige in the Middle East and around the world." However, more could have been said in depth about the "humiliation of occupation" and what now lies in ruins (the Islamic State being the direct result of meddling from the West). *Start anew for Iraq: How?* The United States has not taken responsibility to restore the country it devastated. "In six years they have destroyed Iraq," remarks a voice returning to Baghdad with Women for Women International (W4WI). "It basically looks like we do own it and have created our own kind of hell out of it" (Zainab Salbi).[1] Similarly, in discussing how the country is being cleansed of itself (physically, economically, intellectually, historically) and how Saddam Hussein was reported to have once said "Iraq is one big gutter, and I am the one who keeps the lid on," another voice from the blogosphere noted: "He was right. It turns out that the Iraqi gutter has overflow[ed], breaking the drains, leaking through pipes, swelling over dams, swamping the land and turning it into one huge sewage" (Layla Anwar).[2]

The calamity on Capitol Hill on September 29, 2008, and the dismal handling of the long-predicted financial crisis were not only attributed to the personal shortcomings of a then outgoing commander-in-chief whose imperial presidency was said to be ending in disaster. They were also associated with the comprehensive failure of his leadership show—characterized by a my-way-or-the-highway partisanship, whose alarmist rhetoric and catastrophic performance over his eight-year rule have left his supporting party confused and deeply divided.

The agony of two grinding wars and what has come to be known to the world as the "Western financial hurricane" triggered by the "American downturn" have marked the defining moments of the Bush ineptitude. Time for a long-overdue U-turn, kept on moaning the press, which had come round to calling Bush's "long war" a "failure of monumental proportions" resulting from "ill-advised American policy," and "an Iraq syndrome" akin to the one suffered by Americans in Vietnam a generation ago.

Damned if you don't (get out) and damned if you do. In writing a comprehensive review of America's war strategy for the Obama administration, a former CIA officer (Bruce O. Riedel) kept running into the specter of a war lost and, as he noted, "Vietnam walked the halls of the White House."[3] *And She continues to walk these halls*. The much-abused V- and D-words, as well as the code terms around them, kept on lurking behind every war calculation related to Afghanistan. The resonance was plain and the Vietnam parallels were inevitable in many aspects, despite the obsessive effort to spell out the differences. On the one hand, the Bush administration's official storyline had revived the familiar paranoia of having victory turned over to the enemies. On the other, the exit strategy for withdrawal also raised widespread doubt about what was achievable in Iraq and Afghanistan and what the comprehensive results of the Iraq War turned out to be. The classic double bind wrote itself into every discussion of the "post-Iraq" era of US foreign policy. Despite its new approach to foreign policy meant to help to rebuild the global stature of the United States, the Obama administration's sharp refocus on al-Qaeda and its escalation of the war in Afghanistan only brought back, among both government representatives and antiwar analysts, more vivid comparisons with the war in Vietnam.

Deceive and retreat, wreck and wrap were courses of action in Iraq that had, for a while, threatened to reproduce the chaotic and horrific ending of the Vietnam runaway. No wonder the question Donald Rumsfeld perpetually asked his general on assignment used to be: "When do you get this thing wrapped up?" Well known to the public by now was the ex-defense secretary's "light-and-nimble," short-war plan and his itchiness to push off quickly as the initial spectacle of war grandiosity was morphing into an onerous, cumbersome spectacle of literally nine-million-tons-heavy war infirmity (the weight of military gear shipped to Iraq). "Exiting Iraq: Now or Never?" "Out of Iraq How?" Of course, "nobody's gonna want this albatross around their necks," but no, "You Can't Go Home Again," because the question is not just "to win big, get in a hot air balloon . . . and then, we're out of there." So went some of the representative concerns previously voiced on the perils of pulling out of Iraq quickly and leaving behind carnage and chaos.[4] The Giant would have to learn all over again "How to Walk Away,"[5] for in Now the How inevitably geared its head, and with Again, memories of a past apocalyptic defeat loomed large. Already at the time when the Bush administration vocally held on to its claim of victory over its enemies, images of the runaway in Vietnam took a new lease on life in many of the presses, and the cases of Lebanon and Somalia for the United States or, further back, of India and Algeria for the British and the French, resurfaced in print. Unforgettable examples of endings in the history of imperial wars lurked about, and when things fell apart rather than falling into place, scrambling for the exits seemed to be the bitter norm.

Conservative political analysts were thus led to wondering aloud whether the Iraq war could have become the greatest military defeat in US history and whether America's crave for winning at all cost had not already set it on a path to "imperial decline." Eager to bid good riddance to a politics of fear and smear performed largely to cover up the mess that followed the deceptive cry of victory, a disillusioned American public voiced its afflictions toward "the unwinnable war," "the shameful retreat," "the doomed-to-failure policies," and "the end of victory culture." Some even saw a legacy of "triumphs without victory." Not only "the Iraq war is lost. The only way to get out of it is through diplomatic negotiations," but furthermore "the war on terrorism cannot be won." Not by brute military force. So it has been reckoned among realists and those whose distress ran far deeper than any outraged battles they fought against the pre-emptory militarism of Bush the victor.

Elsewhere, during a lull in the bombings by Israel, which had pounded the town of Tyre in Lebanon, a fisherman warned: "This is a war of nerves. Don't be fooled by quiet. Be afraid of it" (Khalid Mehdi). That silence in between; before and after the blast. One may start out fighting the "far enemy" only to realize the need to confront the "nearby enemy" and face the evermore elusive "enemy within." "Traitors are lurking within the system," and cutting even deeper into the psyche of our times is the banal saying: "Evil may be living just around the corner." In the return of dark-age violence via new technology, it is globalization at its most divisive that thrives as the world is conveniently reduced to winners and losers.

Despite the danger of overacting against an unknown mobile enemy, the heart wavers at the sight of continual televised bloodbaths and hostility makes its appearance in the most trivial instances of routine life. When the flag of security threat goes up, many are made to feel edgy, and if a person screams, everyone runs scaring each other literally to death. Overnight, the entire world comes to be populated with foes. Havens of safety seem to be shrinking in proportion to one's effort to recover them by force. Time to Go Home. One sees a potential enemy everywhere one looks, and one startles at every shade and shadows that come one's way. Going home, one feels no longer at home.

> Perhaps the best way to get down from the big imperial mountain is to walk, not fall.
>
> Wes "Scoop" Nisker, *Crazy Wisdom*

Now time. Sanguineous time. Whenever the face of victory shows up, it morphs to let one catch a glimpse of death in the survivor. Not long ago was a time when, at the height of jubilation over an implied "Mission Accomplished," our victory President G. W. Bush could not say more than a couple of lines without recourse, over at least a dozen of times during his speech, to his favorite word, "victory." Words of triumph emptied of meaning and thoroughly bled of heart-life. The policy of "might makes right" militarism was always busy looking for new scapegoats and new semantic disguises to reassert itself as the legitimate path of the one and only superpower. Since then, the situation has shifted drastically in the lower-ranking sections as official statements on the two wars became strikingly cagier with time and definitions of "victory," manifestly unascertainable.

Analyses related to the end of victory culture strike a painful chord in the history of American triumphalism, for every victory achieved by force of arms by the all-powerful over communities of lesser means ("such an inferior force," as the press puts it, and North Vietnam was certainly "a little fourth rate power" by Henry Kissinger's standard) is bound quickly to collapse with closer examination. As civilians and victims of wars across nations put it, *there is no victor or loser in a war—only survivors.* A headline in the *New York Times* (September 19, 2003) read: "Two US Fronts: Quick Wars, but Bloody Peace." Highly intoxicative, sanguinary power feeds incessantly on sacrificial flesh and blood. In neither Afghanistan nor Iraq does the cry of victory seem to have had a life span longer than the instance of its announcement. Bush's "new war" had not only been a war started with no end in view, it remained at core an endless war.

As a poster noted online, "For George Bush and Dick Cheney Iraq has been and will be (forever) a 'no lose' adventure. They will retire to MILLIONS in 'payback'. . . . The present Iraq is EXACTLY what was wanted by Bush and friends."[6] On the one hand, the war in Iraq was won before it was fought. It was a war of easy triumph and oversize technical power, which needed no withdrawal plan and couldn't be bothered with any possibility of unintended consequences. On the other hand, the war drags on pathetically in its inability to find a suitable ending. Moreover, it has to drag on, callously open-ended, for the benefit of the elites making up the military-industrial complex. ("I told you," reminded G. W. Bush repeatedly, this is "a very long war.") Its profoundly unacknowledged indeterminacy was symptomatic of a dying victory culture *in conflict with itself.*

The "war on terror" would be made to last as long as possible, for the interests at stake are too high; too many livelihoods directly or indirectly depend on the sustainability of the US war machine. *Lovecidal time. Or, when love is suicided* . . . Much has been said about the unequaled role of America in exporting weapons around the world (leading not only in arms sales worldwide but also in sales to client-nations in the developing world). And much has been unveiled as to the comprehensive corruption, among both invaders and insurgents, which the sea of oil waving underneath Iraq has been feeding. Toni Morrison was voicing a rather popular concern when right after the fall of the Twin Towers she warned us of the peculiar smell of money rather than morality that the invasion of Afghanistan carried.[7] And smell was also what led, some six years later, a civilian from Houston to comment: "The Bush Administration has taken politics from the gutter into the sewers." More recently, when asked about the controversial "success" of counterinsurgency in creating a never-ending demand for the primary product supplied by the military, a man who served as chief of operations for the former top commander of American forces in Afghanistan, General McChrystal, replied: "It's not going to look like a win, smell like a win or taste like a win. This is going to end in an argument." Ultimately, even those in support of the general's strategy reportedly knew that whatever he would manage to accomplish in Afghanistan "is going to look more like Vietnam than Desert Storm."[8]

Screen Replay

"Only one thing matters: winning," used to affirm our victor president G. W. Bush. Conquering and defeating by extracting wealth. The war started with no end in sight, for winning in material expansion was the imperial goal, and all that counted in the picture of war glory was: minimal risks with massive destruction, followed by imposition, at all cost, of unification, centralization, and stabilization of the imperial kind—in other words, a government of any composition that would deliver the expected goods. Size matters in all things US, and under the Bush administration we seemed to be addicted to the most facile solution of solving problems in the face of adversity: military action via carpet bombing, advanced technological firepower, and colossal artillery deployment. The smell of money has been haunting the taunted "success" of the surge, as buying temporary loyalty has become the positive measure of a politics taken from the gutter to the sewers. Divide, bribe, and conquer, and as in the movies, blow up everything not of Ours—all for Their own good. Then, the pieces would just fall back to order under the superpower's magic wand. The story would then find its swift happy ending, with Evil being pulverized into awesome fireworks and dust—or cheerfully changing sides.

What mattered in the reiteration of power was the telling and showing of the sensational, the exceptional, the extra-ordinary—in brief, the apocalyptic mise-en-scène of victory ("the most spectacular victory of the century" as some of the American presses saw the 1991 Gulf War). Always seeking to gain exclusive rights on the coverage of an event, the US TV corporate media often ends up copying one another, reproducing to the letter not only the same images but also the same anecdotes, the same sound bites, same words, same biases, in raising and mobilizing the war as event. Far from merely recording and interpreting, the corporate media prescribe political existence and promote social conformity in the name of freedom of speech. The world was thus programmed to feel "shocked" and "awed" at the deployment of power via images of raw sensational destruction, as it witnessed the undiscriminating use of massive force against the slightest signs of perceived threats. Seek and destroy. Bait and kill. Provoke, attack, and invade. So goes the doctrine of pre-emption according to which a powerful nation can attack any other nation (especially of lesser powers) it deems to be threatening—not imminently, but arbitrarily, *sometime in the future*.

> Maybe this was the goal of human beings from the very beginning: to kill themselves.
> Maybe the whole nature of the planet is summed up in one word: suicidal.
>
> Valie Export

Meanwhile, time is watching. Even as reality was said to have caught up with the axis of denial, voices from the highest level of the Bush administration's tower continued until the very last minute of its reign to affirm: "We're not looking for an exit strategy. We're looking for victory." Indeed, as a golden rule of screenwriting decrees, a story ends when the conflict it carries is resolved in the climax. From then on, the action is all on a downward slope, and a wrap-up is expected to bring the narrative to a close as quickly as possible. However, the current wars' script has apparently strayed away from the established path of success and assumed an agency of its own. Structural questions unexpectedly come to the fore, which raise concerns as to, for example, what happens to the story when the climax came prematurely, with no resolution, no denouement, and nothing brought into focus in its aftermath? How is it supposed to sustain unity and interest when the problem lingers on indefinitely in size and significance? Indeed, how would the narrative find its way out when the central conflict keeps on spreading both inside out and outside in, reaping ever more complex backlashes and follows-up, not only for those directly and indirectly involved but also for those merely watching from afar? And, within the Good-versus-Evil setting, what course of action would be needed at this stage for the antagonist to be reconciled to the protagonist?

So far the exits offered to sight appear inevitably clumsy, contrived, and embarrassingly cliché. Although the downward slope of ending effects has long been identified, the war victory narrative remains in dire need of a satisfactory ending. In mainstream screenwriting, a good writer is expected to select first the conflict, working on its climax and resolution, while leaving the middle to be filled in last. In other words, conflict is the essence of the narrative. The rest matters little. To uphold such logic one would have constantly to be pitched against another in combat for the narrative to be. The world becomes a mere expanse of battlefields, and centralized conflict becomes the global norm. Winner and loser find themselves struck by a strange hunger no food can sate.

The ending, like the beginning, turns out to be already somewhere in the middle: there, where the pendulum swings back and forth, between victory and defeat, from one desert, one marshland of hostility to another. Colonialism—by other means—rather than the much-taunted withdrawal, has been said to be proceeding apace. In counterinsurgency operations, the distinctions between trainers, support troops, and combat forces often overlap. There is a growing chorus of voices among war analysts that sees the situation with the United States's projected role in Iraq and Afghanistan as a problem of colonialism in the twenty-first century. Despite President Obama's attempt to realign foreign policy with the moral values and missions of American government—that is, empathy rather than a purely self-interested view in redefining liberty—US foreign policy under what has been hastily called "Obama's liberal neoconservative administration" is moving eerily toward colonialism. With an expansive vision that promises a comprehensive US presence and administrative apparatus (with a stronger emphasis on "civilian programs" in American-led reconstruction "from the bottom up"), needs are also set up and sustained, which make US expertise and guidance indispensable, as they spread into every nook and corner of life in the occupied territories, from the inner workings of the local people's sociopolitical system to the practical details of their local economy.

During G. W. Bush's ending days at the White House, many memorable verbatim statements of the outgoing president surfaced in the press. Aside from the earlier, much-quoted claim to not being able to remember any mistake he could have made since 9/11, he was, for example, recalled as having admitted, "I think I was unprepared for war" in a rare moment of vulnerability, while lamenting the faulty intelligence used to build support for invading Iraq. The Decider, who promised to "rid the world of evil," has brought about the country's dire need for the Undoer, whose expansive view of presidential responsibilities had initially set both national and foreign hearts fluttering with anticipation.

Gone, perhaps, is the hubristic claim to defeat "adversaries at the time, place and in the manner of our choosing." But there are, perhaps inevitably, many echoes of Bush in what appears as change. Grinding on, the wars already outlast World War II in Afghanistan and Iraq. Unsurprisingly, none of what was supposed to be happening at the end, via US and Western interventions in these wars, turned out the way it was supposed to be, despite the more recent claims to a "dark victory" in Iraq and to an "American victory" in Afghanistan after bin Laden's death. With the talk of an "economic reset" to a "new normal," executives expand their 2010 jargon repertory, and "exit strategies" figure at the forefront as policymakers are said to be busy planning ways to withdraw from the markets and companies they have hastily rescued. Again, the occupation continues by other means: "It's Obama's War, Now," "This is not a withdrawal. It is occupation lite," says a voice of Truthdig and Common Dreams, in a text read on March 19, 2009, at gatherings by the World Can't Wait in eight major cities in the United States.[9]

In these times of orchestrated closures and of faked endings, there is, on both sides of war, truly neither closure nor end. While America's longest war was said to be speeding to a conclusion, a *Time* report of July 23, 2012, raises deep concerns for the epidemic of US military suicides that jumped 80 percent from 2004 to 2008 and has increased another 18 percent in 2012. More soldiers (95 percent of whom are male) have died by their own hand since the war in Afghanistan began than have died on the battlefield. The report evokes "the insidious enemy" and calls this dire problem "the ultimate asymmetrical war" that the Pentagon is losing. To which a US Army sergeant's voice replied: "You have to understand that when we come to Afghanistan, part of us never leaves . . . . In the space inside of us where the war never ends, everything [the Army] does will never be enough . . . . There are some torments that all the health care and all the support in the world will not ease. If this war has taught me anything, it most certainly has taught me that" (Alexandra Grey).[10] On the same day, July 23, 2012, some six months after the last US troops left Iraq, a series of coordinated attacks shook more than a dozen cities across the country, killing over a hundred people and wounding twice as many. Raising questions about an al-Qaeda resurgence and shattering US officials' claims that there has been a dramatic change for the better in Iraq these last few years, the bombings and shootings were said to bear, in their scope and boldness, the hallmarks of al-Qaeda. They took place within a few hours of each other and struck mostly at security forces and government offices. Unsurprisingly, the *Economist*'s headline for the event read "Sliding Backwards."

With no real pause for the end, and with the war switching from *Af* to *Ir* then back to *Af*, now cum *Pak*; with Yemen, Somalia, and now Syria lurking on the horizon, already the talk has shifted to the "undeclared war" well underway and to the Next War—the *multiwar*, the cyberwar in the era of Predator and Reaper. Everyone seems to know no decisive victory, no military solution through force and intervention is possible. And yet . . . finding its way back on today's screen of events is a familiar Orwellian comment: what ultimately matters is not so much whether the war goes well or badly but that a state of war should prevail. Not only the war turns inward, but civil space has suicidally become the battle zone in this economy of permanent war. The mindset of militarism thrives on and so continues unabated, a sickness that seeks no real cure. Again and again, the new normal reaffirms itself to be the state of *pending ending*.

twilight walk

no
reality
I
reality
lasts the length of a printed letter

Gray sky no clouds in sight, gray soil no line within view. A shape, a shade; tiny, ephemeral, hardly visible; how it wanders between woman and deer; sky and earth mingling to infinity. All around is gray, the color of mutual reflection. No high no low, far away no bound no ending. Solo, a surface. Expansive, flat, matte, alone with itself. As the skylight dims, images begin flowing, shading toward the shadow screen. Noises recede, stillness slowly settles in. Here and there, a few stray hairs: smoke swirling, swelling, and fading. Scattered into the evening breeze, the fragrance of dead wood burning and of moist earth. Now, no time. A hollow vessel is sitting wide, ready to sound at the slightest contact.

> A journey of a thousand miles begins with one small step beneath one's foot.
>
> *Tao Te Ching*

Now is the time to take a walk in the twilight until darkness meets the walker in her walk. For years, she has been setting out, moving into the moment of encounter, as if for the first time, with antennas all out. Emotional truths often retreat behind events' factual appearances. Already, she's on her way: no, not the routine march of the two lights—or an ending and beginning binary—but the slow return to primal matter through the very light of transition. A multicolored gray whose time resists capture and whose hues defy every black-and-white formation. Wondering what might come her way, she heads forth; walks, stands, leaps, stops short, sees, sees not, and sits on the side of the road, waiting until it etches its way under her feet again. In time, she finds herself unwilling, by necessity, to move fast, always faster, at the accelerated rate of a jet society entrapped by efficiency and productivity. Into the nonknowing of everyday, there where the path remains unmarked amid the deluge of markings, she winds her way. Falling here rising there, again she lags far behind in her own schedule, outstripped by her peers who, more eager to adapt themselves to the winds of the times, trudge ahead into the deepening darkness with no lights of their own.

Beware of the time of terror *entre chien et loup,* when wretched dogs are taken for wolves. She must have tried to tell how, in between two lights, one can't be sure what exactly comes into sight. Sometimes, blessed with the gift of gab she may, deluded deluder, try to make do, postponing the inquest, borrowing from the lamps of others and overlooking the debt owed. But trials on the way seem to know no bounds. If she were to explain it's an error only a human can make in so fine a rhetoric, she would be facing a wall. Not only refusal to admit errors and lies continues to plague our kind, but the words used and overused would also lose whatever power they have left, unless they are given back to silence. Some things remain inexpressible and all-too-well-said, even to the writer in her twilight walk. Specters of reality appear utterly real to the terrified mind, and naming in such a state is often forgetting the game of host and guest on which the name thrives. Every step is a stimulus to train the name. Thus, stripped quiet, without a single word to say it all, the itinerant gropes for her own blue ray to light her steps. Now crying weirdly, now speaking with holes and forgetting some of the basic rules, she feels her way through.

> How do I know the world is like that?
> Because of what is within me.
>
> *Tao Te Ching*

When it comes to the world of forms, humanity's escape from its own gift in darkness is hard to blame, for who is it, who walks by one's side, free and exempt of the debt of time? Losing the knack of resembling all, despite the sustained effort to be just like everybody else, she's compelled to walk aside, out of normal pace, there where her feet take her. As she stares into the growing dark, she catches an unexpected sight of a face staring back—her own. What a shock. Enough to make her flesh crawl, then, to make her fall about laughing to tears. Or so, she wonders. In the twilight of names, shapes, and values, what does one have to say to the other? How long has she let herself be scared senseless by riding the man-made wave of fear? Silence, dust on the road, void. Truly, the one who says it doesn't know. Yet, the possibilities of the word are such that writing, like speaking, often takes the form of a vast Absence, whose telling is telling everything at once, including the telling itself. Sometimes this happens despite herself, not while she's focusing but right when she is simply scratching her belly. Reality unexpectedly bumps into her, catching her on the raw. In mirth and hilarity, the path walks about, and everywhere she turns, it keeps her company. Slowly but steadily it fares, alive in her own pace, flowing through the tips of her fingers, and traveling all the way down to the soles of her feet.

With every step, the world comes to the walker.

Enters the time of winning and losing. Wartime. Suddenly, the screen goes blank and the text disappears. The whole history of inputs and outputs, of updates, repeats and undos seems to be instantly wiped out. So is the writing time at the computer. The mind panics aloud, and already, the machine's memory is being blamed. Can't it be relied on to store what was meant for selective access and creative process? Despite the compulsory continual upgrading of hard-, soft-, and firmware, the digital data cloud remains radically ghostly. Mumbling its way through, reason curses these "deficiencies in the database"—to which our FBI director legendarily attributed all recent abuses and mismanagements by the bureau (its misuse of the Patriot Act by overusing national security letters, for example). Regardless of how much memory power it has, it never seems enough, for what the machine so faithfully stores and unexpectedly deletes must be retrieved at all cost—now. Zero tolerance, as expected in the science of bits and bytes, for that which threatens to dis-remember the human in man. The mind gapes and frets about such a failure to back up, mourning noisily what is thought to be lost. But, with a stroke of luck, the screen is now filling up again. The work has only disappeared to magically reappear in time.

the matter of war

The Oil Stain

> To look at the long narrow road that leads the world to the slaughter house.
>
> Etel Adnan, "To Be in a Time of War"

No television viewers who followed the 1991 Gulf War could forget what they saw in the aftermath of Operation Desert Storm: apocalyptic images of burning Kuwaiti oil fields set alight by withdrawing Iraqi forces. Saddam Hussein has had his own scenario of "shock and awe" more than a decade before the concept (again, attributed to Sun Tzu) was put to use with fanfare in the Pentagon's 2003 battle plan. The spectacular scenes of devastation showed a raging inferno with gigantic lakes of oil pooling in the desert sand and numberless choking walls of flames and smoke rising a thousand feet high into the air, as a reporter on site estimated. Most terrifying was the sight of blazing red and golden yellow at the core of jet-black plumes of smoke that eclipsed the sun and turned day into the thickest, longest night—an event viewed, in these wars where vision machines run the show, as the inverse strategy of turning night into day via infrared technology. The oil went on burning not for hours or days but for some seven months long . . . Half of Kuwait's 1,330 active oil wells were set ablaze, with an estimated seven million barrels discharged, polluting both sea and air along more than eight hundred miles of Kuwaiti and Saudi Arabian coastline. So devastating the damage, so total the despoliation, the waste, the violence done to the land and people, that one could not help (like this viewer who watched the footage in petrified silence) taking in the full magnitude of man's propensity for self-extermination.

Crimes against humanity and crimes against nature often go hand in hand. A film director working obsessively with man-made visions of hell has understood as much in succeeding, with consummate skill, to capture the grandiose splendor of the wreckage. To pay homage to these "Lessons of Darkness" in their full apocalyptic proportions, Werner Herzog did not hesitate to magnify their emotionally operatic impact, using swooping helicopter- and truck-mounted shots with a soundtrack that includes music from Wagner, Prokofiev, Verdi's *Requiem*, and Mahler's *Resurrection*. The sight of the sky turning black as the earth belches towers of smoke; the feel of the sheer madness underscoring such a wreckage; and the power of a camera indulging evil as aesthetics, were enough to give every scene documented a quasi science-fiction look. Strange enough, for example, is the (otherwise common) scene of firefighters compelled to extinguish fires through fires, by hurling balls of flames into the oil geysers. At stake is nothing more, nothing less, than the folly of a world driven by its own need to reignite, indefinitely, the fire of annihilation. "Grateful that the Universe out there knows no smile," Herzog noted with humor in his "Minnesota Declaration: Truth and Fact in Documentary Cinema" (a statement he apparently wrote for a show at the Walker Art Center, April 30, 1999): "Each year at springtime scores of people on snowmobiles crash through the melting ice on the lakes of Minnesota and drown. Pressure is mounting on the new governor to pass a protective law. He, the former wrestler and bodyguard, has the only sage answer to this: 'You can't legislate stupidity.'"[1]

The Western media called Saddam Hussein's spiteful gesture "a last desperate act." As in a bad divorce—when one of the two partners has betrayed the other—if I lose, You've got to lose too. It doesn't matter what the price turns out to be, You just can't win, even if this means I'll have to sink our lifeboat to pull both of us down. Indeed, "*war is the no-win all-lose option*" (Gore Vidal).[2] Whether or not Hussein acted out of spite and desperation, there was, however, much more to the story, for he apparently knew what exactly mattered most to the United States. He knew which wound to inflict that would hurt most his ally-turned-enemy. He apparently knew, as a voice from the very top of the White House put it, "the Middle East, with two-thirds of the world's oil and the lowest cost, is still where the prize ultimately lies" (Dick Cheney). And he apparently knew, if he were not ruling a "country that floats on a sea of oil," as another prominent voice (Paul Wolfowitz) from the Bush administration put it, his deeds would not have triggered such an "offensive" reaction from Washington. In brief, he knew oil was his priceless weapon.

Attempts to explain Hussein's act of destruction, which includes assertions about it being a strategy to cut down visibility so as to thwart US sky power, have at best led to the release of captured documents whose contents simply point to the elephant in the room. Hussein had ordered the oil wells to be prepared for destruction well before the Gulf War had started. Understanding fully how crucial the oil fields were to their enemy, the Iraqi forces had to make sure to prevent their enemy from having access to them. Significantly enough, the captured documents suggest that blowing the oil fields could also be used for its *uplifting* psychological effect on Iraqi combatants and that destruction should be implemented at the last moment *in front of the enemy*. This was part of how they could *win in losing*. There's a world of difference between technical aggression and symbolic challenges. Hussein was attentive to the power of media images and was determined to play the game of ruse and diversion à la Western, complying with and discarding the rules as he saw fit. Indeed, how more ostensibly can he signal to the world what lies at the very core of the bloodthirsty conflict and what, despite all the talk to distract and mislead, remains the obviously hidden face of a betrayal? The "last desperate act" may very well be said to be, instead, Hussein's last laugh of total vengeance.

It was oil, and oil power all along. With the declared promotion of democracy and assertion of US hegemony comes the undeclared need to control Iraqi oil reserves. The subject has already been well covered by a wide range of thinkers. In the Bush administration's cockpit of lies, however, they laughed it off whenever the matter was brought up among concerned citizens from diverse walks of life. They said it was derisive and too simplistic to suppose that the double invasion of Afghanistan and Iraq was about oil. But the writing on the wall speaks volumes of the money-smelling war now that the long-held dreams of US dominance over the Iraqi immense oil wealth start yielding some of the much-coveted outcomes. In the announced Iraqi oil law, Exxon Mobil, BP, Chevron, Shell, and other carbon cronies of the Bush administration were said to be given unprecedented no-bid contracts in sweetheart deals that allow them to be among the first to drill Iraq's untapped (nominally state-owned) oil fields since the industry was nationalized in 1972 and to pump humongous profits from them for decades to come. Now that the United States's grab of some of the largest oil wealth on the planet seems like a done deal, the bottom line is, as a favorite (corporate) American saying goes, what it has always been: *business*.

It was foreign policy as fed, among others, by a relentless imperial drive and by black-gold power. Business is business, and for the superpower, access to the fuel must be gained, at any cost, no matter what it takes in terms of human lives, of economical and environmental expenses. The interventions in Iraq, as in Afghanistan, were wars of conquest to secure control over the key areas of the world energy system in the Middle East as well as new energy resources in Central Asia. Worth remembering, as reported by the *New York Times* and the BBC, was how on the second day of G. W. Bush's 2003 invasion of Iraq, Iraqi forces had set fire to several of the country's large oil wells, and within a week later in the Rumaila oil fields, six dozen wellheads were also set ablaze. The days the choking clouds filled the air again and blocked out the sun were when pillars of billowing flames and of dense, black, pungent fumes spread their writing high on the southern sky of Iraq, fanning a clear, deeply symbolic signal that the US invasion had ignited anew a human and an environmental tragedy. In the second as in the first Iraq War, Saddam Hussein's loyalists blew up the oil fields to expose to the world what they saw as the United States's underlying motives for resetting their country on fire: oil, and still oil. It was a blast for a blast; a show of fire for another show of fire—all done with special effects for the global ear, eye, and nose.

American politics has long held a love-hate relationship toward black gold. Criticism of the lust for oil goes hand in hand with admiration for a tradition of quintessential entrepreneurs wresting wealth out of oil. But when oil demands ever-larger pay in blood and iron, and what happens on the ground matters less than what could be extracted from it, somewhere something snaps, and the hostility harbored toward the sheer money power of the oil families finds its outlet in excoriating the fatal blood-for-oil drive—and with it, the link between oil, arms, and investments—as practiced by the Bush oil dynasty and its allied power factions. Corporate greed and military empire. Nothing new. After all, in the name of higher causes, such as democracy, national sovereignty, and security, and under the pretext of rescuing the country from its post-Vietnam hangover, not one but both Bush administrations have gone to war with the same oil-rich Arab country.

"No Oil for Blood"? But "blood is thicker than oil," came the reply, for "the violence now is primarily Iraqi on Iraqi." With anti-Americanism having spread like wildfire, rather than acknowledging the nation's need for an image makeover "to win back the world," attempts continued to be made by the Bush administration to reassert that despite its dilemma, America remained strong regardless, and the muscular American-dominated, "unipolar" world would hold out: "Still No. 1" (*Economist*, June 30, 2007).[3] Half a decade on, while "Iraq is swamped in blood," noted a voice from Britain's *Independent* (March 19, 2008), "they were busy telling us that things were getting better, that the rebels were mere 'dead-enders.'"[4] In fact, the longer the war lasts, the more immensely lucrative it proves to be for warlord-investors (in arms, oil, construction, and private security, as it has been widely appraised and substantiated). Magnified in proportion with their wealth's prodigious growth is the omnipotent influence of these power elites who have been gorging on war contracts. For the mercenary forces involved, a voice of *Truthout* (January 8, 2007) remarks, the war has "nothing to do with democracy or security or any coherent ideology whatsoever beyond the remorseless pursuit of wealth and power, the blind urge to be top dog."[5]

The fetid odor of blood *money* and *power*, profit and dominion, prevails no matter what, for even and especially as the walk-away was being scrutinized, what some of the strongest representative concerns voiced had been critically emphasizing was the importance of having "the US regain military, economic and intellectual *bandwidth* it once *employed to advance its interests elsewhere*" (*Time*, July 30, 2007).[6] Nothing short of that, so it goes. For, as it is well known, the interests apparently under attack and in dire need of protection from axis-of-evil member nations happen always to be those of the superpower's ruling elites and its allies. When war is conceived in black and white terms, the enemy, created in one's own image, hardly has an existence of his own. For an apparently interminable time, the voices of fear and smear were busy decrying: "US troops are caught in the middle of a horrific ethnic cleansing"; "The violence is among them, we're not the problem"; or else, "We do not trust them"; "They don't deserve us"—since their elected leaders are not doing what we expect them to do; We "stay the course," because "our job is to protect them"; We are there "to help prevent genocide and chaos." Thus, it seems as if (the) Hell (we've unleashed) is always to be found in the Other. As things spin out of control, presumption, under- or over-estimation, and failure to recognize the interlocutor in the enemy—the "ungovernable" in the "vanquished"—have been undermining all efforts at "winning decisively" and at achieving another US grand strategic victory.

Deep in the Red

> May it rebel, that nerve of life, may it twist and throb.
>
> Clarice Lispector, *The Stream of Life*

The war of nerves is also a war of words—an info-war, and a "verbal struggle" as Mao used to call it. A raw, red place where words are bled of substance. "He lied, they died," read an anti-Bush button. As it turns out, the "attack on our way of thinking," a favorite line of the Bush official narrative, is also more distinctly an attack on Our way with words—that which defines our mindset and our relations toward other peoples in foreign policy. What may turn out to be most oppressive in war victories is not so much what they claim at the end of the day but how—the discursive forms through which pernicious power "stays the course" and circulates. A specific worldview is surreptitiously carried into the syntax and semantics of our languages. Whether the war is one of revenge or one of choice, it remains thoroughly invested with a linguistic aura of highly selective legality and self-serving morality.

A long war—of nerves and words. Despite the condescendence implied in every reference to "rhetoric" and "semantics," words, set in motion in the tapestry of voices quoted on these pages, lie at the core of wars. They trigger conflicts and activate peace processes. They matter, for they have the power to destroy and heal. Through the links they create while in use, they ignite fire and blood, just as they burn out and go on independently with their business of tripping up reason and logic. Through them, the political is made possible. Never are words "only words," or rhetoric "mere rhetoric." The globalization of events is both real and virtual, material and immaterial in its scope. To negotiate with what can be said and what remains unsayable in public requires not only careful wording but also different approaches to rhetoric, different assemblages of the sayable, and a differential listening of what appears as the same. "US leaders should stop shooting from the lip," noted a civilian from Massachusetts. After a visit of G. W. Bush to his allies in the region, the *Arab News* commented on his "saber rattling," which they found to be "sad, even depressing." While reporting on how, under Bush, the White House charged Democrats with "trying to win an election by losing a war," a voice of *Time* remarks: "A war of words yields heavy casualties when the subject is war itself."[7]

Deeper in the red, immaterial forces continue to steer strife and conflict. The logic of war, with its warp and woof, has been keeping everyone busily wrapped in programmed darkness. One word more or one word less and the spark of war is set off. Thus, "war spews words. They make up its fog," noted an article in the *New York Times*.[8] And fog there is, plenty indeed, when delusion is accumulated upon delusion and success deceptively claimed through reliance on more military action as well as more corruption and buying power. Trashing and demonizing in a timely, divisively selective manner was part of the strategy of swift and massive destruction. Words, phrases, semantic fragments and with them the power of affective forces, or else the equanimity of the void no naming can fill. While talks about "an end to evil," threats of punishment for "scofflaws," and repeated reassertions of military triumph in a "can't-win" situation abounded, the chance of achieving the war's grandiose objectives retracted with every empty promise of a predicted "complete victory" in the *future.*

> Tet summed up the puzzle that was Vietnam. Victory somehow meant defeat, for to win you had to destroy what you won, and to destroy what you won . . . was to ensure the enmity of those in whose name you fought.
>
> Tom Engelhardt

The future was getting old; the avant-garde was becoming very retro. But it didn't matter. So obstinate was the desire for fiction, so intoxicating the crave for success, that the drums of war went on beating:

"And when victory is achieved," three dots many blanks . . .

Lovecidal, or the suicide of love.

All those fighting on the ground agreed that there was a long way to go and no guarantee of success. But in the political theater, the stage was already skillfully set, and opinions were designed, orchestrated, and calculated for their déjà vu effect: while G. W. expressed "chagrin" at the "pace of success," the Iraq Study Group report in 2006 proposed an exit strategy and depicted a deteriorating state of affairs (or a "lose-lose situation," as the media puts it) in which the problem was adroitly displaced so as to place the burden of remaking the unmade on the natives themselves ("Iraq's Biggest Failing: There Is No Iraq," *New York Times,* December 10, 2006).[9] Interpretations of temporal dips in death toll varied according to political positionings. But the dip in 2008, for example, which was largely due to the negotiations prompted by the Iranians' intervention (leading to the disarming and the ceasefire of the Sadrists—the forces led by Muqtada al-Sadr) but which Washington was quick to attribute to the "surge" of US troops in Iraq, had seemingly held American generals cautiously hopeful, at least for a while.

Having learned the lesson from their former president's premature declarations of certain victory and conclusive accomplishment, these generals became extremely wary of declaring success in their task, and they were always careful, in what they claimed, to leave open the possibility of unexpected blowback and reversals. Until. Already. They consistently refer to the "success" as being "fragile" and have no reassuring explanations, no final false comfort, for what is happening. One of them even wondered aloud, when praises for the surge were at their peak in 2008, whether the surge was really working at the beginning of the year or whether it was just "dumb luck." Not only the "success" was much contested by local Iraqis' and unofficial soldiers' sources but also, as an informed analyst of this war puts it: "The US generals not only said that they can't withdraw precipitously from Iraq—they've said that they can't withdraw *at all* from Iraq . . . . From the point of view of the US remaining in Iraq, the situation is deteriorating, and it has been deteriorating since the beginning of the surge."[10]

"When Will They Be Ready, Really?"

> I am a bleak heroism of words that refuse
> to be buried alive with the liars.
>
> Audre Lorde

When, under Bush's imperial presidency, the chairman of the Joint Chiefs of Staff (General Peter Pace) was asked whether the United States was winning in Iraq, he replied: "Winning to me is simply having each of the nations that we're trying to help have a secure environment inside of which their government and their people can function" (*New York Times*, November 10, 2006).[11] The deceptive, paternalistic overtones notwithstanding, victory has shifted its stance to take on a seemingly more modest, altruistic face. The price paid for any small gain in Iraq has been astronomically high, and occupation had degraded, on both sides, the humanity of combatants who underwent the tribulations of war and occupation. A cover story in *U.S. News and World Report* (September 17, 2007) concluded that, "Not even the best military minds can predict whether America will in the end achieve what most closely resembles victory—a stable Iraq." In taking stock of Iraq at the end of 2007, the same journal cautioned, "the drop in violence raises hopes for progress in 2008, but it's far from a sure thing"; and brushing over "disturbing accounts of intimidation and violence—such as militants threatening schoolgirls without headscarves," it pointed to the difficulties involved in the "tough balancing act" required by the troop drawdown (*U.S. News and World Report*, December 24, 2007).[12]

The "dicey situation" was one in which the blame conveniently fell for a while on the ineffective central government of Iraq, since without American bribe money (a.k.a. "efficient grease"), friction was said to remain the status quo and local political factions to be locked in a battle for power. With Iraq's security environment deteriorating sharply during the first half of 2008, and with the rate of war casualties unevenly climbing and descending on both sides (with American-paid salaries being handed out to former enemies), there was a widespread tendency in media coverage to reduce what happened in war-torn Iraq to a mere clash between Sunni and Shia Muslims and, by extension, to see the whole of the Muslim Arab world through the lens of sectarian violence. A senior US military officer expressed as much when he noted, "the Sunnis need to realize they've lost, and the Shia need to realize they have won" (*U.S. News and World Report*, December 24, 2007). In the shift of responsibility for protection to local forces, the pitiful refrain of the colonial tune of freedom and democracy was played out over and over again: "The locals couldn't—or wouldn't—do the job on their own"; We did our best, but *They did not live up to Our expectations*. Why give democracy to such undeserving peoples? "Can America Save Iraq from Itself?" They took the praise, "but We did all the work." Thus, as the government-fed media frame it, in the eyes of their US partners, Iraqi troops continue to be plagued by incompetence, poor discipline, and, above all, they are deemed to be untrustworthy at the very core.

Although distrust between Us and Them is decisively mutual, the blame comes to fall on Them almost exclusively, whose military forces are "rife with sectarian loyalties." No wonder, for in Our win-win scenario, it doesn't seem to matter much to Us that yesterday's freedom fighters whom We support should become today's terrorists, and those who serve Our interests should suddenly find themselves recast from "terrorists" into "moderates." It seems to matter even less what other peoples, here those from Iraq, think of Us—how, as a voice in Baquba (Abu Taiseer) remarks, by their own definition, "what the US [is] doing in Iraq and in other countries is the origin and essence of terror." Surge, bribe, and kill. What apparently went largely uncovered in mainstream media was the chaos further brought about in the reckless exploiting of existing divisions and the unprincipled buying of loyalties—a musical-chairs game in which money power turned enemy-insurgents into ally-moderates, and only as long as it lasted, foes could temporarily act as friends, switching sides vis-à-vis the occupant-outsider so as to fight the insider. Thus, the question of closure had been accordingly and misleadingly reframed, from "How will it all end?" to "When Will They Be Ready?"[13] or "Are They Truly Ready?" The Almighty's mouthpieces seemed to have run out of targets to blame for this debacle. As Washington worked its way out of its own delusive fog, the more information purported to be unbiased, the further it removed its consumers from the truths of war. Under the disguise of balanced pros and cons, what goes unsaid remains unsaid, and one after the other, recycled veils continue to be spread over it, ultimately working to perpetrate and regenerate the causes of the "evil" those responsible for the occupation's blood and chaos claim to eradicate.

As exemplified in the misinformed war of counterinsurgency and in the highly amorphous war on terrorism, the dominant's license to bully others had become nature: "We're kicking ass," said G. W. Bush, happy to recycle a trite, emblematic expression when Australian Deputy Prime Minister Mark Vaile asked him about his trip to Iraq en route to Sydney. Devising concrete goals, getting ahead, and winning over: everything is tabulated so as to provide new ways of measuring success. Or at least it is thought so. When the gain-or-lose mind dominates, life gets tightly framed around picking and judging; and, driven by the fear of defeat, one forgets to slow down to ask how well one knows one's enemy. Moderates, interested in normalizing relations with Western forces are so-called people with whom "we can do business"; they are paternalistically treated as deficient allies in need of intensive training. Whether solicited or not, military *advisers* and *training officers* are dispatched, first to take over the direction, then to give proper instructions and set the mold for a just-like-us-to-our-taste administration. Eager to *teach* but not really to learn from others, we often *train* them just enough so that they can do "the dirty job" to bring an acceptable closure to our unfinished business.

Mimic or perish. The fact that the occupied country's military remains an under-resourced infantry is part of the strategy to keep the need for American support fully effective. (As heard in his January 19, 2007, floor statement made in response to Bush's decision to increase troops in Iraq, Obama did not hesitate to use al-Maliki's remark that if his army was given better weapons and equipment, American soldiers could all go home.) To meet our requirement of competency, the Iraqi government would essentially have to think like us and do what we want them to do, such as choosing to ally only with those whom we approved (rather than to consolidate its long-term alliance with Iran, for example). Thus, even when asserting their nationalist politics, They said They were ready to take over command and American troops were no longer wanted in their cities, We invariably insisted (under the pretext that all "must depend on the situation on the ground") on having the last word and doing it Our way. Having written a memorandum in which Iraqi weaknesses were detailed in scathing language, a US colonel and adviser to the Iraqi military's Baghdad command bitterly admitted: "As the old saying goes, 'Guests, like fish, begin to smell after three days.' Since the signing of the 2009 Security Agreement, we are guests in Iraq, and after six years in Iraq, we now smell bad to the Iraqi nose."[14]

> We as women know that there are no disembodied processes; that all history originates in human flesh; that all oppression is inflicted by the body of one against the body of another; that all social change is built on the bone and muscle, and out of the flesh and blood, of human creators.
>
> Andrea Dworkin

Until then . . . It doesn't seem necessary to pause and genuinely share with the public why, in our effort to bring such invaluable gifts as "freedom," "democracy," "security," and "stabilization," with attached goods such as "free elections," progressive reforms of many kinds, including even and especially those claimed with regard to women's rights and gender equity, we are consistently met with resistance and resentment by both sympathizers and resistors—as if what we give can only be accepted when it is shoved down their throat. "Why do they hate us when we are so good?" Why do those whom we designate as fit for the task to take over our mission end up being invariably called "weak," "unfit," "incompetent," "puppet government," "failed apparatus of state"—by *both* the Right and the Left, the American savior and the local insurgent? Why, despite the extravagant expenditures on war, these chosen and yet defective ones are being kept under-resourced, being turned into aid-dependent paupers, and made to rely on American all-too-indispensable support?

Friend or foe, the other is produced—in our own image. The enemy, selectively demonized and reduced to an infantile lesser human, if not to a monster of the worst murderous kind, remains primarily an "invisible adversary" (a term all too familiar to Vietnam veterans): indefinable, derided, or despised; held cheap, humiliated, or deprived of existential autonomy, and hence, frustratingly difficult to track down among combatants and civilians alike. Voicing a common concern, a civilian from Missouri remarks: "They [the Iraqi terrorists] can blend in with the population, smile, shake our hands, thank us and take our money one day, then attack us the next. This could go on indefinitely as casualties increase with no end in sight. We cannot win this war." In a victory culture, the all-powerful seems, as it befits his fate, hypervisible and -audible while his enemy remains ghostly: omnipresent and yet unidentifiable, deadly and yet mostly unseen and unheard. Sneaky, treacherous, *they all look alike.*

Once trust becomes phantoms of the self,

> It is not by the head that civilizations rot.
> It is first by the heart.
>
> Aimé Césaire, *Discourse on Colonialism*

Small Cell, Large Cell

Freedom, unachievable by force, has a way of its own. Simply enough, the best way to get out of one's own prison is to "lose" the prison. But one is such a jailer to oneself, and so amazingly entrenched one's mental patterns of holding often prove to be that rather than surrendering and taking action to get out, one often feels more secure hanging on to the powerful fictions of self-imprisonment. The jail-mind of gaining and losing is a self-help system of beliefs underlying the core of our social conditioning. Thus, a prison of one's own could become utterly endearing, despite the discomfort met every time a limitation asserts itself. If defensive living allows one to adapt oneself to dicey situations of many kinds, it also lures one so deep into one's own creations that one forgets one's way out—through dis-creations. To turn the self-jailer loose and let one's delusions undo themselves in the process of unmaking one's prison, spiritual elders of ancient China raised this impasse for the mind (that cannot merely be "solved"): "You have been raising a goose in a bottle. As it becomes full-grown and can no longer fit through the neck of the bottle, you want to get it out without breaking the container. How will you get it out?"

History does seem to enjoy taking a laugh at men's victory disease and information delirium, especially when both the refusal to reverse course and the push to leave in order to salvage America's prestige stem from the same jailing fear of *losing*. (*What's with* your *goose? Live the world from inside the bottle.*) On the reverse face of victory, one sees flaring blue the humiliation of defeat. One catches sight, for example, of the runaway nightmare and its aftermath as experienced in Vietnam (for, in addition to the 1 million displaced within Iraq, over 1.8 million exiles and refugees have left the country, with 3,000 fleeing daily in 2008).[15] And although one may not see well through the Dark Night Policy, one does get an inkling of the loss or reassigning of mighty steel—the nine million tons of military gear shipped to the region, whose moving cost was estimated to be in the eight hundred millions ("Moving Mountains" noted *Time* magazine).[16] And last but not least, one glimpses the folding up and handing over of that largest embassy in the world, the massively fortified citadel in the heart of Baghdad called the safety zone or ironically enough, the Green Zone.

"In Iraq, the decider needs to learn to un-decide," said a voice of *Time* (February 12, 2007), "[Bush is] trying to dig himself out of his Iraq hole and making it ever deeper as a result."[17] Some time ago, when the nation was euphoric over another "easy victory" of the Gulf War, Bush senior already intimated that "if they crack under force, it is better than withdrawal." Desperate for an opportunity "to exorcise the demons of Vietnam" (*his one and only way of goose tending*) and hungry for outright victory, he was set on having, at all cost, his ground war in Iraq. And on February 28, 1991, the day the end of the first Iraq War was proclaimed, Bush senior exulted: "By God, we've kicked the Vietnam Syndrome once and for all."[18] (*Goose's out? Not yet, not quite. Seems like he still badly needs the bottle, for fear no one would* luve *him otherwise. How to get out then without breaking?*) However, skillful enough not to antagonize the combined coalition forces and eager to give a more grandiose interpretation to this victory "for all mankind," Bush senior affirmed in his televised address to the nation the day before that "no one country can claim this victory as its own."

Less prudent than his father, Bush junior was not only paying any price to win but also set on owning victory, turning a blind eye to the ground reality in Iraq and refusing any proposal for "a graceful exit." (*Goose's back in without leaving the bottle.*) On the fifth anniversary of the start of the war (March 19, 2008), he was still making the case for persevering in the conflict with his favorite punch line: "This is a fight that America can and must win."[19] (*No way out. What a perdurable bottle! Goose's well settled, all snug, stuck deep inside.*) The war in Iraq has remained a test in US democratic ideals, which the country was said to have failed rather miserably, as the government paid no heed to the demands of a large constituency of its citizens. Again and again the tune was stubbornly replayed to ears struck by victory disease. "We will never back down, we will never give in, and we will never accept anything less than complete victory," triumphed our professed God-consulting president (G. W. Bush) in a speech at the Woodrow Wilson Center in December 2005.

History, when conceived with no single master narrative, often takes its cues from what accidents and incidents tell us in the margins of official events. Political analysts have widely commented on the danger of having a victor commander-in-chief who sought glory in war with little consideration for the long-term human costs involved. But more dangerous yet was the predatory mission of recasting the world according to his and his surrogates' small-minded view, which continues fatally today to bleed America—economically, politically, mentally, emotionally, and spiritually. (*"By God!" How did we get (in) there? What keeps us all bottled up? How do we get out?*) Some time ago, after having injured two fingers in a mountain-biking mishap, when His ex-Almighty crashed into a police officer in Scotland, G. W. Bush remarked: "I think I've found my limitations." Whew, ordinary mortals averted their eyes in sympathy, while the world breathed out in relief. Such a (banal) statement from the Decider of the most powerful nation in the world seemed oh so reassuring and yet, deep down alarming. Finally, something—no matter how small, partial, and individual—had sunk in. How precarious what is known as the "normal" state can be. For, when wealth, health, power, and invincibility appear as a given from the outset, three dots and many blanks . . .

Civilian voices from across eastern and western America did not hesitate to fill in these blanks with memorable insights. They continue to dot today's gray political landscape with vivid comments and sharp mother wit. The problem with Bush, said a voice from Cambridge, Massachusetts, for example, was that "this president has no awareness of death . . . . Death hasn't entered his field of vision." Emblematic of a zero-death mentality, he was a handicapped man who saw not his handicap, a mortal who had not experienced mortality. It was as if death, that *utter otherness* no name has succeeded even to approximate, had not really entered his field of consciousness. He had not seen its shadowy faces lurking in everyday ("on the ground") reality . . . . For, as a soldier's mother pointedly noted, the very people who pushed for the army, one of whose slogans has been "Mission First, People Always," had not fully understood the slogan. "Under Bush," noted a voice from Fallon, Nevada, "no violent acts against the US have occurred since 9/11. But the cost has been a legal and spiritual 9/11 every day since."[20] "I almost cried. I am not an educated man," said another voice from Guerneville, California. "I have a high school education. I have always taken comfort in knowing that the person in charge of the country—and in many ways the world—is smarter than I am. I don't honestly believe, though I have tried to, that this has been the case for the past eight years. It seems that George W. Bush never really got it . . . . I don't think Bush ever took the opportunity in all his travels to see America or, for that matter, the rest of the world. He was never in touch."[21]

As the saying goes, whether an ending turns out well or badly is all about how the loser loses. To paraphrase a statement made on colonialism over four decades ago, the highest achievement of imperialism may be said to lie in the fact that it is through the show of its intransigence that it intends to last, and it is through this same intransigence that it prepares its fall.[22] Already in 1996, in support of the 1991 Gulf War, a member of the Institute for Defense Analyses set out to give a more complex picture of the fight, arguing that the "victory for all mankind" claimed was widely misunderstood. Rather than embracing the standard explanations that opposed the coalition's advanced technology (precision air and missile strikes and information supremacy) to Iraq's poor training, leadership, and numerical inferiority, the analyst's research showed that "modern warfare provides increasing penalties for error, but little ability to prevail cheaply over skilled enemies."[23] (*See what it's like, this bottle? Instantly returning inside, constantly carrying it on one's back. Oh, how so scared one can be sometimes when walking into the deep of night, knowing not how to let the world enter for fear of going uncaged.*) And, already in 2003, when the nation stood at the brink of war again with Iraq, a US senator (the late Robert Byrd) warned the public of the "crude insensitivities" and the "bellicose language" of its reckless administration and pointed to the disastrous consequences of the latter's "callous disregard of the interests of other nations" in these terms: "We are truly 'sleepwalking through history.' In my heart of hearts I pray that this great nation and its good and trusting citizens are not in for the rudest of awakenings . . . . Our mistake was to put ourselves in a corner so quickly. Our challenge is to now find a graceful way out of a box of our own making" (February 12, 2003).[24] (*There where wings grow, no in no out, no comings no goings. No breaking. Take a step with the world and the goose takes flight.*)

> From the window of my small cell
> I can see your large cell.
>
> Samih al-Qasim, "End of a Discussion with a Jailer"

Living Dead or Suicided? Choose, Please

Widely circulated among citizens blue with disillusion during the presidential election season of 2004, an e-mail dutifully urged:

"There are less than three months until the election, an election that will decide the next President of the United States. The man elected will be the president of us all, not just the Democrats or the Republicans.
To show our solidarity as Americans, let's all get together and show each other our support for the candidate of our choice. It's time that we all come together, Democrats and Republicans alike.
If you support John Kerry, please drive with your headlights on during the day. If you support the policies and character of George W. Bush, please drive with your headlights off at night."

between victor and victor

> How do you get to be the sort of victor who can claim to be the vanquished also?
>
> Jamaica Kincaid

Midway from an entrance to an exit, a river without banks. Journeying into the recent past leads to a crossroads. Now time as not-yet time and as all times infinitely bifurcates from dark to dawn. The universe holding each and all—not in a single two but in many twos—is a generous provider. In the twofold way, falling headlong into darkness with ears and eyes wide open is already engaging in a downward ascendance with ears and eyes wide shut. There's no mere escape toward the light at the end of the tunnel, as habit would have it. Amid all the gloom and chaos of warring civilizations, a transpolitical dynamic lurks.

New instability, new insubstantiality, massive revolts across nations. Nothing is taking shape out of the ordinary: no single proper name, no union, no movement, no uniform organization, nor any centralized counter-system. And yet, something finds its way up from down, round about from out there and in here, the lived sores and sicknesses from burning wounds. Unsparingly, the nerve of life in rebellion, as in survival, twists and throbs. In vital, communal third spaces, neither the blasé nor the cynical prevails, only the imperceptible ordinary, profoundly indifferent to the clash of binaries on which both the governing power and its resistance thrive. The force of life moving through sorrow and struggle continues its course and the widening movement of people's discontent around the world can hardly be stopped. *Time* magazine was merely gathering sea foams from the world sand page when it established "The Protester" as its no-name Person of the Year 2011. Those who embody and see into the vitality of such a collective force have time and again worked at bringing its unshakable spirit alive during the darkest periods of war history.

The Strength to Lift a Hair

In its manifestation, every reality shows not only its diurnal and nocturnal facets but also its between states—a range of subtle, inter-possibilities that defy the tendency to frame the world into neat battling opposites, for imperial interests. One, two. Not one but many twos. Doesn't the "*duo*" contained in "*di*versity" refer to the many and the overly much in Chinese? Doesn't the word itself, materialized in the doubled sign for "evening," suggest many sunsets? There is, so to speak, a world of differences between "victory" and victory.

In the aftermath of September 11, *The Art of War* by Sun Tzu (sixth century BC) had been given yet another baffling lease on life as it entered mainstream American culture and it remains evermore popular. This over-2500-year-old Chinese classic, whose powerful study of military strategy continues, throughout the ages, to influence the history of warfare and to affect certain turns of world events, is even heralded today as the best book ever in the business milieu. "Everything you need to know to make a kill," so it is co-opted and promoted to the business insider as well as to anyone who faces conflict in the civilian fields. The current revival of Sun Tzu's practical art of war remains indicative of a transnational culture of victory in which cunning distortion meets with unabashed recognition.

The book's widespread relevance for military professionalism and its long standing recognition in US military thinking since the Vietnam War seem to be primarily based on the way its principles have been opportunistically misappropriated by warmongers. So thoroughly were Sun Tzu's principles abused and misused in its alienated, modernized interpretation, that they have been credited with influencing a most eclectic range of not only eminent war leaders across times and regimes (such as Napoleon, Mao Tse-tung, Võ Nguyên Giáp, Bill Clinton, G. W. Bush, Saddam Hussein, Osama bin Laden) but also key business executives in pursuit of success and media celebrities eager to fend off screen competition (not to mention us all, ordinary wannabes caught in the winner-versus-loser game of everyday existence).

Both officials from the Bush administration and members of the insurgent forces in Iraq and Afghanistan are said to have referenced at length *The Art of War* to justify their actions. Yet, a careful look at the book, whose lasting power lies in the complex and concise call for multi-dual applications of its principles, could yield a contextual reading radically different from the one(s) opportunistically popularized. To mention one example: prevailing through the precepts of *The Art of War* is the strong emphasis laid on how knowledge and strategy are only at their peak efficiency when *conflict is made altogether unnecessary*. "To subdue the enemy without fighting is the supreme excellence";[1] in other words, to win without fighting is the art of bloodless victory. A product of experience gained through historic events and battles fought during the author's time, *The Art of War* is, paradoxically, *a book written to undermine war*. However, despite all the proud references to Sun Tzu, what seems to thrive on in America's current wars is the persistence with which, one after the other, the rules expounded in Sun's treatise have been repeatedly broken. It is therefore against the grain of mainstream warspeak that one could listen to the way the book's two-millennia-old voice of male wisdom still uncannily resonates in today's warscape of Iraq and Afghanistan.

Commander and military strategist Sun viewed the ravages of war in its extreme form of incendiary attack and siege as a mass cannibalism of human and natural resources. Victory over others by forced battle is consistently reproved. As "it does not take much strength to lift a hair," he wrote, "to perceive victory when it is known to all is not really skillful." Moreover, "the general rule for use of the military is that it is better to keep a nation intact than to destroy it. It is better to keep an army intact than to destroy it." Among explanations and prescriptions gathered in succinct form and powerful rhythms are such advices as: "*It is never beneficial to a nation to have a military operation continue for a long time*. Therefore, those who are not thoroughly aware of the disadvantages in the use of arms cannot be thoroughly aware of the advantages in the use of arms. Those who use the military skillfully *do not raise troops twice*"[2] or else, "know the enemy and know yourself; in a hundred battles, you will never be defeated. When you are ignorant of the enemy but know yourself, your chances of winning or losing are equal. If ignorant both of your enemy and of yourself, you are sure to be defeated in every battle."[3]

To turn Sun Tzu's light around is to see how his principles could eloquently apply to explain the delusions of the wars in Iraq and Afghanistan and to ascertain the extent to which America's tactical and strategic mistakes have sped its decline: while Iraq was "a dumb war," Afghanistan is "a folly" that continues structurally to raise the specter of Vietnamization, with analysts calling the political failure in Kabul a "Saigon déjà vu." The futility of the latter war was, as mentioned, amply and meticulously exposed by the leaked war logs, which revealed it to be "mired in an escalating stalemate" (Daniel Ellsberg)—a striking replay, as in Vietnam, of a set of allied forces' corruption and incompetence. Colossal strength deployed to lift a hair underlies the hyperpower's spurious claims of invincibility. Its "might makes right" military policy reveals imperial leadership to be riddled with blind spots, as it so readily lets itself be *awed* and *shocked* by its own deployment of massive firepower. The logs also speak volumes as to the arrogance of the high-tech combatant and the glee taken in exerting godlike sky power, zooming in for the kill and bringing death from above (all as if psyched up on a musical reprise from the Vietnam War film *Apocalypse Now*, with its exaltation of destructive powers).

During World War II, J. F. Kennedy soberly wrote from the Pacific, "All war is stupid." Perhaps after all, the very nature of Sun's brilliant approach to warfare—in which military force is based on a skillful play with the visible and the apparent—profoundly invites distortion and misappropriation of his principles. Said to rely as much on messing with the enemy's head as on slicing it off, such an approach was linked to an anecdote popular memory persistently associates with Sun's leadership skills: namely, his legendary attempt to train the King of Wu's 180 concubines in the art of war. Apparently, the challenge the king issued to his general concerns not only the latter's ability to command an army but, more tryingly, his ability to control and discipline a battalion of women. Since the women kept on not behaving themselves and falling about laughing wholeheartedly instead of following his orders to wheel and march, Sun ended up, per military laws, having the king's two favorite concubines beheaded, whom he had appointed as leaders. As the story goes, after the decapitation, the rest of the concubines silently fell into file and became "exemplary soldiers." Right, left, and about, they turned without a single mistake, as if they were born to the military code.

To the male "awing and shocking" threat of "decapitation," female disorder efficiently retreats in silence. This was how war and death were brought into the realm of laughter and unconformity. Military drilling meter and measure unavoidably trigger laughter among women—a laughter whose nature turned out to be unsettling and mutinous to the threatened ear of a master. Thus, military command is what decapitates the feminine, forbidding her to speak her speak. In a male economy, women either lose their heads on their own by conforming or the head(s)man decapitates them, as patriarchal society much prefers their bodies and has no use for their minds. Thinking and questioning aloud, or simply tittering and tattling in response to male (warring) order, would so disrupt its power that women who hold on to their heads would have to veil them, literally or figuratively, in negotiating their place in society.

Both "awe and shock" and "decapitation" are terms attributed to Sun, which have been made household words by the Department of Defense during the second Gulf War and popularized by the media when the United States was pursuing its targeted killings of Saddam Hussein and Osama bin Laden. "Decapitation" has become a dominant strategy in the war on terror, and "leadership decapitation," "decapitation thesis," and "decapitation operations" are all key features of counterterrorism policies. It is well known, for example, that G. W. Bush and the allied commanders launched more than one "decapitation strike" on Hussein in their attempts to remove the Iraqi regime's leadership and that the Deputy National Security Advisor, John Brennan, referred to killing bin Laden as "decapitating the head of the snake known as al-Qaeda." If, in Sun's story of decapitation, division ran mainly along the gender line, with the stain of cultural stereotyping in current media reports, the discrimination runs gleefully also along the lines of race, ethnicity, and religion.

Today, the question as to why beheadings have been made a key element and a sensational spectacle by Islamic militants (the Islamic State, or the Islamic State of Iraq and Syria) in their campaign would appear redundant when contextualized with the above strategic use of decapitation in the war on terror. Such a question could easily be turned around to find its partial answers in the transreligious, manly war ritual of seeking glory by exhibiting rival heads and in the transversal, competitive escalation of psychological warfare. (As with the previously discussed Californian photo showing the Statue of Liberty holding up the severed trophy head of bin Laden with red splashed and dripping underneath, the "barbaric gloating" that follows the shedding of blood from the decapitation of an enemy could apply to both sides of the war divide.) From one context to the other, language rapidly moves from the figurative to the literal. The gorier the images of embodied violence in the propaganda campaign, the more effective they are thought to be in stirring anti-Western or anti-ISIS sentiments. What appears to characterize our times in the recent spate of beheadings attributed to ISIS reign of terror is not so much the decision to kill by decapitation as the choice to record, in real time and in its messiest gruesome allure, the act of beheading on video and photography. The disturbing images would then be widely distributed via social media, often with the killers posing to be seen with the decapitated heads on display. Decapitation seems here to be used strategically at once as homage to and comment on the power of the illicit image. Such a power, obtained by capturing in graphic details the sensational horror of killing, continues to be thoroughly exploited by the American entertainment industry, whose claim to serve a consumer society steeped in violent media has kept its producers busy indulging in ever-more brutal forms of homicide on screen.

Lovecidal. So they have suicided love.

Stories shared from people's experiences often tell of military firepower as a sign of imminent self-destruction and firearms as tools of ill omen. Such a prediction is all the more acute when these are deployed, whether in faraway lands or in the homeland, against an ill-defined enemy, whose "elusiveness" keeps on shifting the boundaries between friends and foes, loyalists and traitors. The danger of hubris loomed large when in foreign policy, the Rest mattered little to the West, and wielding American power was tantamount to willing a form of nationalistic myopia blinding the doers to their own doings: "We're an empire now, and when we act, we create our own reality," a senior adviser to G. W. Bush was said to have affirmed while dismissing criticism from "the reality-based community."[4] Seeing ourselves as the navel of the world, indulging in this ancient affliction beautifully named the omphalos syndrome, we work at convincing ourselves the world goes the way we think it should.

To win global domination would supposedly give us the license to woo the rest of the world. And, since power grows in proportion with hostility for it, why bother with all the loathing and bitching about when, as with our immature youth, straight anti- and against-stances are ultimately forms of dependency, if not of plain envy? The Other is just a bad kid. (Just a *foreign* cause, a *minor*'s case, or "a bunch of *lefties*.") So go hand in hand the stoic voice of Reason and the obscure Desire for sanguinary power. Those invested in governing the world by force through willed paternal myopia hold on firmly to a relationship of Us and Them in which the world in its entirety continues to be appraised in the light of what We know (according, for example, to that European tradition of Enlightenment, which lies at the foundation of Our exclusionary humanist view—how, in our need to humanize and animalize as we see fit, we perceive, translate, evaluate, and legitimize Our reality as the One and only one deemed universal), with little concern for other ways of knowing and often no hint as to the existence and value of other possibilities of apprehending the world.

> We must go to learn from them [the colonists], the art of conquering without being in the right.
>
> Cheikh Hamidou Kane, *Ambiguous Adventure*

Twin Victories

In the cold light of winter 1991, a decade before the fall of the Twin Towers, television publics around the world were treated with a deluge of well-subsidized war-deploying images from the golden Arabian Desert. Fresh activities across the extensive theater of war operations were supposedly "zapped live" into our living room through a twenty-four-hour news network. As the nonstop cheerleading, military-glorified coverage was boasting the end of the war in the month of March, millions of Americans who tuned in to their television sets to follow the daily and hourly montage of the programmed Gulf War witnessed the most amazing dual claim to victory. It was one of those moments difficult to forget in media reportage. Until then, until this phase of double victory, a false transparency in the war was promoted and viewers were lured into thinking that, despite the news' full dependency on the Pentagon, what they heard via TV correspondents' reports on site was the unfolding of war-related scenes in real time, neither pre-edited nor precensored—in other words, military planning as media reality. As the airwaves were filled with talks about the war drawing to an end thanks to the swift "victory" of the American-led coalition forces, and as the mainstream media were busy praising and cheering the glorious results of Operation Desert Storm, the televised news surreptitiously showed images of Iraqi people celebrating their own "victory" of the war.

Since the "war" itself went largely *unseen*, "real time" TV coverage of the event was then losing itself in a host of trifling speculations, personal accounts, and technical details, providing relentless images of meaningless instantaneous television information. What the public got were techniques of war processing, and what they saw once the air campaign moved to the ground campaign was a carefully filled Absence: since the press was *not allowed to see* what was happening, for fear they would report atrocities committed by our troops as during the war in Vietnam, "embedded" journalists living with the troops ended up reporting on themselves struggling with the odd physical and psychological conditions of desert acclimatization. Raising the stakes, playing up the tension, and hyping every piece of information released by the US government, they speculated on the turn of events as they randomly bore witness to soldiers' routine activities. The same statements, the same visuals were recycled from one news channel to another. Anticipation formed the core of their war reporting and the public was kept in a state of adrenaline surge, sanguine about what *was likely to happen in the immediate or near future* and swooning over the cool power of technology on display. In the move toward smarter, computerized fighting, the affective impact of warfare took over its operational force, as all focus was on the *strategic production of war* in its building-up of force via the parade of high-tech-looking weapons.

Endlessly replayed was the same footage of Iraqi soldiers surrendering, which showed them entrenched in the desert, apparently dazed, confused, or grateful, emerging from creases of the land and hidings in the sand, sometimes waving a piece of white cloth, giving in largely without a fight, and hence stripped of their role as real combatants. White, the color of emptiness, viewed in war contexts as the color of no nation, or of neutrality, submission, and defeat, strangely also affirmed itself in this no-real-war scenario as the color of nonparticipation. By not fighting and turning their back in response to the parade of power, the soldiers seemingly denied their American adversary the opportunity to fight and win as real victors, thereby deflating the glory of the latter's force and ultimately "deactivating" the TV war.

Emptily, the commented televised sequences repeated themselves, while much of the action of the war took place beyond the gaze of the camera. The public got a view of the wreckage only once the pounding from the air was over. But, far from conveying the glory of liberation, the procession of burned Iraqi vehicles and incinerated bodies famously dubbed "turkey shoot" on the "highway of Death" led widely to public revulsion, as with all scenes of carnage. (This footage of the trapped forces withdrawing from Kuwait along the road to Basra seemed to have fallen through the cracks of censorship, for all outtakes of the war likely to show the bombing of bewildered and helpless Iraqi soldiers being graphically "blown to pieces" by unseen attackers as a mass execution rather than a war were never released by the military.)[5] It was amid this rerun footage of mutual indignity that viewers were also exposed to flashes of images from the Arab televised news showing jubilating Iraqis and elated youth making peace signs to the camera upon receiving news of *their victory*, while incredulous, the US reporter's voice briefly stated how, in proclaiming victory on his side, Saddam Hussein continued to mislead his people.

A Legacy of Inflation

The effect was stupefying for all parties involved—those affiliated with the ones being scorned as well as those associated with the ones doing the scorning. The overkilled TV buildup was for naught, and the whole event could be seen as a tragic farce. For both sides, the much-feared tiger turned out to be a mere paper tiger. It looked as if the oversized military power was running after its own shadow, with no real adversary in sight. Caught in the very game of power he initiated, the Giant has been led by a trumped-up threat to show off his might and is lured into a ghostly war, reacting to a danger of his own creation and fighting a projection of his own fear. To paraphrase and readapt the fatal ending of a well-known children's classic, it may be said further, that while the toad was strategically swelling itself to death to size up with the cow, the latter, too eager to win, immediately took the swelling for the "only thing that matters" and, in fear of losing the match, was driven competitively to puff itself up to overblown, destructively suicidal proportions.

Information and disinformation seemed to go hand in hand, and it was difficult to tell in the thick of raised Storm dust which side of the two warring parties was winning the race in reveling in delusions. After all, it was during the gray predawn hours of January 17, 1991, that the United States–led forces, involving a broad coalition of nations, attacked Iraq in what came to be known as the Persian Gulf War. In this conflict—also called the American War, the General's War (Bernard Trainor), "a sort of in-house TV war" (Robert Fisk), "total television," or more radically, the No-War (Jean Baudrillard)—war itself is in crisis, having lost its meaning and credibility. A ghostly war, despite the exorbitant cost in taxpayer's dollars, the blow on our Bill of Rights, and the tragedy in human lives. A fake, deceptive war, whose long-term consequences continue to wreak havoc, fully registering in the way we define "American interests" today and relate to the world.

On parade were two shows of force, two bluffs, and two "victories." With the Iraqi media claiming victory for President Saddam Hussein, Baghdad Radio trumpeted: "The allies of Satan and its accursed leader have been taught a lesson" (BBC, February 28, 1991). "We won! We won!" Hussein said, firing a pistol into the air to celebrate, when the cease-fire left him and his men in power. He then took the opportunity to reiterate that "we will never lower our heads as long as we live" (a position he defiantly kept until the very end, until when he was hanged). Ten years later, in an address to his people to mark the tenth anniversary of the conflict, Saddam Hussein provocatively recalled the "victory over enemies" of the Arab world in the 1991 Gulf War, which he saw as a battle between "those who made Satan their protector" and those "who had God as their protector." While he emphasized "the will to defend right against falsehood" and the need for his country to remain "unyielding to exploitation," Deputy Prime Minister Tariq Aziz confirmed, in a televised speech, that his country was stronger than ever and that "we believe in what we said 10 years ago: We are victorious . . . . Victory can be achieved through the strategic results of any confrontation, and we are confident that we gained victory in that struggle, which lasted 10 years and is still going on" (CNN, January 17, 2001).

The parallel "victory" shows surreptitiously broadcast on US TV appeared to have stunned American reporters in their representative, righteous views of right and wrong. Western media quickly dismissed such a claim for "victory" as a lie, a subterfuge, and a desperate attempt by Saddam Hussein to hide the stinging, face-losing blow inflicted upon him, whose dictatorship seemed to have thrived on shameless falsification. The claim was made, so it was said, because he needed to protect his image and to cover Iraq's military weakness vis-à-vis his neighboring countries, especially his former enemy Iran. But the lie was so blatant, the dictator's speech so obviously assertive and obstinately confident, that one could not help but puzzle over the very nature of victory—or, more specifically, of the two media-made, media-claimed victories.

Today, the question is all the more relevant with the uncanny reversal of war logic, as one recognizes across contexts how the same words, the same entrenched rhetoric, the same intransigent assertions and negations with the same lexicon of violence keep on shuttling across the Us-versus-Them divide, closing the gap between Evildoers and Gooddoers and interlinking the two adversary ex-heads of state in their howls for war victory. The resonances between Hussein and G. W. Bush in their hubristic war speeches and moral claims tell volumes about their mutual dependency for validation purposes. In their apparent enmity, they work as a team. Verbal memory seems to replay itself indifferently across opposing fundamentalisms. The Iraqi dictator may be dead, but his reiterated words of victory amid defeat still resonate in occupied territories, as they had found a staunch parallel and had taken on a new lease on life under Bush's imperial presidency.

In today's "new wars" where the transient line between winning and losing is opportunely muddled and opportunistically repositioned from within, there is no longer any loser. It is apparently only between victor and victor that the fight unfolds—all to the benefit of war and its longevity.

she, the wayfarer

All see and nohow on. What words for what then?

Samuel Beckett, *Worstward Ho*

It all begins again with the darkening hues of the evening. Walking on in dusk light, never quite leaving semi-darkness, slowly a line from Samuel Beckett comes in her way: "Ever tried. Ever failed. No matter. Try again. Fail again. Fail better . . . . The no face bad. The no hands bad. *The no*."[1] The night is young, a character of his play would say; *take heart*. Fail again, fail better. With one tone of gray surreptitiously passing into the other as the sun capsizes, the time has come when her eyes tell her far more about the scripts of our quaint reality when half closed than when wide open. But rather than merely going after what is easily recognizable—the prelaid, pre-envisioned tractable path—she's delving into what is windingly in the making.

The more she tries to see, the more her normal sight fails. Eyes dimming, sweat oozing out, tearing she wonders: Why this sudden flooding? Has the dis-ease taken over physically in its psychic charge, or is the body simply cleaning up as it goes on releasing? Patiently, writing grows unpredictable. Slowing down, taking detours, and widening out with small wild turns, often catching the writer by surprise as it goes about on its own. Walls keep on rising, blocking the view in untimely ways. There's no lack of ideas, however. These may neatly line up, all ready to go, but even when the space to be filled remains blank, they can't be forced in. Biding their time, they somehow find their way in, uninvited. As she waits for the words to surface while walking, she marvels at how many miles long it has taken her to enter that voice from afar, honed to the art of failing. Fail not to fail, fail as many can—and as no one dares.

No analysis can fill in the blank gaping at she who's staring outside-in-all-out blue. Unfinished and incomplete, the ephemeral voices quoted form a fabric of fragments thriving on the blanks of their beginnings and endings. The world on the move writes itself, setting in motion the rhythmic threads of cited words whose insights, instabilities, and resonances across oppositional contexts become part of the process of giving ear to both what the media perpetually recycle and the way they tell what they can tell: rumors, opinions, comments, reactions, judgments through imposed or internalized censorship.

With each step, the mind threatens to stray off, going literally berserk with the prattles of war as the body quietly takes in the dark energies of a victory-crazed world. Needless to say, when it comes to poison, don't ask who the enemy is, spit it out, vomit all of it. Don't let it spread and take effect inside while one tries to take revenge. In surviving mode, the mind goes blank. The waiting allows her to suspend and go on. Side by side, she and her Double thread on, steeped in silence. The walker speaks not, but one of them does anyway. Gray, in its infinite tones, does. It keeps watch as it discolors. Mercilessly, beginning over again and again, the mind tosses words around. It plans, amplifies, argues, blames, yells, and threatens, but also tricks, trips up, betrays its own kind, or else sets out to seduce, cajole, pardon, surrender, and even sing songs . . .

In differing keys.

Walking with the Disappeared

> The blue mountains are constantly walking . . . . If you doubt mountains' walking, you do not know your own walking.
>
> Dogen Zenji (quoting Daokai of Mt. Furong)

The heart goes on listening. Spectral voices re-emerge. "They die for a lie." So the signs on the road read. "Till they all come home," said a magnet stuck in between two bumper stickers of a mother's car. Or "Walk in Their Shoes," urged a public installation of shoes of all sizes from the dead in Iraq. Sadly, "it didn't really end"; "it never really was over," murmured disconcerted soldiers' voices in echo. While lying in the night of Baghdad, when neither beginning nor ending could be sighted, another voice recalls: "I kept hearing one of the squad leaders tell my team leader to help him ID the bodies of his guys." The Irish metaphor for the term "battle" comes in her way, notably showing a "web of men" killing one another and dying. A tangle of bodies, whose actions are primarily driven by pain, fear, terror, and the ominous presence of death—manifested in the immediate return to anonymity of the fallen bodies.

"It's this strange thing. He came home, but he's not home at all," commented a soldier's wife. "Murder is a crime. What's war?" asks a Women-in-Black placard. "Stop torture," cried a banner dropped above a freeway. "Don't tap my phone. The eye is watching you and others"; or "Defend the constitution," "End the violence," "No Love in Occupation," read other banners unfurled on the go. All around the country and across nations at war, CODEPINK messages read: "Mothers Say No to War" for "No War Is a Good War"; "Women Say Pull Out"; "Stop the Next War Now!"; "No Spying"; "Diplomacy Not Drones"; "Ground the Drones!"; "Surge: Big Mistake," or else, "Democracy Is a Feminist Agenda," and "Peace Is Creative." While a broad cross section of Americans continue to voice their resistance to the war mind-set, and military moms no longer shy away from raising questions loud and clear in public, on the other side of the battle line, fresh enemies are being continuously created, who vow to match insanity with greater insanity. Such are, for example, these vows by an Iraqi soldier (Mohammad Sidique Khan) on an Arab TV channel: "Just as they made rivers of blood flow in our countries, we will make volcanoes of anger erupt in their countries . . . . Our words are dead until we give them life with our blood."

Meanwhile, three dots linking many blanks . . . History yawns.

> They all lie in a row,
> No line between them,
> I recognize that each one was a soldier.
> But which is mine? Which one is another's?

> This man was White now he's become Red.
> Blood has reddened him.
> This one was red now he's become White.
> Death has whitened him.
>
> Marina Tsvetaeva, "Swan's Encampment"

Stories of wounded humanity are told many times over, and yet they remain illimitable. Traders of blood. Blood of death, blood of life. Crazed, chaotic, enraged blood. When the invisible fluid becomes visible, when it starts boiling to the surface, hot-headed leads rapidly to hard-headed, and not only seeing red asserts itself as the common symptom, but everything around feels enflamed as if ready to incinerate any itinerant who happens to venture a bit too close to the heat. Suddenly verbs, adverbs, nouns, adjectives, and especially conjunctions—all the linking verbal devices—lose their reason of being, and one after another, they go missing on the screen. No, not mere words of vengeance but *the vengeance of words on the move* . . . Too much time at the machine and the world itself turns into a portable computer screen, always prey to the white light of disappearance and forgetfulness and hence likely to be lambasted at the slightest sign of *failure* to respond.

In frustration, disruption prevails: a casualty writing necessarily suffers when the words that guide, the language that arrives, are accordingly those of fragmentation, spacing, and awaiting. Beneath the Almighty's foot: nothing. No master narrative, no totality pre-exists that cannot be pulled apart and returned to the blank beginning or ending of the fragment. A gap, a lacunae: manifested in the loss not so much of the ever-growing threads of thought pursued as of what tightly connects them to one another so as to keep them from falling away. A gap, a break: experienced quiescently whenever the mind subsides, letting stillness emerge from the cracks of discontinuity and allowing writing to find its unsought rhythm—the feel from down below, at the tip of one's toes.

The time of uncertainties is also a time of daily bewilderment over what matters most to civilized people. As the hyperpower has been struck in its heartland and revenge has become the deceiving verb of the day, terror continues to stalk the world, intimately, indefinitely. One is reminded of the animal energy that makes a man bark ferociously every time a stranger or a foreign-looking passer happens to walk by. History seems to be nothing else but conflicts of unstable bloods. War after war, and all these "war on . . ." and "war against . . ." as if life is all about killing—and lying on top. Exposure to the unnamable in sorrow and suffering leaves the mind at a loss, grieving for the undead and reeling from the senseless loss of blood in the world's hemorrhage. Life appears then in a string of less-words: visionless, stateless, homeless, hu-man-less, and, above all, heartless. The hope of getting somewhere for a better life hangs by a fragile red thread. The world one runs away from also runs away from oneself. Knowing not who isn't the *refugee* in today's political conscience, one mourns the loss of one's own ability to dwell: *on earth, under the sky, before the divinities, among mortals, with things*—in cyberspace.

When millions of people walked for peace in February and March 2003 in cities around the world, an old Gandhian saying resurfaced on their banners: "An eye for an eye and the world goes blind." The giant wave traveled across nations and the massive turnouts caught many practitioners of nonviolent resistance by surprise. Power of the people or sheer necessity to release the energy of a guilty conscience? On the one hand, the White House contemptuously dismissed the wave, saying it was only a puny stir within the silent majority, and our then commander-in-chief (G. W. Bush) happily used it in his public reactions to legitimize his war—invoking antiwar rallies as examples of exactly the kind of freedom of speech enabled by democracy, for which the United States was fighting on behalf of the Iraqi people. History is caught flagrantly repeating itself as the same argument as the one much exploited during the war in Vietnam prevails: "the great silent majority of my fellow Americans" (Richard M. Nixon) versus a "noisy minority" (or "nervous nellies" who break ranks, as Lyndon B. Johnson put it). On the other hand, failing can expose the system in its failures, and learning from failing remains a strong survival skill. The "failed movement to prevent the war" precisely showed "the crisis in our democracy, the crisis of the two-party system, the crisis of a dysfunctional opposition party,"[2] in which neither one nor two functions as such. Successes, like failures, come in cycles, and in every success, a failure already lies hidden. Indeed, what would a struggle be that neither puts itself at the risk of failing nor recognizes the possibility of failure? Despite all the frustration and the feeling of powerlessness, the walk for justice has massively gained in size, partly thanks to cybernauts' activism and the growing list of alliances among social movements and communities of peoples from all walks of life.

Circle of Love: Pink, White, and Black

> We're already walking around in a polyrhythmic kind of way. Music is an art form for recognizing the vibe that is the ground of life.
>
> Rachel Bagby

On March 8, 2003, International Women's Day, the White House was unexpectedly given a color and encircled in pink. Over ten thousand participants came to celebrate a global peacemaking force initiated by a women's grassroots movement. While the administration's color-coded alerts have been based on classified degrees of manufactured fear, the CODEPINK alert, which calls for people to "wage peace," takes as its base of action kindness, compassion, transnational alliances, as well as *humor and creativity*. The color—a seemingly universal girly color—may at first appear as heavily gender-coded and harmlessly decorous. To resist an administration on the brink of war then, women stood up in PINK, reclaiming the diversity of a hue they have long discarded to make their statement for peace. As with all stereotypes whose taken-for-granted stories fall apart upon scrutiny, it suffices to dwell

longer with the functions and affective impact of pink to realize anew its transformative potential. Pink comes in many tints and tones, and as long as it manifests itself, the question remains, politically: Which pink? How, when, and where. "With fire in our bellies and love in our hearts," the Women in Pink said, they are rising up—across borders—against bloodshed and destruction. Laugh while you act. Laugh in between shouts. March, protest, provide if you can, and care. Pink, in its multiple tints and hues, has undergone many trials. Gathering both the male and female energies of white and red—the colors of purity and passion or of new beginnings and strength—pink in its deeper shades has proven to be most effective (in prisons and police cells for example) in defusing aggressive and destructive tendencies arising from fear and friction. Which pink? And how pink?

What does mature pink feel like?

Feminism is the new funny, so it is said by those involved. The movement's manifold activities differ according to circumstances and contexts. They run anywhere from the usual acts of civil disobedience—massive die-in, teach-in, sit-in, chanting, marching, and holding vigils for peace (one of which lasted four months in front of the White House)—to wearing pink of many shades, festive hats, and bright gloves; delivering pink slips to the administration's highest-ranking warlords who fail to serve the people; distributing certificates of shame to the Dirty Dozen, those congressmen and -women who had the worst pro-war voting records; dressing as pink nurses and doctors for peace to demand healthcare instead of warfare; sending a Pink Badge of Courage to Jimmy Carter for his efforts in actively seeking a solution to the conflict between Israel and Palestine; visiting the memorials of Lincoln, Roosevelt, and Jefferson in pink party clothes, while chanting and holding dead Iraqi civilians' photos; moving in vibrant parades in front of the Justice Department, the Internal Revenue Service, and the Capitol, asking to "Restore the Constitution"; paying tribute to mothering around the world on Mother's Day or to fathering on Father's Day, while fundraising to alleviate the dire conditions of Iraqi women and of the millions of Iraqi refugees; and, last but not least, offering workshops, eight-week-long activist training and action camps at their

DC Pink House during the summer. Despite the vicious attacks it has undergone (including that of nurturing Red) CODEPINK has, since its creation in November 2002, become a worldwide network of workers-walkers for peace and social justice, with an impressive and creatively expansive range of program areas (including peace delegations to Iraq, Israel-Palestine, North and South Korea, and Burma), and with 250 active, decentralized, local groups around the country and the world.

A culture manifests itself in the way it manifests love.

Ooka Makoto

The power of Pink as initiated by women in the United States seems to carry at its core a long history predating their formation. It calls to mind the struggles of bereaved mothers and grandmothers around the world, such as the renowned cases of the Women of Juarez and Chihuahua cities in Mexico and of Las Madres de Plaza de Mayo in Argentina. Here, in a reverse scenario of color energies, the silent walk around the plaza, started on a historical Thursday afternoon in April of 1977 by a group of fourteen mothers in search of their missing sons and daughters, and it has continued ever since to become a vital part of Argentina's modern history. The recurring scene is at once familiar and strange: to challenge their government, women young and old persist in walking quietly together every week for half an hour, wearing white bandanas to represent the diapers of their missing babies; covering their heads in white scarves to symbolize the doves of peace; or dressed in dark colors with conspicuous plain-white-gloved hands as a powerful symbol of their fight against the so-called Dirty War (La Guerra Sucia 1976–1983, a term much contested, which a court of law replaced by that of "genocide").

Las Madres, whose sensuously striking marches for over three decades are known to the world, were thus encircling and dotting the Plaza de Mayo with white signs of motherhood, peace, and integrity, right in front of the vividly pink presidential palace in downtown Buenos Aires. Although practical reason explains it as a vernacular technique of wall finish that mixes paint with cow's blood, wasn't La Casa Rosada's color also said to have been chosen by President Domingo Faustino Sarmiento to defuse political tensions as it symbolically blended the red and white colors of his nation's official opposing parties? It was in plain sight of the Pink House that Las Madres made their silent suffering public. Learning to deal with lies, verbal abuses, dog attacks, and tear gas, and outwitting the police who worked at breaking their demonstration, they continued to care, search, put their lives at risk, and walk. It was their love, courage, and steadfast endurance in sticking single-mindedly to their one initial question "Where is my child?" that ended up changing Argentina's political course by setting an unusual precedent for other political dissents to make themselves heard—until the military government itself toppled.

Today the mothers' walk reaches far and wide, attracting visitors from around the world. In a much-advertised tour of Southern Exploration, tourists are informed that "if you arrive at the plaza on a Thursday afternoon during your Argentina tours, you may meet Las Madres and buy T-shirts and other items that support their efforts." It is significant that the walks continue to happen around the obelisk at the Plaza de Mayo—a place at the heart of the country where Argentinian Independence was proclaimed in 1810. In fact, Las Madres's work has not reached an end under the rule of the civilian government for, although the military admits to nine thousand cases of unaccounted kidnapping, until there is a full accounting of the missing, the weekly marches will persevere. During the dark period of the Dirty War, thousands of citizens vanished—tortured, imprisoned, or exiled—and among them were many with no involvement in any political activity. The whereabouts of these *desaparecidos*—the "Disappeared"—remain largely unknown and the search for the bodies of the thirty thousand killed continues. Las Madres as a struggle that has grown in size and in scope now involves not only the Línea Fundadora (Founding Line), whose members keep to their original goal of locating the remains of their children and punishing those responsible; but also the Asociación Madres de Plaza de Mayo, whose members carry forward the political agenda of their abducted children, and the Asociación Civil Abuelas de Plaza de Mayo, whose members further trace the whereabouts of their grandchildren—the offspring of the disappeared—so they may be returned to their birth families.

> going and coming
> their traces disappear
> but they never
> forget their path.
>
> Dogen Zenji

The call of the Disappeared continues to haunt and move women around the world. It gains in new resonances as it spreads and intensifies across the continent, leading the way to the Mexican cities of Juarez and Chihuahua—the killing fields for young women and the site of over four hundred unresolved femicides. On November 25, 2002, more than a thousand women clothed in black marched through Mexico City, mourning the deaths of the innocent female victims and protesting the indifference, or rather, the collusion, of the authorities involved in the investigation. More recently, on International Women's Day 2008, mothers of femicide victims and their supporters again took to the streets. Objecting anew to the inefficient response of the authorities and demanding an end to such "a climate of impunity," they marched, filing past the cross monument raised in honor of murdered women at one of the entrances to Ciudad Juarez from El Paso. Despite the promises of public officials and the rooting out of large amounts of suspects, some of whom were policemen, more disappeared bodies continue to turn up in the desert. Again, it was through the tireless digging of the mothers searching for their daughters and the tenacious struggle for justice of the victims' families that national and international attention was drawn to the situation, which governments on both side of the US-Mexico border have been trying to cover up.

Each time a new victim emerges to visibility, the wounds open anew and the trauma deepens among terrified mothers and relatives of the disappeared. "When are we going to see an end to femicide in this region?" they agonize. Despite the horrific nature of these crimes (about a fourth of the victims were kidnapped, raped, and strangled in a similar way), hundreds of cases of femicide remain unresolved a decade and a half after the first grisly murder spree that started in 1993, and only one thing seems certain with the situation: women are in danger on the streets of Ciudad Juarez, and the fear of carnage gripping society has spread farther south, into Chihuahua City. In Juarez, thousands of women live in terror in shantytowns and work in *maquiladoras*, the factories on the US border that produce for export, mainly destined for the United States.

Whether carried out in 1993–1996, 2001–2003, or 2008, the slayings coincided with violent upheavals within the ranks of organized crime. Here both sexually tortured and killed young women and male victims of organized crime often turned up in clandestine graveyards at the same location. Again, the May 2008 e-mails and cell phone warnings of spectacular bloodbath on public thoroughfares, as well as rounds of death threats against women's rights activists, members of Juarez's Nuestras Hijas de Regreso a Casa (May Our Daughters Return Home), came amid an unprecedented wave of narco-violence in the area. With body counts increasing (although no two sources agree on the death toll of the young women) and little protection from the government, Ciudad Juarez, the bustling city across the border from El Paso has become a festering wound in itself. It has come to represent the "contact sore" between two mutual corruptions and exploitations, two cultures *unequally* bound in ruthless material production, plunging headlong into social regression through an economical border-system that ends up devouring itself.

The Red-Blue Divide

Again, during the 2004 presidential elections of the United States, the banner-loving media resorted to an astonishing image of the two Americas. On the evening of November 2, watchers huddled with friends and neighbors in front of television sets had a unique opportunity to witness the Red invasion minute by minute of the US map. Despite the prevalent hope for change, even if slight or lamed, the divide turned out to be even more intensified than with the previous elections: red swept across the South, the Great Plains, and most of the Rocky Mountain West, while blue remained confined to New England, the Mid-Atlantic, and the West Coast. The color line mattered more than ever and it was, still is, on this line that the future of the Free world is being bet.

Later, bemoaning the fading of blue, a *Time* magazine quote read: "In now standard red-vs-blue political short hand, the high court lacks a deep blue liberal in the mold of, say, Thurgood Marshall or even Harry Blackmun. It lost another gradation last week: Sandra Day O'Connor's neutral (or flickering) gray." The forecast then was for more red, but nobody could imagine how gaudily red the political shade of the country went on looking to the outside world.

In the midst of a historical presidential race that would help determine the color outcome of the new patriotism, readers of this same magazine were regularly treated with a page featuring the results of the campaign on a scorecard that told us what the winning hue of the week was: red or blue, depending of the performance of the candidates for each round. But as the media denounced, it did happen that a reliable red state like Colorado underwent a mixing-color process and ended up in a hybrid camp.

The 2000 color-coded electoral map was used to cast the United States as a fifty-fifty, bipolar nation whose political divide seemed to have hardened with time. But, at the end of spring 2008, as Barack Obama was about to win the Democratic nomination, the American electoral battlefield reopened with hot questions concerning the way the US map may end up looking in its color dominance. A wrap-up by the Economist reads: "Under George Bush, red states were red and blue states were blue. This year the map could be drenched in purple."

thriving on a D-stroll

A Hole in the Heart

> The characteristic of many modern illnesses is that they are cooling, debilitating, hardening and chronic . . . . In our society, you're not well paid for having a warm heart but for being smart. We have to be cool and efficient and above all we must not show too much warmth and enthusiasm. Those who do are quickly considered a little nuts or over the top. It's a sign of our times.
>
> Oncologist Robert Gorter, on the healing power of love in cancer treatment

"Bring Them Back Alive." As they march with these words embroidered on their kerchiefs, Las Madres feel very close at heart to their children. In the Mothers' circle of love over death, it is ultimately the search for life that prevails. The power of the Disappeared lies in the uncertainty of their deaths and the very elusiveness of their whereabouts. Those under threats sometimes survive; those thought to have vanished into invisibility bide their time to re-emerge into visibility; and, rather than appearing as emotionally wretched bystanders, those mourning in public have empowered themselves to become suddenly a moving force that extends into the world. The mere act of grieving collectively and the courage of taking a national trauma on a regular walk reveals a silent potency, a dormant antipotency, and a diffuse agency that remain ungovernable by nature.

The Mother effect has a humanizing impact that continues, through love, to inspire a kind of mad courage across borders and nations. Again and again they dig in the earth and search there where no one in their ordinary mind believes it is realistic to go any further. Known to endure through highs and lows, mother love enables the ordinary person to do the impossible. Refusing to give in to physical threats and other intimidations, she remains dauntless, with no concern for her own safety. Such continue to be the situations of women in many parts of the world, who, by the sheer force of love for their lost ones, have learned to turn grief into struggle—a quietly persistent work for justice and truth that, more often than not, looks like a beating of one's head against the wall. The Tiananmen Mothers' costly act of remembering in China is an example. In their call for a process of truth and reconciliation, mother courage demands not only apologies from the government for their children's deaths, and a full investigation and public accounting of the shootings, but also *the right to mourn peacefully in public*, to accept humanitarian aid from inside and outside China, the ending of persecution of victims related to the dead, and the release of all people still in prison for their role in the 1989 protests.

Formed by a growing network of some 150 families who had lost their sons, daughters, and other relatives, the group was officially launched in 2000. It is led by Nobel Peace Prize–nominee Ding Zilin, a retired university professor of Beijing's People's University (initially a party training school), whose only son was among the first to be killed by government troops during the slaughter of workers and residents that occurred not far from Tiananmen Square (in the adjacent avenues). The story of the teenager's death turns out to be at once painfully common in its mother-son dynamics and strangely telling in its political symbolism—a troubling foretoken. On the night of June 3, 1989, Jiang Jielian was said to have left the family home in defiance of the curfew and of his mother's insistent plea. Eyewitnesses told Ding that as he made his way to Tiananmen Square, Jiang was shot in the back, through the heart, by the People's Liberation Army troops and left to bleed to death. Since then, six times, the mother has attempted suicide.

Despite the world press coverage of the bloodbath and of the troops and tanks moving in to clear the student-led demonstrations in Beijing's Tiananmen Square, despite the local witnesses testifying to soldiers killing and injuring of a large number of unarmed civilians—workers, activists, and students (two to three thousand as reported by the Chinese Red Cross), officials claimed that the massacre did not happen. According to the official version on Chinese TV on June 4, the soldiers were simply defending the capital from a "handful" of "hooligans," and no one was killed. Former defense minister Chi Haotian, for example, shrewdly affirmed in the United States: "Not a single person lost his life in Tiananmen Square." Needless to say, the question that inevitably arose with the discrepancy between the seen and the said was: What kind of puny-numbered "ruffians" or "hooligans" would require such a Goliathan troop deployment? Indeed, Tiananmen Square might not have been the exact killing grounds that night, for the slaughter, which did happen nearby, was not specifically aimed at the students (despite the deaths and the merciless crackdown on them in the aftermath) but rather at the dissident intelligentsia and working class—a popular uprising that blocked the path of the People's Liberation Army on its way to Tiananmen Square.[1] Many people of different walks of life had joined the demonstration in the dark. Many had been outraged at the government massacre. But when the lights came back on, no one dared to claim any involvement in the demonstrations.[2]

Virtual Monument Censored

The government's denials were cleverly deceptive, and the small rhetorical nuance allowed them to hold their ground righteously over the years, hoping to cover up the massacre with a series of oppressive measures—arrest, material confiscation, extensive intimidation, arbitrary detention, and excessive sentencing of those involved. Overnight, the student protests changed name; what was initially called "a patriotic movement" by the governmental media later became a "riot" in the *People's Daily* newspaper editorial. Shifting language so as to legitimate violence is a common practice of oppression. Ding Zilin, who, in her own words, "uses her tears to wash her face" everyday for a decade long, not only refused to be silenced by such a maneuver but she also never stopped challenging the government's claim that the prodemocracy movement was "counterrevolutionary." Even as they sought to strike a private deal by saying instead that "all the people who died were unintentionally wounded," Ding diligently worked at exposing the deceitful nature of their denials and has been collecting the names of those shot dead by the troops. The number she was able to document on her own has reached at least 203 by June 2012—a hard-gained finding she considered to be only the tip of the iceberg. The government has forbidden hospitals and crematoriums to issue any figures, making it quasi impossible for investigations to come closer to the true number of deaths, which Ding estimates to be approximately three thousand.[3] And so, the search continues.

The June Fourth event's victims—whether departed, detained, tortured, or socially discarded—continue to dwell in people's hearts. Twenty-three years after, on June 4, 2012, amid a sea of candles and a rallying call for justice, an estimated 180,000 people in Hong Kong are said to have attended the annual vigil to commemorate the Tiananmen crackdown. Given by the organizers, such a number has more than tripled the 55,000 estimated in 2007; it certainly speaks to the steadily growing (rather than dwindling) interest the event has been generating. (Mainstream narratives claim that Chinese youths either have forgotten it or have no consciousness of it, since they have never seen photographs or read reports about it. Thus erased from collective memory, Tiananmen remains unknown history in mainland China.) The scale tolerated of such a public commemoration within China's borders remains unique, for the broad spectrum of mourners attracted ranges from the elderly directly affected who came every year to the young generation born after the event who volunteer their services to "never forget June Fourth" (unsurprisingly, Internet access to both terms, "never forget" and "six four," were blocked by the authorities on this date) to stand up for their rights and contribute to the democratization of China's political system.

Nowadays, hundreds of thousands of people reportedly persist in holding their own commemorations for the Tiananmen victims, despite Beijing's censorship and efforts to suppress its history. Resisting government efforts to erase the nation's memory, Murong Xuecun, a novelist, blogger, and former student of the China University of Political Science and Law who announced his intentions to turn himself over to the authorities after the arrest of his three friends (a former researcher at the Chinese Academy of Social Sciences, a professor of the Beijing Film Academy, and a human rights attorney) on May 6, 2014 in Beijing, remarked: "Beijing has been in denial for 25 years . . . . On the surface the government appears stronger than ever, with over 80 million Communist Party members, millions of soldiers, and nearly $4 trillion in foreign exchange reserves—yet it is actually so fragile that its leaders lose sleep when a few scholars meet and talk in a private home."[4]

It was in a similar spirit that a few years earlier, on May 28, 2008—the eve of the nineteenth anniversary of the Tiananmen Square crackdown—despite years of repeated harassment from the authorities—phone tapping, close surveillance, detainment, and house arrest preventing them from holding any public memorial or protest—Ding and other Tiananmen Mothers launched the group's official website, created as a virtual monument in honor of the 188 dead. The site brings to the public the fruit of the group's nineteen years of painstaking documentation. It features two maps, one showing the route along which the killing took place and the other indicating the hospital locations where the victims spent their last moments. The site lists the names and bios of the dead, as well as the eyewitness accounts and testimonials from members of the group on their tortuous ordeal. The Mothers, as Ding voiced, had hoped the information given on the web would help both educate a younger generation of students likely to have forgotten the event and "awaken the conscience of the Chinese authorities."

To the *audacity* of the Tiananmen Mothers' *hope*, the government's hard-liners issued a swift response. Only three hours after its launch, the Mothers' website was blocked in China, just when Beijing was scrupulously working at improving its image to the world by relaxing (albeit just a trifle) its grip on the press and Internet censorship in the wake of the earthquake in Sichuan Province. As Ding assessed, "The Communist Party relies on two things to rule China: lies and the police."[5] She realistically noted that she may not live to see the day when the officials would revisit the Tiananmen event, but "what is important is the process, and we have tried our best. Since we have already started, we cannot give up. We must press on because we have done no wrong."[6] No wrong, no regret. As common sense decrees, beware of the blind power of the blade, for those sticking their neck out risk having their head chopped off. What hope is there that the callous system will do anything other than continue indifferently to call the protest a "counterrevolutionary riot," deny the full extent of the slaughter, cover up the deaths, and ostracize those who dare to speak out? What conscience can the Tiananmen Mothers expect to awaken in their documentation? Ding Zilin reminds us that what the students and the people opposed, that led to the June Fourth crisis, was *corruption*. "The people tried to influence things. The government not only didn't accept this, but brought about a massacre," said Ding, who vowed on, "We'll never waver . . . . we will use our letter, and use the language of the relatives of those who were killed to continue their legacy."[7]

So long as the authorities keep on covering it up with minor changes in the official version, the June Fourth event (an outcome of the prodemocracy April-June–1989 movement) will remain a gaping wound in the history of China. Every year Ding's phone and Internet connections were cut off in the days around this date, but no matter what . . . We'll never waver, the Mothers say. Anger may wane, but fires survive. We must press on. Each, no more than a simple messenger of hope, a current of mother love, and a lamp that lights up in lost, forgotten corners. We cannot give up. As with those fun candles that never fail to provoke peals of laughter among children and adults alike, try to blow them out and they'll relight all by themselves . . .

Miles of Strangeness

> Walking forward does not obstruct walking backward
> Walking backward does not obstruct walking forward
> Walking beyond and walking within are both done on water.
> All mountains walk with their toes on all waters and
> splashes there.
>
> Dogen Zenji

With every step, the world comes to the walker. The Disappeared live on.

The more a government tries to sanitize yesterday's, today's, or tomorrow's reality, the more profoundly insecure its system proves to be. Fear breeds fear, distrust engenders distrust. Discrimination, distributive injustice, selective dispossession of rights and of dignity may be said to characterize the daily battle the government carries against its own people in the streets, in their homes and businesses, in schools, subways, buses, and airports, in virtual reality and cyberspace—just about anywhere they can get them through unconstitutional, often unlawful attacks, seizures, and detentions.

The problem is all along, very close to home. Despite the harsh criticisms voiced toward the crazed dreamers who work with their own hands and feet and dare to believe in their own force to change things, it is the trust born among strangers walking together and their propulsive generosity that makes a difference. When issues lived in public turn life into a carnival of regenerative potentials, fun easily mingles with fear, and the spirit of new alliances on the making prevails over that of crippling isolation and alienation. The democratic project ultimately feeds off the resistance of the "noisy minority," whose challenge to the so-called silent majority and its self-proclaimed representatives contributes to keeping democracy alive. The call of the Disappeared from afar is a constant reminder of the battle for truth and justice at home, around civilians lost to sight under similar diets of humiliation: blanket detentions, random searches, racial profiling, and arbitrary prosecution of those who look suspect to our eyes. The application of different standards to different people, the attack on foreign- and queer-looking members of our society, their secret and indefinite confinement, have led to an oddly regressive social phenomenon:

That of the disappeared in the land of the brave and the free.

"The Days San Francisco Stood Still," as the *Bay Guardian* put it (March 26, 2003), were the days when a series of massive marches, some drawing nearly a hundred thousand participants, led to the shutting down of the city, whose loss was estimated to be in the millions of dollars. Protests against the war spread in some eight hundred cities around the world and the peace march in Rome involving about three million people was remembered as the largest antiwar rally in history. Rather than being limited to specific ruling figures and nations, the audience it now addresses is often of global dimension and the walk simultaneously picked up by participants across communities has become a world manifestation. Each step taken is a link, in the history of walking, with those who took the act into the political sphere vowing, as did a woman widely known to the world as Peace Pilgrim, that she will remain "a wanderer until mankind has learned the way of peace." Walk she did, 25,000 miles on foot and beyond, until her death, dropping her ordinary name and safer existence as an American "farm girl" to become a walker among walkers. What may sound like a romantic vow in this age of cynicism turned out to be an act of life endurance and resistance. Alone she went, together she moved, appealing for world disarmament, for freedom, and for the sheer pleasure of feeling oneself alive.

With globalization and ecology enforcing the reality of mutual dependence, the concept of Us versus Them makes as little sense as that of setting up one's left hand against one's right hand. And yet . . . "In older times, when peoples lived separately, and more or less independently from one another . . . the concept of war, the idea of an enemy to destroy and of a victory to gain for your side was a real possibility," said the Dalai Lama in his untiring attempts to discourage his people from calling the Chinese their enemy, but "today, the world is different. The survival, success and progress of each are tightly related to the well being of others . . . . destruction of your enemy is, in reality, destruction of yourself."[8] The walk is the tie that binds. As strangers meet, memory and stories grow in size and in scope: always larger than one's own and yet made vibrant through one's singular experience. When judging the impact of Peace marches, there's a tendency to focus exclusively on the receiving end—the general public, the government, the local and national institutions under scrutiny, the individuals in charge—rather than focusing also on the performing end—the walk and the walkers themselves. As an inveterate wanderer puts it, "only long miles of strangeness can lead us to our home" (Kenneth White). Thus, in the midst of a general "Who cares if your own kind dies?" someone strides on, like this other doer, Doris Haddock, a.k.a. Granny D., the eighty-nine-year-old great-grandmother who walked across America to gather support for campaign finance reform. Spreading doubts about the big D-word in a way that resonated with a broad section of her fellow people, she remarked: "It is said that democracy is not something we have, but something we do. But right now we cannot do it because we cannot speak. We are shouted down by the bullhorns of big money."[9]

Light Weight

Toward the end of his journey as an invincible victor, having reaped from innumerable conquests, the aged emperor Kublai Khan, as Italo Calvino envisions him in his *Invisible Cities*, proudly watches the boundless extension of his territories only to remark melancholically how, by growing needlessly too far outside and neglecting to grow within itself, his empire is being crushed by its own weight—the weight of walls and towers, abundant riches and ponderous hierarchies. "*The triumph over enemy sovereigns has made us the heirs of their long undoing,*" notes the voice of consciousness.[10] Form and emptiness constitute the double facet of every reality; and when the coin is tossed up, it swirls down, showing on one side the empire as the sum of all possible acquisitions of wonders and revealing it on the other as endless, formless ruins. Growing wiser and shifting his interest away from weight, Khan then dreams of a city, which the moon has granted not only the power to grow infinitely but also the privilege of *growing in lightness.*

the mole's empire

> In this world
> we walk on the roof of Hell
> gazing at flowers.
>
> Kobayashi Issa

What has been recorded as a matter of a few sporadic happenings of our times can unfold its narrative unfittingly and stare inside out with unblinking eyes at the walker who dares to stride on when the road disappears. Once the path has gone up so high, to the very top of the mountain, there's nowhere else for it to go but down again. For those, like Calvino's Kublai Khan, who have experienced the crystal clarity of the mountaintop air, the descent may be quite lonely, but it is a descent fully assumed *in light-ness*. As the outer (no real outer) road leads to a dead end, the one extra step one stakes one's life on may prompt one to turn about radically and to thread that deeply neglected other road often called "inner" (no mere inner). With each step, time slows down and ripples out. Constantly turning is the one single movement of in and out: the further the involvement inward, the wider it opens outward onto the everyday vistas of existence.

The Other Victory

> The line dividing good and evil cuts through the heart of every human being.
>
> Alexander Solzhenitsyn

Winning by force and weight has its costs. "You Have the Watches, We Have the Time," said a *Newsweek* headline (October 2, 2011). The expression, often attributed to a captured Taliban fighter, was used to sum up the US-Afghanistan conundrum. Here, the insurgents were said to show no interest in numbers, statistics, or schedule (quantitative references dear to Western media's criteria of evaluation), for they were confident of the ultimate victory on their side: "Your watch's battery will run down, and its hands will stop. But our time in the struggle will never end. We will win."

Some time ago, as the quest for the man "somewhere out there"—al-Qaeda's "dark genius" (Osama bin Laden)—foundered for almost a decade, Afghanistan reappeared on the news during the last year of G. W. Bush's presidency as *this other war that's still not won*. More recently, it was claimed as the just war, the "war of necessity," whose focused, declared goal may be "to defeat al-Qaeda in Pakistan and Afghanistan and to prevent their return to either country in the future" (President Obama's speech on March 27, 2009) but whose latent objective is apparently also to turn these two countries into colonial outposts of the US empire. Mentioning al-Qaeda repeatedly continues to be the best way to sell the war at home. Already in the renewed mission by America and its allies, echoes could be heard of the sinking logic behind the "dumb war" or the "war of choice" in Iraq. Ironically, NATO's commander in Afghanistan did not hesitate to compare his troops' acting to that of a *powerful but stupid* bull lunging after insurgents.[1] The coalition forces and the government of Afghanistan had failed to win over the people they claimed to protect, and the fight against an opposition called "the Taliban" continues to be deadlier than ever, with casualties in the country exceeding those in Iraq since 2003. Again, the lack of credible partners in Afghanistan and Pakistan was convincingly invoked, and the failures have been widely blamed on Hamid Karzai's government installed by America in 2001 and ineluctably disqualified since then, in many British and American presses, as "untrustworthy," "unpopular," "inept, corrupt, and predatory."

Thus goes the unending replay of an old mind-set—*déjà vu, déjà su, déjà tu, déjà* . . . (Already seen, known, kept silent, already . . .). The longer the stay, the worse it smells. The war in Afghanistan "will not be quick," warned our president Obama, for unsurprisingly, the costs are expected to be high and the outcome uncertain. As the Western forces struggled to maintain their weak hold on the country, their ambitions conveniently scaled down and their aims became drastically more modest. "The generals need more troops," we were told; and of course, the military imperative has always been to win, not to lose a war. But despite the then-newly announced "clear, hold, build" AfPak strategy—meant to win Afghans' confidence and support—cautious analysts of the war came up with reports bearing titles such as: "NATO's Mission Impossible," "Afghanistan: The Growing Threat of Failure," "Losing Afghanistan?" "United States Bogged Down in Afghanistan," "Why the Taliban Are Winning—for Now," "From Saigon to Kabul," "Remember Vietnam?" or "Could Afghanistan Become Obama's Vietnam?" All sounded dreadfully familiar. Critics talked about a quagmire with a "muddled mission," of Obama's choice between being a "Failed War President or the Prince of Peace," and many also hastened to add such hackneyed affirmation as "victory is difficult but still possible." With the escalation of war, however, the mood remained bleak, for the size of the US force bred its own discontents, and the foreign troops were said to create more conflict than they could possibly quell.

More than ever, the analogy of Vietnam found its way back in war experts' analyses and the Afghanistan War has repeatedly been said to look fundamentally like the one in Vietnam. *Frontline* producers who went backstage in the war called what they uncovered "the Vietnam poltergeist," the specter of a war lost. Despite the president's pointed rejection of such an analogy (saying it "depends on a false reading of history"), the parallel of policy in Washington is said to be frightening, and "leaving Afghanistan is like leaving Vietnam." People hear distinct echoes of Vietnam in the Afghanistan War, and as they remember the tragedy and lessons of the war lost, they have come to state the evident: "It's all too easy to go into war but not so easy to get out." As in Iraq, the longer the foreign guests stay, the worse they smell to Afghans' noses. Afghans have undergone a serious "crisis of confidence," and as a villager in Paktia put it: "We're caught in the middle and we are sick of it."[2] When asked by a commander of a company of British troops whether he should fear the Taliban's force more than the commander's troops, an opium-poppy farmer in Afghanistan was said to have replied: "You will come down and fight, and you will win. But you will win only for one hour. Then you will go back to your base. The Taliban will return."[3] Due to steadily increasing resurgent violence, the growing illegal drug economy, and fragile state institutions, as of 2008, Afghanistan was ranked seventh in *Foreign Policy* magazine's index of *failed States*. Despite the widely declared Afghan victory, an overlooked and revived-for-replay war continues with no end in sight.

> After all, the man who officially started it all is theoretically gone
> We could declare victory, Toto, and head for home.
> But why do I think that, on this score, the malign wizard is likely to win?
>
> Tom Engelhardt, "Osama, Dead and Alive"

In a special report on al-Qaeda on July 19, 2008, the *Economist* asks the indelible question: "Winning or Losing?" The legend of the Western world's most wanted man, who dominated popular iconography since 9/11, told how in going underground, he left an awe-inspiring trail of militancy stretching from Afghanistan, Pakistan, and Iraq to Indonesia, North Africa, and Europe. The precise reach of his power remains indefinite. It took nearly a decade of manhunt, hundreds of thousands deaths in Afghanistan, Iraq, and elsewhere, and some trillions of dollars spent on counterterrorism before the United States got Osama bin Laden, the al-Qaeda leader wanted "dead or alive" by the Bush administration. Although bin Laden's messages on the Internet did not make headlines in the mainstream media in the last few years before his death, the man happily thrived online, issuing over two dozen video- and audio-taped messages to his followers, with doom-laden warnings to the West. Through shadow work, he subsisted, calling for attacks on enemy targets in the region and beyond. Slick propaganda on DVDs were said to flourish in Afghanistan, such as the one urging followers to carry on a "global jihad" against "oil-thieving Christian crusaders."

The *Economist*'s analysis emphasized, on the one hand, al-Qaeda's forte in using the tools of globalization to gather a networked movement around a single worldwide cause—jihad against infidel and evil

America—and, on the other hand, a hubristic America walking into a trap of its own making by invading Iraq, thus providing the jihadists with a popular cause against occupation in the heart of Muslim land. The analysis spoke of "the virtual caliphate of cyberspace" and of "a hydra-headed monster," which, cut down in Afghanistan, was growing back on Pakistan's borderlands.[4] Ironically enough, while al-Qaeda intended through its big and small victories to destabilize the West from within as well as sow discord between Western countries and their local allies, analysts of the West were betting on al-Qaeda's propensity to kill indiscriminately to aggravate further in-fights with "near enemies," leading ultimately to self-destruction. Meanwhile, the struggle against al-Qaeda's resurging threat continues. Both al-Qaeda and Taliban militants had made a strong comeback, on Afghan territory as well as from the Pakistan side. Mullah Omar had, in the past, promised "more Afghan war," declaring in one of his rare announcements (published in the Afghan Islamic Press in February 2008): "If foreign troops leave Afghanistan, that will be a victory for the people of Afghanistan."[5]

In today's battles across the world, if on the side of the occupying forces, "victory" is short lived and accordingly defined down with time—meaning, at most, preventing catastrophe—on the side of those fighting against occupation and colonization, victory remains defiantly linked to strategic outcomes. As long as battles à la David and Goliath persist, there will be claims for David-versus-Goliath victories and gleeful stories of heroism woven around them. The myth will continue to live on, often with sling and stone changing hands, and those playing David readily shifting role to become Goliath in the rise to power. In resorting to all kinds of subterfuges and excuses to justify their invasions, modern Goliath nations tend to pick on those smaller nations and communities they know they can easily dominate militarily, to make a show of their invincibility and fulfill their colonial quest. Hence, having neither the size nor the weight—the numbers and the technological might in armed forces—the latter need not win a conventional fight to succeed. It suffices, instead, that in their deeds, they *outlast* the will of the dominant forces.

Endure, persist, resist, and exist. Much to the irritation of Goliathian powers, Davidian victories tend to remain indelibly etched in people's collective memory. As "common sense" decrees, in asymmetrical warfare, the test of victory is bound to be asymmetrical. Memory recalls, for example, the case of Hezbollah's claim to a strategic, historic victory over Israel at the close of the 2006 "July War" in Lebanon. While Israel launched an extensive air and land military campaign against Hezbollah with the aim of eradicating the organization, and failed to achieve it, Hezbollah sustained defenses on Lebanese territory and fired a record of some 246 rockets into Israel. Following their leader's public declaration that victory would mainly consist of surviving, Hezbollah held on, and *survive* they did, despite the devastation, the ruins, and the loss of a large amount of their best fighters.

"All that we need is to persevere, stand steadfast, and confront them united," said Hassan Nasrallah, Secretary-General of Hezbollah, in an address to the Lebanese nation (July 14, 2006), and in his own words, "to every Palestinian, Arab, Muslim, every free and decent person in this world, every oppressed, tortured victim of injustice." Some of the Western presses frowned on what appeared to them as a "crowing about victory amid the ruins," but if in the aftermath of the UN-brokered cease-fire, there were some disputes over who really won and mixed responses on who, in the end, had gained most in the war; there was also a clear consensus on Israel's "strategic defeat" (a term also used by the White House). "Shortcomings," "failings," "failures," and "lost" were the very words spat out by angry leading figures within Israel, whose administration suffered pressures and staff changes as a result of having lost to a "very small group of people" of no match whatsoever for Israel's defense forces (Moshe Arens). Having survived this asymmetrical military conflict, Hezbollah, to the eyes of many (including the *Economist*), emerged with a military and political victory, which some eight hundred thousand supporters gathered in Beirut on September 22, 2006, to celebrate.

Of great relevance to this July War were the Israeli soldiers' accounts of how their air crews often hunted in vain for the sources of Katyusha rocket fire and how Hezbollah fighters seemed to burst out of the ground to loose off a rocket-propelled grenade only to disappear quickly into the earth again. After Hezbollah yielded security control of the area to a UN peacekeeping force as part of the cease-fire agreement, Israeli troops discovered and dynamited some of the camouflaged underground bunkers and fortified firing positions, whose elaborate network was built over a six-year period, deeply burrowed in valleys and hilltops throughout south Lebanon. Nasrallah's men thus lost possession of a number of well-equipped strategic bunkers that honeycomb the hills for miles near the Israeli border. These subterranean tunnel structures proved a major stumbling block for the thirty-four-day Israeli offensive and were key to Hezbollah's ability to survive Israel's onslaught during the war. In this battle à la "hawks versus moles" (terms popularized during the American war in Vietnam), it suffices that the latter persist in their resistance, for the Israeli army to lose its aura of invincibility. Meanwhile, despite Hezbollah's ostensibly acknowledged claim to victory, their great hero, Nasrallah, went back deep into hiding: as is widely known, he is "the underground mullah."

Terrorist Sightings

In the months following the September 11 event, in a dogged attempt at locating Osama bin Laden, the US special operation forces began scouring the mountains and attacking systematically the entire cave complex at Tora Bora in Afghanistan. While the quest for the man "still out there" continued unrelentingly without any sign of bin Laden or of the al-Qaeda leadership, "some folks" back home were empathetically carrying out their own version of the search. Keen on helping, they were most eager not only to report any actions deemed suspicious from Arab-looking persons (a.k.a. the "Brown Threat" in which are often conflated Chicanos, Latinos, South Asians, and Middle Eastern Muslims) but also to track down the precise whereabouts of the enemy in their very midst. The FBI was thus said to be bedeviled by a continual barrage of spurious reports on the accused terrorist mastermind being spotted walking among the innocent populace, each of which they had to investigate.

This was the time when feeling vulnerable in their own home, "folks" startled at the sight of anything foreign to White America and barked hard at the shades of their own projections. Terrorized, some did not hesitate to revert the terror by abusing both verbally and physically all perceived "rag heads" and "sand niggers." This was hence also the time when, feeling unsafe in the streets, American Muslim citizens and many brown-skinned people stayed home for fear for their lives. Some even changed their dressing and shaved their beards when they had to go out. Spreading wide, for example, were news of passengers on an airliner refusing to let it take off unless an Afghan family was removed from the plane or of a Louisiana congress member declaring that any airline passenger wearing "a diaper on his head" (sic) should be pulled aside for questioning. Simple actions easily appeared ominous when carried out by any outsider. Saboteurs seemed to lurk not only in the city but even in the remotest sites of the American desert. Living in a climate of fear, made to feel the enemy's ubiquitous threat, one often forgets portents of death do not look any different from anybody else. However, while giving a face to evil may help to make the menace at once more real and more familiar, everyday folks had often proved the contrary in their eloquent reports on the dread enemy.

Most noteworthy were the sightings recorded in the *Salt Lake Tribune*, in which federal agents voiced their surprise at how many Utahns apparently believed bin Laden to be living in the Salt Lake City area. Speculations ran high as to why, of all states, he would choose Utah as his hiding place. And believe it or not, as rumors have it, it was because of his predisposition for polygamy (an apparently discontinued practice still attributed to Mormons) and his infatuation for the majestic beauty of Utah's desert whose variedly complex landscape, associated with the desert landscape of his homeland, could fully provide him with adequate means of concealment. Sightings of bin Laden in Utah were said to surpass by far those of Elvis, and the West Valley City Police Department had to check every cave in town with no success of catching him. The man "still out there" was spotted everywhere in public spaces—on the freeway, in a mall of Salt Lake City, and last but not least, at McDonald's eating a Big Mac and fries.

Power of the Unseen

Being a hero is being prepared for a gift in time.

Deng Ming-Dao

The present conveniently obliterates the past, but the latter keeps on returning to haunt the very consciousness that seeks to forget it. Staying firm and mobile rather than weighty and static. Learning, on the move, how to read and receive the gift of time. Persevering, waiting, confronting. From a long and yet not-so-distant past, the strategy, as construed here, brings to mind the wars fought in Vietnam against Chinese, French, and American imperialisms. The scene of repeated battles "between a heavy-weight and a feather-weight—lumbering force against light agility" (Bernard Newman),[6] Vietnam was an open wound—both a protracted colonial war and a major international conflict, whose specters bide their time to loom up again in current world crises. The fall of Saigon in 1975 was the fall of not only the government in South Vietnam but the two centuries of Western ascendancy in Southeast Asia and, further, of the invincibility of any modern Goliath's military machine over peoples of lesser means.

Memory recalls the name of Điện Biên Phủ—the historic battle fought in Vietnam between the French and the Viet Minh in 1954, which ended the First Indochina War, inflicting on France a massive colonial defeat. The French High Command had attempted a momentous gamble and strategically selected the valley of Điện Biên Phủ, a village in northwestern Vietnam, near the Chinese and Laotian borders, as a site for a showdown with the enemy. But, instead of being lured into the set-piece battle as the French would have it, the Viet Minh reversed the situation and made it a killing ground for the French who, caught in a noose of their own making, became a "sitting target" during the fifty-five-day siege.

The loss of human lives on both sides was staggering. (Numbers differ widely from one report to another, but the approximate estimation was: 7,700 casualties, 10,000 captured [of which only 3,000 came back alive] on the side of the French, whose army included the Foreign Legionnaires [Algerians, Moroccans, Tunisians, and Senegalese] with the best of the French Expeditionary Corps; and 4,000 dead, 15,000 wounded on the side of the Vietnamese, whose army also suffered huge losses of their best men.) Despite the superiority of the French firepower and the valiant fight they deployed until the very end, the "little men in oversized uniforms" had beaten the white man at his own game. France's nine-year-long dirty war (*sale guerre*) ended with the decisive victory of the Viet Minh.

It was the first time a non-European independent movement that began as guerilla bands before becoming an organized army succeeded to defeat a modern Western occupier with one of the largest Western armies, supported by its powerful US ally. Even as of today, French administrators and intellectuals of the older generation, still feeling the sting of this slap in the face, tend to react viscerally at the slightest mention of French occupation in Vietnam. Unable to digest the outcome of the Điện Biên Phủ battle, some of them became irate at the thought that they had been trapped because, as they said with contempt, "*we should not have educated them.*" Discussions on the subject easily degenerate into angry insults or physical affronts among participants, who otherwise are impeccably civilized individuals. With the Geneva Accords of July 1954, France formally renounced its civilizing mission in Indochina. Already then, Vietnam was a source of great pride in the developing world. The fact that a small Asian nation had defeated a colonial power changed history.

General Võ Nguyên Giáp, who led the Viet Minh's strategists, recalled how, a few days into the battle, after his army had suffered heavy human costs, he renounced any attempt at a "swift attack" toward a "swift victory." Rather than conducting human wave raids to precipitate the outcome as his men started out doing, he delayed these raids for the final phase and meanwhile decided to besiege Điện Biên Phủ, developing a strategy that has proven useful, across wars, to all forces defying sky power: resorting to the buried strength of the earth and the underground in response to the dominant's economy of air and above-the-ground display of might. Claiming a different kind of space and of "earthy right," digging and hauling endlessly, the Viet Minh built an elaborate system of trenches and tunnels, not only to protect themselves and their artillery pieces, which they continually moved to prevent discovery, but, more important, to get closer to the enemy, slowly and invisibly tightening the noose around their neck. It was through protracted warfare that Giáp secured victory for his troops, and his winning motto was: *"đánh trắc, tiến trắc"* or "Strike surely. Advance steadfastly."

With the Viet Minh's military success, Giáp was credited with a modern model of revolutionary warfare, in which size and sophistication did not guarantee victory. In July 2004, on the fiftieth anniversary of the Geneva Accords, France's most widely read newspaper, *Le Monde*, reserved an entire special issue to commemorate the battle of Điện Biên Phủ, giving voice to the Vietnamese's or the colonized's side of the story. Of great relevance was the recognition given to the impact of the event on the fall of the French empire and its determining role in the colonial world. History recalls, for example, how only three months after the Geneva conference, the Algerian uprising broke out, marking a new beginning of the Algerian War that, despite France's claim to military victory, ultimately led to Algeria's political victory—its independence with the Evian Accords in 1962. As founding events, Điện Biên Phủ and the Algerian War left long-standing scars between colonizers and colonized. If their outcomes still deeply affect certain segments of the societies involved to this day, their reputations spread far beyond the countries directly implied.

> Even in Camus—this fondness for heroism. Is there perhaps no other way? No, even to understand already implies heroism. Is a man unable then simply to open his door and watch?
>
> Clarice Lispector, *Chronicles*

From the substantial visual, oral, and textual documents bearing witness to Điện Biên Phủ, two surreptitiously striking incidents among others marked the end of France's struggle for Indochina. Remembering the final moments of the battle, a French combatant told how he sought shelter behind a barricade of dead bodies, which he and his fellow men had built to protect themselves. As a massive burst of gunfire spattered out all around, the last impression he was left with before the surrender was his vivid feeling of "the wall of corpses shivering" in front of him. On that same closing day of May 7, 1954, as Bernard Fall related it, the last words exchanged between two combatants representing the French and the Viet Minh forces were, ironically but expectedly enough, *in French.* "C'est fini?" (Is it over?) called forth the Viet Minh soldier. "Oui, c'est fini," (Yes, it's over) said the French colonel from a slit trench near his command post. And as the firing ceased, as bodies of friends and foes alike began to crawl out of their hidings to rise to their feet and stand erect for the first time in fifty-four days, *the silence was deafening.*[7]

feeling the way out

The Crawl to Peace

> Let me say, at the risk of seeming ridiculous,
> that the true revolutionary is guided by great feelings of love.
>
> Ernesto "Che" Guevara

When silence appears, it appears in silence. With no warning and no siding. The profound symbolic scope of Điện Biên Phủ's ending moments as related earlier grows with time and resonates anew in today's prominent world events. At the time of the Franco-Vietnamese conflict, all across nations, among peoples struggling against colonialism, eyes were turned toward the challenge of the Viet Minh. Pervasive concerns as to whether they would hold out against the definitely superior forces of the French Expeditionary Corps were anxiously voiced among leaders of African and North African resistances, who had been following closely the unfolding events and had rallied to the cause of the Viet Minh.

Despite the massive slaughters, destructions, and displacements associated with wars for independence or for democracy, it all comes down to this decisively simple, *weightless*, and almost trivial ending between two nations, two armies, or two individuals: "Yes, it's over." Intense but short-lived was the joy of beating them, aggressors, at *their* game and telling them in *their* own language, *it's finished. Time's up.* Years of unspeakable cruelties and bloodshed ultimately led to this *true ending* moment of *lightness*—and deafening *silence*—when all enmities unexpectedly died down and recognition among worming subhumans of what the war did to us all came before any cry of victory, any nation's flag, any existential divide, had yet a chance to interpose. The crawl to peace was a crawl out from protracted life in darkness and a return to nothing more remarkable than ordinary standing, and walking, human status.

The French subsequently acknowledged their defeat (albeit fully so only fifty years later); the Vietnamese bore no resentment and turned it into an investment. *There're no victor or loser in a war*, so the ground reality says, *only survivors*. As a woman civilian from Vietnam put it: "don't lose sight; always focus on the victims, not on the winning or falling government; we did not fight to replace one set of dictators with another." France's ending also marked the beginning of America's involvement in Vietnam, whose protracted war came to a sudden close some two decades later, again, with a cataclysmic defeat to "those faceless little men in black pajamas." If the outcome of the Franco-Vietnamese conflict was a contagious model for many colonial peoples, Điện Biên Phủ remains "a symbol for all time" (Alain Ruscio). Its shadow will continue to haunt today's superpowers, including the United States, Europe, and China.

> The erect posture remains an utopia in our animalistic society.
>
> Valie Export

As war analysts have come to see it, Điện Biên Phủ was a test of wills and "a sobering premonition of the US future military defeat." History seemed to repeat itself—not in details and appearances but in outlines and substances—when a decade later, American involvement turned the violent conflict into a "Second Indochina War." American soldiers were then thrown into what they saw as a hell so bizarre as to leave them, while in the midst of action as well as years after they pulled out, too shocked and scarred to be able to heal overnight from the trauma of such an experience. There where they fought, they had to go down, way down under, to fight a subterranean war deep in the tropical night, in a very "mean place"—the thick, smelly, and *neutral* jungles of Vietnam that made no discrimination between army troops and guerillas and transformed hunters into hunted. Aside from the ordeal of living on edge, often unable to distinguish friend from foe while combating an elusive enemy—fleeting figures that disappear into the dense forest as fast as they reappear from nowhere to inflict damage—the survivors also cursed the abominable conditions of living with the smell of death and rotten vegetation and the painful or lethal bite of slimy, sticky leeches and poisonous snakes. Not only the war had to be waged deep in the undergrowth but the enemy was also said to be fighting as "war fleas," making numberless hit-and-run attacks to bleed the enemy dry. Exploiting fully the shield of darkness, they frightened their opponents by carrying out surprise attacks and making swift withdrawals from the scene of action.

In this war against the United States, again the invisible enemy relied on *duration* in time, while introducing *rhythms* into their deadly tactics. Against an enemy that privileged sight above all, they used the power of remaining unseen. And thus, rather than fighting to win immediately and occupy territory, they gained nightly control by repeatedly killing and disappearing, effectively using a strategy known as "one slow, four quick"—slow, careful preparation followed by organized groups movements, quick attack, retrieval of the dead and wounded and their arms, and withdrawal. (Here, withdrawal is always scrupulously part of the plan.) Taunting and confusing their American opponents, the vanishing forces renewed their strength by retreating into underground complexes. Again, resorting to an economy of burrowing and concealment in response to the opponent's economy of visible display of high might, the Viet Cong developed the skill and endurance to live a subterranean life, carrying their daily activities in a vast labyrinthine tunnel complex deep below the undergrowth of the jungles.

Started during the resistance against the French, the tunnel system spread and expanded during the war against Americans. It was ingeniously built to house sleeping, cooking, meeting, and storage spaces, complete with, for example, a first-aid station, a water well of its own, and even a cinema. Thus, the system was skillfully set up to continue by other means the war above the ground: equipped with concealed entrances, undetectable trap doors, false tunnels, and apparent dead ends to deceive, lure, and blow away those who dared to venture uninvited into the underground world. The multileveled tunnel network could stretch for hundreds of miles, allowing large units to move around undetected and linking districts and provinces from as far as the Cambodian border to the outskirts of Saigon.

At the core of the hellish warfare waged lied the Viet Cong's ability to fight with *the invincibility of the ghostly and the disappeared*. Mobile and light, highly skilled in the art of disappearance, they were always ready to move out at a moment's notice and vanish from sight. The embattled experience was literally referred to by Americans as "the walking nightmare," for every inch of ground in the war zones threatened to maim or kill, and every step could turn out to be the last one for the walker. Life amid the septic jungles was, however, not any less debilitating for the other side, or for these "human moles" (as General Westmoreland called the Viet Cong) who, aside from having to cope with the great B-52 deluges during the late sixties and beginning seventies, lived as "hunted animals," an existence of hiding and preparation, slithering and always on the go, which demanded constant watchfulness.

The path for independence has been a long, arduous one filled with ways of being often at odds with what, in normal human time, is viewed as the "four dignities"—Lying, Sitting, Standing, and Walking. Instead, flitting, crouching, creeping, crawling, wriggling, slinking, and cowering in wait are some of the terms borrowed from the survivors, which may best describe their subterranean mode of living during the long war years. Operating in a state of semi-starvation and feeding on a jungle menu of kills of every kind, they also had to cope with the stress, fear, tension, and moments of sheer terror that accompanied their every waking moment. But worse than the terrifying air strikes, and the snakebites that proved to be a plague to the guerillas whose sole footwear were rubber thongs, worse than the far enemy (American soldiers) and near enemy (South Vietnamese combatants), was, in fact, nature's army of light, puny, and deadly dwellers: the mosquitoes.

As incredible and yet dramatic as it may sound, for the guerillas, these bloodthirsty insects were the prime enemy, and malaria attacks were what they called their "jungle tax." Very few escaped the disease, which was reckoned to have also ravaged the North Vietnamese army (more than one in ten died of malaria) in their journey down the Hồ Chí Minh Trail and, ironically enough, to have killed North Vietnam's minister of health during the very study tour he took in an attempt to devise preventive measures. Today, the complex tunnel systems in southern Vietnam still partially bear witness to the harshness of the guerillas' life of constant hiding and endurance; moreover, they have become a source of investment, and the ones in Củ Chi remain a popular example. The hand-dug subterranean stronghold is a war memorial—one of Vietnam's most famous battlegrounds and, in the flourishing industry of war tourism, a prime visitor's attraction. Some called this underground village, with its labyrinth of interwoven tunnels achieved with utmost endurance, one of the marvels of the twentieth century. Tourists eager to have an authentic feel of the 'Nam experience are invited, as greeted by a sign at Củ Chi, to "please try to be a Củ Chi guerrilla [and] wear these uniforms before entering the tunnel." Black pajamas, pith helmets, rubber sandals, old rifles, and even snake juice and other food as the Viet Cong had it are part of the exoticism of war in the tropics.

When the General Cries

> By what road
> does the scent of the cinnamon flowers
> come to us at the end of the day?
>
> Trần Thái Tông

Animalizing the human other goes hand in hand with humanizing the animal. In the dense jungle of events, doings, and happenings, history comes in interrelated fragments to be smelled, tasted, and touched—sniffed out, tracked, swallowed, held on to, or vomited while walking for survival. Pauses, interruptions, and reprises: there's an odd rhythm to this long, spatial stroll on foot. One slowly burrows one's way through the fissures of history, not by eyes but by ear, nose, tongue, body movements, and contortions. As a Vietnam journalist and historian (Bernard Fall) noted, literally speaking, "the Americans are walking in the same footsteps as the French although dreaming different dreams."[1] What seems like a great dream to invest in often turns, as it approaches, into a dreadful, torturous experience of failed or unwanted investment. "The walking nightmare," which persists in haunting many combatants for the rest of their lives, resuscitates in vivid details the sleepers' worst walking fears. The terror-inducing dreams are so many road signs pointing to an intimate and yet collective failure to respond effectively to a situation of conflict. Unwinding in long-lasting series, these recurrent nightmares speak volumes of the tormented wandering in the dark, from a world of lived terrors to another, of no less real terrors.

Each step forward hurts, and the joy of being able to return to the normal everyday remains profoundly mediated by the grief for every spark of life lost in combat. The slow slide back to wakefulness carries with it all the suppressed wounds to which friends, family members, and acquaintances are directly or indirectly subjected. These bide their time to resurface, thriving on as a national trauma and wreaking havoc in the pain-body, just where they are thought to have disappeared. Today, the question remains as to who these war dreamers truly are, and what their dream portrays, both individually and communally. War somnambulists, unaware of their strange and terrifying sleepwalking, can act overconfident in their future-telling, pretending to foresee with their eyes closed while asleep, and forgetting when awakened, the spooky nocturnal activities they have been carrying out.

Lionhearted during daylight, but often so very scared at sundown, while walking into the night, combatants find themselves caught raw and frozen in terror at the fatal roar of war. Something neither human nor quite animal or machine. For a brief eternity, the heart stops beating. Body and mind drop away and the screen goes blank. Again, in, out; on, off. Resuming its course, the recurring rhythm of 1 and 0, being and nonbeing, has both an unsettling and pacifying effect. For intrepid warriors, it may take more than one missing beat to see themselves in what fills them with terror. But to the ear ready for that missing beat, war offers its "lesson of darkness" as an irreversible gift of death. Intimately intertwined are medicine and sickness, living and dying; and as a tale of ancient China tells, no man-made inventions come out of the blue. When a man seeking to purchase the most venomous philter to end his enemy's life eagerly double checks: "What could be more lethal than the fastest of the deadly poisons?" the poison maker replies: "the human heart."

In a television interview with the four-star army general Norman Schwarzkopf, Barbara Walters noted how some of her questions had brought tears to his eyes. "Generals don't cry," she pried while affecting surprise. Schwarzkopf—whose reputation as the bravest of the brave peaked during the first Iraq War and was intimately linked to his success in commanding Operation Desert Storm—responded not only by admitting the tears positively but also by affirming, when asked whether a general can cry, how scary, indeed, the thought of a man who could not let his emotions or his tears show up was for him. In this interaction between a (super)woman and a (super)man, a heroine of the press and a hero of the military, an apparently most banal answer to a most banal question takes on a strange resonance. What seems of trivial matter in normal circumstances and of "natural" occurrence among certain members of society suddenly becomes a newsworthy and extra-ordinary event. With changing times and circumstances, and with an ear for the implied but unsaid dimension of gender, the mere question of shedding tears—in public—further takes on a bizarrely exhibitive value in the promotion of today's images of expressed manly sensitivity.

Oddly enough, the discussion about whether or not one should stick to the *boys don't cry* motto hasn't quite died down yet, and societies across cultures tend to frown on any display of strong emotions other than, for example, anger, disgust, rage, and certain forms of admiration, heroism, or patriotism from their male members. Furthermore, there seems to be a particularly sacred time when men are not supposed to well up in front of others. Only the lesser man—the unmanly, the weak, the coward, the abnormal, the sick, the handicapped, the *effeminate*, and, of course, children and women—weeps, for example, at the spectacle of war. Among numerous stories to tell, David Halberstam, a well-known reporter of the war in Vietnam, chose the very following anecdote—another seemingly trivial instance of verbal interaction—to relate in a published letter to his *daughter*. A Marine general in Washington had apparently falsely spread, via the mediation of a *female* journalist from Washington, the news that Halberstam had burst into tears upon seeing a photo of "a bunch of Viet Cong bodies." Considered to be indicative of the changes he went through, the anecdote tells how his reception of what he saw as one of the most memorable charges leveled against him by Washington's employees has shifted over time. For him, the initial gravity of the matter lay not only in the fact that the story was untrue but also in the fact that manhood was particularly valued among war correspondents, and the Hemingway hero, who cried not, was still widely cherished in this milieu. As Halberstam wrote, the charge implied was that "tears were for women, of course, and not only had I wept, but I had wept for the other side."[2]

> O eye, you cry for others:
> sit down awhile and weep for yourself!
> the bough is made green and fresh
> by the weeping cloud for the same reason
> that the candle is made brighter
> by its weeping.
>
> Rumi

"*Tears were for women, of course*," and yet . . . It was only a year later, when another correspondent, Jack Langguth, publicly claimed the same incident to be a symbol of a changing America, that Halberstam saw clearly into it the truth of his personal journey and concluded, like Langguth, that the story ought to have been true for him as well as for others, even if it was not. "I was simply a part of a great national interior debate taking place throughout the country; we were reexamining not just America in Vietnam, but America itself."[3] From A to A, America, the "still No. 1" superpower ought, as Halberstam urged, to have respected rather than shamed those who have cried. At the sight of fallen bodies on both sides of the combat lines, America ought to weep for America—then and now. Not mental tears but the tears of salty water. And not only the tears that flood the eyes, noses, and mouths of mothers, daughters, sisters, wives, and widows, but above all, the tears that well up from a heart broken open at long last to receive the gift from the wounded, the disappeared, and the dead.

Washington's Visual Scar

> The feminine is always an untidy fit in this present world.
>
> Susan Murphy, "All the Unknown Women"

Anyone visiting the Vietnam Veterans Memorial in Washington, D C, can, together with some three million other people who come to visit it each year, bear witness to the healing power of such an infinite moment, when war survivors of all walks of life and grief-stricken relatives of fallen soldiers face the wall of engraved names and weep openly, caring not who sees them nor how they may look crying their hearts out in public. They just stand there, weep, and weep. At one with the polished black granite wall where their own reflections appear with the names of their loved ones. So uncanny was the dark presence of this visual scar in the landscape of Washington that at first some Vietnam veterans were said to be afraid to approach it. Preferring to keep their distance, they stayed by the trees a hundred meters away and stared at the memorial wall for hours. Some other observers, yearning for a traditional figurative war monument that emphasizes manly glory in action (conventionally pictured in stone or bronze statues of human figures) rather than quiet contemplation in mourning, did not hesitate to call this meditation in black "the wall of shame" or "the black ditch."

The night-in-day quality of the monument resides in its understated play with light and visibility. The initial controversies around the wall came as a structural supplement to those that had underscored one of the most divisive wars in American history. Perhaps most disconcerting to these negative observers, whose expectations of what a monument should look like have been dashed, are the very features that constitute the memorial's unique strength in its bold simplicity: that it remains indifferent to winners and losers and inscribes on its face only the names of those killed and missing in action; that it offers a tactile experience of collective mourning and a space for public display of suffering and reconciliation; that it expands horizontally on terra firma rather than rises vertically into the sky as with the Washington Monument to the east and the Lincoln Memorial to the west; that it presents itself at once as a wound in the earth and an opening, sloping down below ground level, so that visitors reading the names in ascending magnitude, merge into the space of the dead following the wall's descending course; that it becomes not only a site of memories but also one for pilgrimage in which past and present meet through new alliances; and, last but not least, that the artist and architect who conceived such a memorial turned out to be indelibly "marked" in terms of gender. "Tears are for women only, of course," and in designing the project, Maya Ying Lin clearly believed she "never would have won" if the submissions for the competition had not been judged "blind," with entries identified by number only in order to preserve the anonymity of their authors.

Have things changed in the last few decades? Apparently, yes. Has America changed with Vietnam, as Langguth affirmed? Apparently, yes. Now that according to both scientists and spiritual leaders, the lack and loss of heart, its cooling, hardening, and malfunctioning seem to account for humanity's core problems and modern illnesses, even warmongers know they can't win over the people's hearts unless they learn to shed tears in public. Among famous examples of political wet speeches, it is again worth mentioning those of not one but both Bush presidents. Television watchers may recall how immediately before, but especially after, the "surge" G. W. Bush helplessly choked over his lines in public speeches to display his emotion when mentioning, for example, the courage and sacrifice of the nation's fallen soldiers. And before him, Bush the father also "lost it quite a bit" during the speech he gave in honor of his son (December 5, 2006), when apparently unable to control himself, he sobbed over his lines, exhibiting his emotions in their red swollen rawness and bursting out in tears twice, leaving his halting sentences unfinished as he proceeded to praise his son's deeds and, more particularly, the latter's handling of "victory."

Both Bush presidents have had their onstage emotional moments during which they successfully look like Everyman, or perhaps as media logic would have it, Everywoman. Who would not feel like welling up at the sight of another person's tears? And yet. Endearing is the one who tries to speak in the throes of sorrow. And yet. Recent studies from members of Penn State University and Purdue University suggest a change in attitudes toward men who cry in public. While choking wet in front of others has become more acceptable for men, it is less so for women. If shedding tears is often equated with honesty and truth, and is now judged more positively when performed by men, it is not so with women. Rather than translating a genuine emotion, a woman's tearing in public is viewed as conformity to a gender stereotype, inclination for overreacting, inability to control emotions, self-indulgence, or even downright deception. (Margaret Thatcher's famous crying upon leaving office was widely suspected to be an artifice deployed "to make the men in gray suits look like bullies.") A man in tears still stands as such a rarity that these are apt to carry much more weight, whereas women's feelings tend to be largely discounted in the currency of emotions. Again, this particularly applies to the realms of affective politics, where a male politician may work at shedding an occasional tear to show a vulnerability that hints at depth and sincerity, while in order to succeed, a woman politician may choose to "use her head" and hold back her emotions, offering, instead, an appearance of toughness, rational competence, and icy self-control.

Have things really changed? Yes, *apparently. Tears are* still *for women, of course,* but temporary role-reversing in gender politics helps to set the researcher on a sidetrack. The stereotyping ultimately holds, despite the shift in the reception of appearances. *Generals don't cry*, and Schwarzkopf, who considered himself to be neither dovish nor hawkish but rather "owlish" (both wise and ferocious), didn't allow himself to cry during battles, so he said. However, the mere fact that he admitted to having done so afterward, like all these "old tough guys who cried when they returned from war" at the loss of human life, made his media popularity both as a military hero and a well-rounded family man soar high. If, in today's American culture, we are said to be clearly "on the wetter swing of the historical pendulum," and tears have become fashionable among politicians, then Now is the time to cry a different cry.

Whether in victory or in defeat, now is the time for the generals and their armies to weep. Not only for the victims on our side but *intimately*, for one's own loss and for humanity's victims: victims of occupying forces; victims of the oppressive powers in each and all; victims of victims; and moreover, victims to a victim order—the systematized laundering of all forms of wretchedness, which capitalizes on human misery and masks a profound malady of indifference. Now is the time to absorb the truth of the eye's liquid function and to let the tears guide, as great power conflict returns and imperial expansionist policies continue to drive governmental abuses in the name of national interests and security. Seeing not how in their very intransigence, they are preparing their—and humanity's—own demotion, competing resurgent empires are again flexing their muscles at savage human cost.

> Something, or an infinite number of things, dies in every death.
>
> Jorge Luis Borges, *Dreamtigers*

the world is watching

Lotus in Tears

> Shatter my heart so room can be made anew for limitless love.
>
> Sufi prayer

Sadness may be state-mediated, as writers in Vietnam readily concede, but tears are a gift. When asked about the current situation of Vietnamese literary production, they note with quiet laughter that they have at long last "gained permission to be sad" and "can now weep without being gagged." The emotion has proven to be particularly dangerous—especially when felt for the "wrong victim" or "counterrevolutionary" cause. Like the right to freedom, the right to sadness is to be earned. In Vietnam's cloudy state of freedom of expression today, where the government has been working at muzzling political dissent since late 2006, intensifying Internet control and stepping up crackdowns on cyber-dissidents, at least forty activists, journalists, trade union leaders, underground publishers, poets, and novelists—including a dozen women—have been jailed, detained, or placed under house arrest during the years 2009–2011, for example, on charges of "disseminating 'reactionary' material," "causing public disorder," or "infringing upon the interests of the state."

For many observers, such a crackdown has been the harshest in some twenty years, especially after the government gained membership in the World Trade Organization (2006). Emboldened then by international recognition, the Vietnamese authorities moved to suppress all internal challenges to its one-party communist state. In these times, marked by increased instability and resurfacing crises among world competitors, people are, again, being locked up or made to disappear for merely giving word to their views. And clearly, it is not only in speaking truth to power but also in simply mourning its loss that independent thinkers are taking risks with their lives and livelihoods. The regime has banned, harassed, and imprisoned its citizens for expressing political views online, while encouraging mutual spying and self-censorship among Internet users. Required to inform on their customers, Internet service providers and popular Internet café owners have plainly functioned as "police auxiliaries." Thus, it was also no mere coincidence that not one but eight Vietnamese writers were among a diverse group of awardees from nineteen countries around the world to receive the 2008 Hellman-Hammett grants administered by Human Rights Watch, in recognition of the courage they showed when facing political persecution and human rights abuses.

Tears are a gift. In his analyses of the paintings and drawings exhibition *Memoirs of the Blind*, held at the Louvre Museum, the late French philosopher Jacques Derrida invoked the experiences of tears by Friedrich Nietzsche and Saint Augustine and noted how "deep down, deep down inside, *the eye would be destined not to see but to weep*." It is in the veiling of sight, the welling up and the very coursing of water, that an essence of man's eye is said to reveal itself. Through the action of tears, the eye's essential function is that of causing what lies buried or forgotten—that is, the *truth* of the eyes—to surge up: "to have imploration rather than vision in sight, to address prayer, love, joy, or sadness rather than a look or a gaze . . . revelation is the moment of the 'tears of joy.'"[1] Thus, rather than darkening vision, tears' veiling induces a form of blindness that, neither seeing nor not seeing, "implores" so as to open the eye of eyes.

If there are many great blind men portrayed in the Louvre, Derrida asked, "why so many weeping woman?" With no explicit answer, the philosopher went on to suggest that in drawing those who weep, "one is perhaps seeking to unveil the eyes. *To say them without showing them seeing*." One can always see but not weep with a single eye, for "*it is the 'whole eye,' the whole of the eye that weeps*."[2] And, not so naturally, one can also hide and weep without tears. Here, the question arises again as to whether the lack of tears in representations of weeping could be attributed to the artist's desire to describe specifically men's crying. The gender gap remains visually open, for the difference being made is not only between sight and eye but also between eyes and tears, saying and showing, seeing and weeping—a difference apparently dissolvable only when from the same weeping eyes run the *seeing tears*.

> Tears are signs, not expressions. By my tears, I tell a story.
>
> Roland Barthes, *A Lover's Discourse: Fragments*

March 27, 2008. In tears they cried out against the lies. Chronic lies, all lies, always lies, they said. Unexpectedly, they pushed their way into a news briefing and blurted out a stream of protestations, speaking hurriedly in spurts as if fearful they would not be allowed to finish their sentences. All at once they turned, uninvited, toward the microphones, cameras, and media witnesses to vent their visceral grievances. On the silent surface of repressed suffering, passions suddenly flare up, anguished voices erupted, choking up on forbidden words. Without warning, again, the Great Dam broke, and for a briefest moment, the flow was let loose to run its own course.

It was at the Jokhang Temple in Lhasa that, walled in for two days and forced to be part of the decoy meant to show the world the return of ruling order, some thirty of them—not women, not nuns, but young monks—upstaged the scripted tour by weeping and voicing dangerously unscripted lines. In the midst of irruptive emotions, a few broke down into sobs in between bursts of outpourings, crying out that "Tibet is not free!" and that the Dalai Lama was not responsible for the wave of protests spreading across Tibetan occupied territories and beyond since March 10, 2008—the day when the Tibetan people commemorated the forty-ninth year of their historical uprising against Chinese oppression. The scene was broadcast on YouTube, viewable worldwide—except in China. The monks spoke up in two languages—theirs (Tibetan) and the dominant's (Mandarin)—thereby making sure what they had to say would be understood by the foreign journalists. They spoke up despite the risks incurred, knowing well what each word released meant in terms of punishment—which was not only prison but also sustained, deadly physical and mental tortures. Rather than conforming, they dared to disrupt a carefully set up tour organized by the Chinese government for a select group from the international press to promote the official version of the unrest in Tibet.[3] Moreover, they gave tears to the world. They cried to tell their story. They spoke up, to *implore*.

Tears are shallowly thought of as blurring the truth. But peoples of prayers across spiritual contexts value the gift of having one's heart shattered so as to open out to love. May the eye of eyes open. As the heart moved forward, their eyes leaked, their truth surging forth. The seeing liquid dissolves sight to restore sight, and access to the heart of reality previously invisible to one's normal eye is oddly gained. The (womanly) giving of tears sets in motion the flow of *heartfelt* links and connections. As the eye weeps, feeling surreptitiously erupts to the surface, and the call to come closer to see for oneself powerfully draws all witnessing presences into a binding core. *To have imploration rather than vision in sight, to address prayer, love, joy, or sadness rather than a look.* Here, all eyes on Tibet: a stranger's tear makes itself heard as a cry to see intimately, from one's heart. What do the monks have in sight that finds its liquid way out? What do they know and let it be known that clear, rebelling dry eyes tend to repress or ignore? Ready-made answers to these questions abound, but in the translated words of the Dalai Lama, the man whose loving spirit the Chinese government finds so threatening, "a relationship can be established without any difficulty, from heart to heart, rather than from the tip of one's lips . . . . Ignoring populations in distress does reveal how—despite our intelligence and impressive power when it comes to exploiting men and destroying the world—we are truly dispossessed of tenderness and love."[4]

"I Am the Reality"

> Have you noticed how trees respond under the axes of their enemy? They keep their dignity till the end, falling straight, without ever bending their spine.
>
> François Cheng, *Le Dit de Tianyi*

"Tibet is not an issue," asserts a voice from Beijing, insisting further. She's a pure invention—"a fiction of British colonization." The centuries-old debate continues to flare up in the latest developments of the conflict, offering no satisfactory resolution and remaining deeply divisive among all parties concerned. While China apologists remain fond of recalling the CIA's involvement in Tibet's history of resistance, and while they angrily question the use of such terms as Chinese "colonization," "occupation," or "invasion" as applied to Sino-Tibetan relations, Free Tibet advocates fervently point to the elephant in the room as the Tibetan people continue to be subjected to serious human rights abuses under Chinese rule. Even when all across the region, people rose up in protest at the risk of their lives, Beijing (via Hu Jintao) continued to deny that Tibet is an ethnic, a religious, and a human rights issue. The scripting of two intertwined imperial trajectories, one Chinese and the other British, has unavoidably complicated analysis of China's control over Tibet. The challenge lies not only in the differing use of the modern concept of "sovereignty" universalized through imperialism and decolonization but also in the common abuse of theories of anti-China conspiracy, with the appropriated image of the West as violator of Chinese sovereignty always looming large. But no matter what the argument is, Tibet remains more than ever an "extremely delicate" and "sensitive *issue*" for Beijing.

On the one hand, the damage done to Tibet in the name of Liberation and Modernization has become increasingly difficult to disguise, and the spread of Tibetan resistance can no longer be conveniently distorted and dismissed, as informed netizens from China have keenly reminded. On the other hand, civil unrest has been sweeping the globe these last few years, and as reported by Human Rights Watch, since the Arab Spring the situation with human rights in China has steadily deteriorated. The Chinese authorities' perception of the threat did not lessen with time, and certainly, with the recent wave of public self-immolations (130 recorded by the Central Tibetan Administration and the International Campaign for Tibet from March 16, 2011 to April 2014) in protest against Chinese policy, Tibetan resistance has tragically flared rather than faded. Never before have so many Tibetans resorted to such a drastic mode of dissent, sacrificing their lives by setting themselves on fire to draw the world's attention to their condition. Arrests, detentions, and disappearances of dissidents or of merely outspoken netizens kept on multiplying in China, and the message issued at the beginning of the Dragon Year (2012) clearly showed no tolerance for any discordant voice in politics.

"There is no freedom in Tibet!" After the brief detour on the historical scripting of the Sino-Tibetan dis-harmony, a return to Jokhang Temple, March 27, 2008, with the tears and the cry "Tibet is not free!" irrupting anew. Hasty, perfunctory, and trite, as all slogans are, the words blurted out said nothing that the international press did not already know. What struck the ear was the words' poverty in relation to the enormity of the risks taken to utter them, or more inclusively, to the immensity of the people's tragic plight. They used words not to say so much as to show, or else, *"to say them without showing them seeing."* In signaling the Tibetans' dire ongoing conditions under the Chinese regime's oppression, these verbal shortcuts found their echoes around the world. There was neither time nor space for subtleties. But instead, the raw weeping instantly made their implosive, decades-long silences at once audible and intimately seeable. Discriminated against, humiliated, tortured, patriotically re-educated, and "severely punished" for continuing to listen to their heart of hearts. Fifty years of struggle and of unending bottled-up emotions. Then, on this day, this time, this place, suddenly: their pleading shameless in public. *Imploring*. No matter the age of the body in dissidence, through it leaked indefinite decades of longing for the return of the beloved leader. (As the Dalai Lama puts it, under Chinese oppression, "they were thrust into such depths of suffering and hardship that they literally experienced hell on earth.")[5] The tears and sobs saw them all, and when heard by a person of heart, the wounds admitted to all opened wide across strangers' bodies—bleeding, liquefying for inflicted loss, and, unsurprisingly, *ripe for healing*.

Undone by grief, they cried, and cried out. Despite the tight surveillance, a few lines did seem to have made their way to the international presses' ears. Such were those by the monks warning them of the chronic official lies and of the deceptive presence of fake, false-hearted monks whom the Chinese authorities had planted in the monastery for the occasion: "Do not believe them! They are deceiving you, they are telling you lies!" "For *love of truth*," the monks affirmed, they accepted to run the risk of their actions' serious consequences. "After the Olympics, they will surely crack down on us. Nothing we can do. Let them come. It's useless to be afraid . . . . *We will never change our heart*." Authority defied. Words unleashed, freed of the one who says them, quickly dispersed and returned to emptiness in the wind of the times. Yet, no matter how trite they often are, their mere sound so threatens the dominant's ears that it never fails to draw the worst of irate acts of punishment (including that of forcing electric batons into the dissenters' mouths). Those who went through hell and survived continue to tell the world their gruesome detainment stories, in which their most basic human rights were ruthlessly violated.

First-hand witnesses' stories of the authorities' unchecked brutality in Tibetan prisons have been piling up for decades. Having risked their lives to make their position known to the world, prison survivors continued, upon their releases (despite their being threatened with dire consequences if they ever talked about what happened inside the prisons), to put theirs, their relatives', and their friends' lives on the line. Those who had no choice but to escape their homeland did so only so as to further commit their life's work to exposing the injustice of Chinese oppression. The task is endless. A political prisoner, who had been repeatedly arrested, tortured, and sentenced to forced labor, thus affirmed: "I want people to know that on paper the Chinese government may treat Tibetan people alright but *I am the reality*."[6] In the dominant's terms, peaceful demonstrations are, as the transnational clichés go, crimes of "endangering state security," and prisoners detained for political and religious reasons are consistently renamed "lawbreakers." Punishments of distorted proportions are thus inflicted on the dominated for any politically nonconforming gesture or speech act.

Rather typical, for example, is the case of Takna Jigme Sangpo—the eighty-two-year-old primary school teacher who became the symbol of Tibetan resistance, having spent nearly thirty-two years serving in various prison camps without losing his spirit of independence. In his address at the eighth session of the Human Rights Tribune (June

4, 2008) he revealed how, for having taught the history, culture, and language of Tibet, he was first accused of "corrupting the mind of children with reactionary ideas" and sent to a work camp in Lhasa. Then, for having refused to write to the Communist Party a letter condemning the former Panchen Lama's letter in which the latter asked for Tibet's independence and detailed the crimes made against the Tibetan people, he was further sentenced to three years of hard labor. Later, being falsely accused of being a member of a "criminal" movement (the Tiger-Dragon, a group of young people arrested with a photo of him on them), he was condemned to carrying for nine months an iron brace that made it almost impossible for him to eat and to move. After this, he served in a stone quarry, making bricks for seven years. He was later put back in prison for having written a poster calling for Tibet's independence. Then, for having held that every Tibetan on earth would dream of independence when interrogated, he was again stripped and severely beaten. Moreover, for having shouted "Free Tibet! Chinese go back to China!" to a Swiss delegation (International Committee of the Red Cross) visiting the center, he was put in solitary confinement in a black hole for a year and eight years were added to his sentence.[7]

"Five years is 1,825 days. It is 43,800 hours. To have to spend the best years of your life in a dark prison cell . . . ." Thus it is poignantly reckoned, in another case of milder offense, by a friend writing a letter to Norzin Wangmo, a woman in her thirties sentenced for five years in prison (November 3, 2008) for passing on, via phone and Internet, news about the situation of Tibet to the outside world. Midway into a life's springtime. Brought to a stand by five, eight, and over twenty years of incarceration for leaking news, for shedding "counterrevolutionary" tears and walking the heart's path. In brief, for grieving and mourning—*inappropriately*—over "a long lost love". . .

In the Night of Becoming

> If you stand up, you bump your head,
> If you sit down you bump your arse.
>
> A Tibetan nun

Tibet is an international issue. Although a taboo question at the UN, She is, in human-rights representatives' jargon, "a file that continues to come before the attention of the world." With her turbulent history and unique position in the world, She stands out as one of the most sensitive security and political issues for China, though one that is usually kept in low profile and remains almost invisible in certain parts of the Middle Empire (especially in its more-developed cities along the east coast). Within and beyond the Great Wall, She is China's—and the UN's—Big Denial. The Chinese authorities have sought to represent the unrest across the Tibetan plateau as one "violent riot" by flooding the media solely with images of the events of March 14, 2008, in the capital of the Tibet Autonomous Region. However, the emotions spilling over in Lhasa and the mass uprising across Western China in the spring of 2008 was a strong reminder of the Tibetans' continuing struggle and a heartfelt response by a genuine popular movement that spread like wildfire to the neighboring provinces of Sichuan, Gansu, and Qinghai, as well as beyond Tibetan areas. Half a century of oppression has not worked. Harsh attempts to stamp out Tibetan identity and to quash Tibetan yearning for independence have failed.

The resentment of the Tibetan people across generations has long simmered just below the surface. Following the demonstrations by the three hundred monks from Drepung Monastery on March 10, 2008, spate after spate of peaceful protests—over 150 mentioned by the official Xinhua News Agency—broke out in at least fifty-two county-level locations in Chinese-occupied Tibet, as well as in Chengdu, Lanzhou, and Beijing, where Tibetan students held a silent vigil for those injured, killed, or disappeared in the crackdown. The exception to these peaceful manifestations was the outburst and escalation of violence in Lhasa on March 14, after the government's brutal crackdown on Drepung and Sera Monasteries and apparently a day after China's Ministry of Foreign Affairs deceptively told reporters the situation in Lhasa had stabilized. When a people's groaning is forcefully dimmed out, will their crying be remembered? "Who will write the history of tears?" asked Roland Barthes, a passionate researcher in semiology and cultural politics. "In which societies, in which periods, have we wept? Since when is it that men (and not women) no longer cry? Why was 'sensibility,' at a certain moment, transformed into 'sentimentality?'"[8]

Fear often trumps reason. Small gestures of disobedience, limited acts of nonviolent protest are automatically met with the "iron fist." At the slightest sign of noncompliance, disproportionately massive troops were deployed and a state of martial law was unofficially imposed in cities, towns, and villages across the Tibetan high-desert plateau. Reinforcement soldiers sent to these areas a year after the spring of 2008 to prepare for the worst on the fiftieth anniversary of the historical uprising against Chinese rule were said to have met mostly with nothing but empty streets and intense silence. Tibet was again and again locked down and tightly sealed off from the world. In their colonial intransigence, the Chinese authorities seemed particularly intent on dealing with their unarmed protestors primarily through the use of unrelenting, excessive, lethal force, which they long expected would break the Tibetan spirit. The politics of fear and smear continues its steadfastly blind course. During the protests, antic were both the way the governmental propaganda machine was set to operate in full gear in steering and inflaming Chinese nationalism and the way nationalist public attitudes swelled out of control, threatening to backfire (with Tibetan-hating netizens venting their anger against "those ungrateful minorities" or calling for a move to "kill" and "exterminate them all!"). While intensified "patriotic education" was deployed as a main tool in the vilification campaign against the Dalai Lama, the call was also to "strike hard" and "crush" at their sources, all signs of love and longing for the Tibetan leader.

"I am really shocked by the language they used concerning the Dalai Lama," said Liu Xiaobo, a Chinese civilian critical of his government, "They are talking about a 'people's war.' That is a phrase from the Cultural Revolution."[9] Liu, a political commentator, university professor, and human-rights activist further noted how the true nature of the government, which "hasn't changed at all," showed up during big crises. He recognized, through their attacks on the Dalai Lama and the censorship of state news media coverage, the same strategy as the one used during the Tiananmen Square demonstrations in 1989, when pro-democracy leaders were jailed as "black hands," news of killings was blocked, and televised video footage of soldiers firing on students, residents, and workers was absent or carefully edited out. As acutely feared by a number of readers (including this reader) who have been following his writings for years, Liu Xiaobo himself ended up paying a steep price for his sharp tongue and pen. Having previously spent five years in prison and in a labor camp, he was again detained in December 2008, formally arrested in June 2009 for "inciting subversion of state power," and sentenced to eleven years in prison on December 25, 2009. Such an exemplarily harsh measure, meant to dissuade other Chinese citizens from following his path, seemed to have brought about unwanted results as well, as Liu became, a year after his arrest, the absent recipient of the prestigious Nobel Peace Prize. This despite the extraordinary campaign waged, at both the national and international level, by the Chinese government media and spokespeople to discredit the award. Particularly worth noting in the stream of vitriol unleashed on its sponsors were the warnings that attendance at the ceremony in Oslo would be "a black mark" on relations with China.

Try as they might to advocate a "harmonious society," the Chinese government could not convincingly gloss over the failures of its discriminatory social and educational policies toward the people it claims to have "liberated" from serfdom. Working at downgrading the Tibetan cultural and spiritual legacy with a virulent propaganda offensive against the exiled Tibetan leader, the administration has been engaging in a comprehensive cover-up of the round-up of civilians, the arbitrary arrests, torture, killings, and enforced disappearances that have taken place across Tibet since the people's uprising of spring 2008. In the ensuing crackdown, all major detention facilities in Lhasa were filled to capacity. With a shortage of space, prisoners were sent to neighboring provinces and unoccupied buildings, such as military garages and train stations, were temporarily converted into barracks to accommodate the influx of detainees. The authorities have been tightening their control by sending in the People's Armed Police to reinforce the regular policemen already at work in Lhasa. With whole units stationed at major temples and armed men ostensibly posted at every block in the city, the military's control is omnipotent. As Tibetans wrote online or told reporters from Al Jazeera, the already harsh condition in Lhasa has since been "very desperate," "very, very tense," and "very, very bad."

> In the name of Hippocrates, doctors have invented the most exquisite form of torture ever known to man: survival.
>
> Luis Buñuel

China has been carrying out its own Dark Night Policy. Over a thousand Tibetans of all walks of life have disappeared (twelve hundred by Chinese official statistics), and as the International Campaign for Tibet reported, since spring 2008, almost every Tibetan household in Lhasa has a disappeared member. People still sleep in their clothes, fearful of the abductions in dark night raids, when the security agencies combed each and every house to round up all former political prisoners and arbitrarily arrested hundreds of Tibetans. Once the army moved in, the round up of civilians, the detentions and interrogations, the physical and psychological tortures all took place in the dark. When the lights came back on, as with the Tiananmen Square event, the victims would be out of sight, and his-story thoroughly sanitized. During the months preceding the fiftieth anniversary (March 10, 2009), Tibetans continued to "disappear," often being taken from their homes in the middle of the night to face inquisitorial brutality in "black jails." Ad hoc detention centers have sprouted in great numbers in recent years. The surge of blacklisted, "black hands" detainees, the deepening secrets of the notorious "black houses" or "black jails," say it all. So do the peculiar names given to these unofficial activities of abusive power. The growing network of illegal micro-prisons for common people held without trial or charge, often with the full knowledge and backing of the government (on paper, arbitrary arrest and detention are against Chinese law), are the newest weapon local officials use to prevent aggrieved citizens and "troublemakers" from leaving black marks on their bureaucratic records.

As the Tibetan Center for Human Rights and Democracy informed, nearly six thousand Tibetans were subjected to early morning raids over a three-day period in January 2009, for example. The spike in numbers of political prisoners since the 2008 protests is likely to be the largest increase that has occurred in Tibetan areas, and the highly intensified campaigns directed against Tibetan culture and religion mean that virtually any expression of Tibetan identity not directly sanctioned by the state can be branded as "splittist," "separatist," "reactionary," or "counterrevolutionary" and penalized with heavy fines, or else, with beatings, torture, and prison sentences blown out of proportion. (Known cases against cultural figures include, for example, those of the musician Lhundrup; the comedian Dabe; the head of a literacy project for nomads Palchenkyab; the singer, feminist writer, and activist Jamyang Kyi; and the singer and nightclub owner Drolmakyi, who were all detained with no formal charges in 2008.) Any act viewed as a hidden call for freedom can be condemned as an "incitement to subversion of state power." Any cultural or historical documentation of the Tibetan ancient heritage—be it in the form of a book, a photographic record, a song, or an oral transmission in teaching, for example—can easily be framed as a crime of "endangering state security" and, if smuggled abroad, as an "espionage" activity and "a premeditated attempt to overthrow the government" that is all the more reviled as it is, so to speak, "supported by powerful anti-China groups." (Such were the cases of the history teacher Dolma Kyab at a middle school in Lhasa; the monastic dance teacher Gendun at Yulung Monastery; the documentary filmmaker Dhondup Wangchen in Siling [Xining]; or the exiled musician, ethnomusicologist, and filmmaker Ngawang Chophel—to mention just a few.)

A wide range of cultural workers—writers, teachers, musicians, and other performing artists, for example—have been detained under a new drive against cultural activities that may inspire other Tibetans to think along "unofficial" ways (like what it means to be Tibetan) or adopt a "suspect" ideological approach (such as Tibetan performers addressing the audience as "Tibetan brothers and sisters"—a speech act considered to be "subversive" to the "unity of the nationalities"). Singing songs of longing that linger on "a long-lost love"—an indirect way to refer to the Dalai Lama—remains a particularly incriminating activity. And when the authorities find no proof as to what they view as security-endangering intention from the detainees, they spend weeks or months interrogating and humiliating them in order to come up with other reasons to justify the arrest, such as contact with an activist of the Tibetan government in exile or a link to "an organization of a certain foreign country." The stale and overused official conspiracy theory always demands other threats and other scapegoats—"outside," "foreign," "anti-China," or "Westernized" elements of corruption with "ulterior motives." The trumped-up reasons for arrest have at times been so incongruous in their charges that they usually backfire in heightening the reputations of the artists and thinkers detained. Ironically, as the history of Tibetan resistance since 1959 tells, the dominant's violent oppression has most effectively contributed to sustaining the widespread growth of nonviolent protests in occupied Tibet.

Small Acts on the Roof of the World

> We who engage in nonviolent direct action are not the creators of tension. We merely bring to the surface the hidden tension that is already alive.
>
> Martin Luther King Jr.

When Big Insects Eat Small Insects . . . says the title of a book on the fate of Tibet.[10] Divide and conquer; discriminate and incriminate; control and slowly eradicate . . . Each and every old colonial trick has been put to use in today's Tibet, no mater what their previous status of independence and incorporation within China was. As it has been noted by those directly involved, Chinese imperial policies are matchless when it comes to the questions of domination, subordination, and forced (or induced) assimilation. Ho Chi Minh, the founder of the Vietnamese Communist Party once said, "It is better to sniff French shit for a while than to eat China's for the rest of our lives" (even though he was ultimately compelled to turn toward China for support). Always lurking is the specter of the Cultural Revolution—an infamous wound in Chinese history (1966–1976) and "a long-term leftist mistake" (in party-speak), whose mind-damaging impact can still be found in ruling practices marked by vestiges of its smash-the-Four-Olds policies (old customs, culture, habits, and ideas) and its party's rectification-cum-mass-re-education campaign. Effects of the Cultural Revolution's rhetoric linger heavily in the official language and in the way the authorities handle the issue of marginalized nationalities.

Chinese policies geared toward maximal economical productivity and designed, by the light of Han domination, to eradicate the "weeds" of indigeneity often show little understanding of the spiritual dimension largely underlying the current Tibetan struggle. Forcing, for example, monks and nuns to trample or spit on an image of the Dalai Lama (too moronic a gesture to effect the *change of heart* sought for) is contributing, at best, to deepening Tibetan alienation and, at worst, to reinforcing the image of "China" as a vast kindergarten, with partyism as an obsessive-compulsive disorder—a leading cause of disability worldwide. Having neither the size nor the weight—the numbers, the material, and technological power of the mighty military machine—the Tibetans have learned not to rely on the way of the fist. (Attempts in the past at conducting traditional guerilla warfare were unsuccessfully pushed to their limits, with isolated fights lingering until 1969 in the history of Tibetan resistance.) What can be viewed as battles à la David versus Goliath in other contexts of oppression cannot quite apply here, for the Tibetan struggle can be said to be largely carried out without "battles"—not even with the threat of a sling and stone. Words, prayers, songs, silent vigils, a flag, a yak, a banned image of their exiled leader are the small means by which they assert their rights to differ and dissent during their half-century-long resistance.

"Never give up, no matter what," say the posters on the walls and trees of the Tibetan Children's Village in the Tibetan exiled community. Of the many words and advices the Dalai Lama has been giving his people, these are the ones they choose to recall in their daily activities. Not losing the spirit, not succumbing to fear, *just holding* keeps the struggle going. Endure, persevere, and *exist*. Strangely enough, for the oppressed, merely to hold on is enough to arouse ire of the most destructive kind in the oppressor. Winning by force and weight continues to be the dominant's blind way of ruling. The policy of "might makes right" military prevails over all other long-term costs to the people. Again, it looks as if the oversized power of armed forces has been running after its own shadow, with no real adversary combatant in sight. Caught in the very game of power he initiated, this Chinese Giant has been led, through a self-inflicted mistrust, to feeling compelled to show off his might at every shade and shadow of dissidence. Thus, lured into a ghastly no-end conflict, he continues to overreact to a danger of his own creation and to fight high and mighty a projection of his own fear. Again, much to the irritation of Goliathian powers, the test of victory is bound to be asymmetrical in asymmetrical "warfare." The question as to whether the all-winner truly wins or not remains elusive. In the call for "Bod Gyalo" (Victory to Tibet), every small act of protest has its own definition of "success." Stories of the no-sword warriors' courage

in risking their lives for peacefully exercising their basic human rights tend to remain indelibly etched in people's collective memory.

Under the plight of occupation, communist policies are confronted with protest actions mainly informed by Buddhist practices of nonviolence. Aside from reportedly peaceful demonstrations, what the authorities find so threatening to the security of China are, for example: "singing about things we couldn't talk about" (said a Tibetan entertainer); mourning the dead (in resistance) and holding silent vigil; praying for the long life of the Tibetan leader; refusing to calumniate the (tenth) Panchen Lama or to defame the Dalai Lama during re-education campaign sessions; keeping the latter's pictures in secret; surreptitiously replacing the nameplates of government building (Chinese authority symbols) with pro-independence posters; distributing leaflets, posting information materials calling for the respect of human rights or protection of a people's spiritual culture; reading and circulating the Universal Declaration of Human Rights; and while accepting the charges they (the detainees) are accused of, admitting to having no regrets of their deeds, because "my acts are peaceful and nonviolent." Some would go a few steps further, *pleading* that all charges and penalties imposed on their friends should be transferred to them instead (as with Jigme Gyatso from Gaden Monastery, who was sentenced to fifteen years). Silence, hunger strikes, and other gestures of noncompliance and noncooperation with the authorities are often carried out as so many self-assumed, lone manifestations of a collective spirit.

A range of well-known nonviolent acts of resistance defines the Tibetan struggle, which researchers have found to be mostly spontaneous, highly symbolic, but loosely organized. The Chinese authority's need to accuse the Dalai Lama of "masterminding" the impromptu waves of protests, and to attribute any small, individual pro-independence assertion to the existence of a premeditated, systemically organized conspiracy (a trumped-up charge tortured detainees have consistently been forced to assume) is indicative of a profound inability to grasp the core of Tibetan resistance and empowerment. As researchers noted, under the constant surveillance of the extensive Chinese intelligence networks, most protest activities are initiated on the spur of the moment by two or three people who come together on short notice and are joined by others as the action unfolds in public.[11] The small-scale and improvised nature of these protest gestures have time and again frustrated the Chinese forces, which could not always anticipate or prepare themselves adequately. Despite the lack of coordination, of organized mobilization and large-scale provocation, a dynamic common spirit and a sense of interconnectedness seem to draw the countless small acts of resistance together and to seal them wordlessly across the full extent of the Tibetan-populated areas.

> Win by sensing the opponents' rhythms and knowing where they break down.
>
> Miyamoto Musashi, *The Books of Five Rings*

> One cannot comb different kinds of hair with the same brush.
>
> Yin Fatan, on the question of Tibet

When asked what kind of pressures Tibetans could put on Chinese repression, Dhondup Dorjee, vice president of the Tibetan Youth Congress (an exile organization promoting independence from China) replied: "The pressures will come in any form." Zealous nomads galloped on horseback into a schoolyard in Amchok Bora, ripping down a Chinese red flag and hoisting the Tibetan Snow Lion one, shouting "Free Tibet!" amid the roaring support of witnesses. Two boys in Toronto managed to scale the wall of the Chinese embassy to pull down the Chinese flag and raise the Tibetan one, to the sound of ecstatic cheering and laughing from the thousands of viewers who gathered to see the footage in the exiled Tibetan community of Dharamsala.[12] Three days later, another pair of youth repeated the same gesture in Brussels while the crowd whistled, howled, and shouted "China, Out Now!" Then, when ordered to remove the Tibetan flag at the Sera Monastery in Lhasa, the monks naturally asked why? "Since it is *not ours*, why should *we* take it down?" Elsewhere on the plateau, the Chinese flag was further spread on public roads where passersby were regaled with the rare privilege of *walking on it*. These sound images circulated in reports or broadcast on YouTube (blocked in China) have been widely associated with the Tibetan struggle for freedom. Despite the high price paid (when carried out in Tibetan areas), beating the odds and swiftly replacing the Chinese flag with the banned Tibetan flag remains one of the most popular gestures of protest within and outside Tibet. Since the manifestations of spring 2008, a similar fate had befallen the Chinese flags of numerous local schools (such as those of Rekong, Malho prefecture, Qinghai Province, Karze prefecture, Sichuan Province), and it was said that thousands of them were so replaced by the Tibetan flag in protest incidences across the Tibetan plateau.

Alongside the more classic instances of resistance, examples of more creative incidences abound, in which the Tibetan people cunningly turn banal everyday activities into acts of freedom. Memory recalls the visually striking *circles of love*—by nuns, monks, students, old men, women, youth, and sympathizers of all walks of life—built on the familiar Tibetan ritual of circumambulating a holy site (*khorra*), during which incense was burned, butter lamps lit, and written prayers (*windhorses*) released to float in the wind. Images from the Tibetan exile community bring to mind candlelight vigils with thick snakes of people moving slowly in full, hour-long circumambulations. Such group activity offers an opportunity to draw the largest possible circle around the Tibetan community and hence to participate in a common endeavor while partaking in the ceaseless movement of the universe. A conventional religious merit-making act (allowed under Chinese policy) as well as a commemorative event is here transformed into a powerful political action and performed as a public protest whose crowd of participants keeps on growing with the circumambulations.

Lighting a light and switching it off take on their full dimension when the spiritual and the social, that is also, when creation and resistance, link up in the everyday of politics. Of great significance during the 2008 period of unrest were, for example, the acts of monks forbidden to leave their monasteries, like the hundred monks of Rongwo Monastery in Tongren city, who dared to break their confinement by climbing a hill behind the monastery, where they set off fireworks and burned incense to protest the crackdown in Tibetan areas. During the opening ceremony of the Olympics in Beijing, despite the Dalai Lama's good wishes for the event, Tibetans decided to switch off lights of their houses for two hours in protest of China's policies. Showing solidarity toward the suffering of the people in their homeland, Tibetans residing in Dharamsala gathered at their main temple at McLeod Ganj with their faces covered with black cloths at the time when the Olympics inauguration ceremony was scheduled to begin; they also switched their lights off for one hour every day from 8 P.M. to 9 P.M., for the entire duration of the games (August 8 to August 24, 2008).

Constituting the unseen silent ground on which the more visible manifestations thrive, a creative range of quiet resistances of this kind continues to define the Tibetan struggle. In the weeks before the fiftieth anniversary of the National Uprising (March 10, 2009), the Chinese government stepped up levels of intimidation and proceeded systematically to un-voice dissents. Despite the authorities' endeavors to persuade Tibetans to make merry so as to give the impression of normalcy, many Tibetans across the region decided by unified choice to abstain from celebrating their "Losar" (Tibetan New Year, end of February), mourning and honoring instead those killed and disappeared for their roles in the protests. Since then, No Losar has become a widespread movement not only inside but also outside of Tibet. With the rising number of Tibetan self-immolations these last few years, many, commemorating in silence, continue to refuse to celebrate "a grand and prosperous Losar" the way the Chinese authorities had been compelling them to do under accusations of "separatism."

> Fear, coercion, punishment, are the masculine remedies for moral weakness
> But statistics show their failure for centuries.
>
> Elizabeth Cady Stanton

Anything that has sap has singing, so goes a saying. But oddly, making music in prison could incriminate or even cost musicians their lives. In

1993 a group of fourteen nuns in prison secretly recorded songs and poems in tribute to their homeland and to the Dalai Lama. To add insult to injury, they succeeded against all odds to have the cassette tape smuggled out of prison, and the lyrics ultimately traveled on, beyond Tibet, to the international community. "May No Others Suffer Like This," says a song title; "Seeing Nothing but the Sky," says another; and so go some of the song lines: "In the direction of our homeland / We sing a brief song of truth / Oh wind, if you are conscious, / Carry our song to our birthplace . . . / Do not be sad. The time will come for our reunion." Although the nuns insisted the recording was intended to commemorate their days together in prison ("We recorded the songs to let our families and the Tibetan people know that we are still alive, about our situation and our love for our country"), their individual sentences were each extended between five and nine years, and they were condemned for having circulated "reactionary Tibetan songs . . . with the aim of countering the revolution." Prisoners of conscience all jailed for peaceful resistance to Chinese rule in Tibet, they have become known around the world as "Tibet's singing nuns," "the Drapchi 14," or the "Drapchi nuns." While Lhasa's Drapchi Prison, considered to be one of the world's most feared prisons, is notorious for its abusive and extreme, inhumane treatment of prisoners, its nun-prisoners were reputed for their staunch comradeship and solidarity, as they often put their own lives in danger to shield their cellmates.

Sap they have and singing they dare. It was through songs that they *held on*—flowing from within and telling the world they were still alive, for their spirits had not been broken. In 1997, despite the five-day hunger strike of seventy women inmates, two nuns, who sung Tibetan songs during their New Year, were beaten and put in solitary confinement for two years. In 1998 protests inside Drapchi Prison broke out on May 1 and 4, during a Chinese flag-raising ceremony when prisoners began to shout "Free Tibet" and "Long Live the Dalai Lama." The ensuing beatings, torture, and severe maltreatment of the participants led to the deaths of eleven prisoners, five of whom were nuns, all in their twenties. One of the "criminal" nun-prisoners who participated in the 1998 protest and endured extensive torture, Ngawang Sangdrol, had a total sentence term of twenty-three years—a result of three sentence extensions on top of her original. The Chinese authorities denied the existence of the 1998 Drapchi protests. But, in the sentencing document, the nuns' determination and refusal to submit to prison officials was recorded and their "attitude to confession" qualified as "abominable." As a result of intense international pressure however, Sangdrol was released for medical reasons in 2002, just a few days before Chinese President Jiang Zemin visited George W. Bush's ranch in Crawford, Texas. Her cellmate, Phuntsog Nyidrol, the last (that is, the one given the longest sentence) of the fourteen imprisoned singing "criminals," was released in 2004.

Nuns are considered to be powerful political enemies by the Chinese authorities, who have expelled them in droves while trying to weaken the nunneries and their spiritual teaching by imposing strict rules, planting informers, and devising schemes of political indoctrination. Bold and creative actions of protest continue to be carried out by women, youth, and elderly from all walks of life. One of the historical events during the 1959 uprisings was the spontaneous coming together, twice, at Drebu Lingka, the ground below the Potala Palace, of an estimated three thousand (March 12) then five thousand (March 18) Tibetan women in revolt against Chinese oppression. Many of the peaceful demonstrations in Lhasa were initiated and coordinated by nuns, and numerous were the incidents of dissent from nunneries across the plateau. A Tibet Information Network report in July 1993 showed that in the previous six years, nuns led 49 out of the 120 known anti-Chinese protests in Lhasa (40 percent). Despite their ambivalent status in Tibetan society, they had spearheaded the pro-independence movement and played a critical role in the uprisings. Warrior nuns, as they have come to be known, they are often invoked for their gentle tenacity, their inner motivation and unflinching convictions, refusing to bend to Chinese governmental will and surviving in prisons under unspeakably harsh conditions. More recently, in a single instance in May 2008, for example, more than eighty nuns were imprisoned in the Tibetan area of Kardze, Sichuan, for peacefully protesting against the violent crackdown and calling for the Dalai Lama's return to Tibet.

Many of these victims of human-rights abuses thus ended up spending substantial years of their youth in jail, deprived and tortured for their heart-singing crimes. The stories of the nuns in Tibet and the survivors of Drapchi Prison remain exemplary of both the resilience of the human spirit and the futility in the long term of all-seeing state power.

Arms and physical coercion cannot vanquish Tibet's heart. What sustains its spirit of resistance are, apparently, these initially small acts of empowerment and survival, of affirmation of life and singular *living forces* that give agency to each and all, with no elements of glory necessarily attached—in other words, its people's inner strength. In the sphere of *subtle* reality—both within and beyond the symbolic—where the struggle thrives on, the question is not to attack the system through a unilateral power relation. Instead, everything is based on an intuitive strategic insight; and everything lies in the instance of outbidding—often enough, with one's own *life*. The liminal symbolic gesture dares, defies, and challenges by catering to the fear of the dominant, raising through its small consummate deeds the projected possibility that every ordinary no-doer and naysayer could contribute to "overthrowing" the Giant's system of power. The oversized military war strategies fail, in many ways, to measure up to such a defiance of systemic violence and material power through a refusal to play the Master's game on his terms. The whole of visibly displayed superpower can do nothing much to eradicate, once and for all, the tiny symbolic deeds each individual dissenter is capable of initiating. Again, all this *strength to lift a hair* . . . Victory over others by forced battle was emphatically reproved by the very Chinese military's ancestor, Sun Tzu, whose two-millennia-old voice of male wisdom in *The Art of War* still eerily resonates among strategists of both East and West in today's warscape . . . After all, as the "singing nuns" put it, "it is not very big, what we did. We just sang songs, peacefully, for the love of His Holiness the Dalai Lama and for a free Tibet," and they puzzled aloud: "They say we want to destroy the government, but how can songs destroy a government?"

> The advent of an idea is not so much the first appearance of its formulation as its definitive incubation, when, received in the powerful warmth of love, it blossoms forth, fecundated by the heart's force.
>
> Jules Michelet, *Les femmes de la révolution* (*Women of Revolution*)

The heart goes on bleeding, singing, healing . . . and refusing to be jailed. It sees, imprisoned in every man of iron a frail man of flesh wildly gesturing to be set free. In today's political battles and economic strategies, such power of life continues, in its multiplicities, to challenge the unilateral might of the power over life. Through simple, ordinary acts of life, such as that of carrying a tune, opening up a stifled voice, affirming a (one's) melody among others—in other words, being in touch with rhythmic realities in their everyday—the incarcerated reappear from their disappeared status. Alive, still they remain, even when they're not meant to. They live to tell. But how? No lurid stories of the nun's conditions in prison are disclosed in the songs. Instead, what is manifested through them is the singularity of their mode of resistance and existence: how they stay tuned, connected with the ground of life through the way of vibes. When asked for a message to send to Tibetans inside Tibet, four of the nuns now in exile were quoted as saying, "Keep the spirit alive, know the world is watching, and don't be disheartened."[13]

*
* *

walk for rain

The world comes to her with every step.

The darkening evening shades have gradually spread, dissolving daylight in their course. She walks on into nightfall, listening to her footsteps slowing down. When language recedes, a blue of the bluest light flares up on the shores of no-thingness. Quietly, she takes in the rhythm of the land. A river gently babbles close by, drawing her into its cleansing flow. There are tiny flowers blooming near her feet. A thousand springs seem to rise from the depths of the earth, conferring peaceful inspiration on she who quenches her thirst by them. Who is this wanderer, really? Walking side by side with her shadow, sinking wider and wider into shared silence, she sometimes rests in stillness, feeling what it is like to really stand on her feet, breathing. In and out, in in out and out, so she goes in an imperceptible play of holding and releasing. Breath keeps on moving with Mind until she finds a beat of her own and lets her bodily rhythm guide her steps. Joy comes at unexpected turns, so does sorrow as she re-turns—to the open wounds of a world deep at war. When she lifts the soles of her feet to walk again, up and down, up up and down and round about, she loses herself in her walking—grounded and set free, with no pressure or central directing force.

A handwritten sign on the road warns: "Beware of Walking Dead." The sounds of society faintly come and go, receding further as she veers off again, meandering alone on precarious territory, with no ready-made map. She goes forth to wherever her feet take her and errs as she loses herself for what appears to be an endless time in the dark. Small trails, large trails, they all seem to branch out and disappear, only to reappear where they are least expected. Sometimes the darkness seems to close in, and the night sounds fill her senses with fright. Wrestling with her nocturnal fears, she turns and re-turns and heads straight when the trail seems to curve or go round in circles. History often forgets while claiming to remember. To buy time, it keeps her spinning wild. Now and then a familiar tune yields a quaint note. Urging her to listen again to the resonances of events, to how repeatedly "they win the battle, but lose the war." What are people saying? What has suddenly caught her ear?

. . . Isn't every war already a defeat? The critical turn of the inquiry happens when a Kiowa proverb unpredictably comes in her way: "*Walk lightly in the spring; Mother Earth is pregnant."* She marvels at the invaluable gift of walking with both feet. Hers. She's not merely going somewhere. Rather, she's swallowing each step, feeling it with mouth, hand, feet, sole, toe, the whole body in motion, while noticing how thoughts arise, condense, stray, scatter, and return, always ready to concoct stories and even eager to get lost in the process. Now and then, the solitary walk carries her to a strange, collective site: at once emptied from the noises of everyday squabbles and wide open to the call of world events, living intimately abroad at home. Here, immersed in the madness of the day; there and elsewhere within here, voided of her very thoughts and feelings, drinking free from the providing universe around her.

With each step the world comes to the walker.

It is now steep uphill and she starts sweating. Walking gets harder and harder, but there's a subtle magnetism in the path ahead. Wherever she stumbles, an impasse fully assumed could swiftly turn into a passage. The slippery pathways she dreads happen to provide the very links she seeks. Suddenly, out of nowhere a teardrop forms, wetting her eyelid, clinging to the lashes, and blurring her left eye's sight. The tear's swelling seems to take forever to finally fall. Quietly, she notes it's not a tear of sorrow and wonders: What is it then? What's wetting her left eye? A fine rain begins to fall and drop by drop in the mist, she could feel the nocturnal landscape becoming utterly alive in the wetness. Slowly the water turns the ground beneath her feet into muck. Now trekking in the mud, she schleps and sloshes, hearing with every step forward her shoes squelching and getting stuck in the mire. As if this is not enough, she then realizes she is also treading on something that smells awfully like dog shit. In panic, she finds herself skipping, tripping, and slipping in the rain, landing squarely on her face, no longer knowing how to walk.

A tune by Charlie Chaplin takes her slowly back up, sitting and feeling the vibrations from the ground in her body: *"I always like walking in the rain, so no one can see me crying."* Regaining her inner balance and wiping away the mud with the rainwater, she bursts out laughing, puzzled by all her striving in the slush. Smelly or fragrant, she is mud, water, and crumpled grass. She is the dark and the walking in the dark. Drenched by now, rather than merely dampened, she may as well slow down, let go, enjoy the drizzle and the soak. Kicking off her shoes she treads the path anew, feeling the wet earth with all ten toes' sensors spread wide. There's a keen enjoyment in feeling her bare feet kneading and sharing the clay with the grass and the trees. *In the end of the day, do you know Your walk?* Sometimes when it rains . . . a recurring scene at a marketplace near Enampor where she stayed while living in Senegal comes back to her. It was one of these hot and humid days when the sun was hitting at its hardest. Dazed by the heat and oozing sweat as she bought a drink and sat down under the thatched-roof veranda of the store, she looked out blankly at the pace of nearby activities. Suddenly, she felt a commotion among the passersby and caught sight of some *toubabs* (white people) running for shelter while others hastily took out their umbrellas. Giggles burst around her and a voice called out in Jola: "Look, look at them!" The spectacle never failed to draw laughter from the local people, for despite the abrupt, torrential force of the downpours in this part of the world, the villagers walked on leisurely, being in no hurry whatsoever, amazed at the outsiders' reaction to the rain. Here and in much of rural Western Africa, when it poured, outsiders sorely stood out, for the only ones who ran were white people, city dwellers, and foreigners like her.

> The moon sets at midnight. I walk alone through the town.
>
> Zen koan, *The Book of Serenity*

Rain, said the wise, is the falling apart or the breaking open of a cloud. Love it or resent it, as it suits you. For many people living in areas hit by severe drought, waiting for raindrops is akin to waiting for healing and nourishment from above. "Oh, come beautiful rain," goes the song of a Sweat Your Prayer event that gathered some time ago a large community of dancers in Sacramento. These came together to "pray with their bodies" when the city broke the record of longest consecutive days without rain—a persistent problem in megadrought-dry California. Sweat, tears, blood, and water—it's all the same, they said. The dry fields cannot weep and the unseen flowers cannot bloom unless they are blessed with nature's showers. Being rained on while walking alone in the night makes her shrivel and tremble the way a whole forest shivers every time a tree leaf falls in the wind. It tells her, who is dripping wet, of the fertile soil where dreams are planted and creativity grows wild. The cloud-water washes away, calms, and clears the ground for imagination to prosper anew. Listening to their intimate voices, she wonders: In what tongues do rain and wind speak? In what keys do they sing? And how do they keep their touch alive, caressing and lashing accordingly? Perhaps the unseen color of this shower in the dark is pink. Not black or purple but pink rain. For, whenever the scent of rain and moistened earth arises, writing emerges with every virtual step. And it's everywhere when one doesn't go looking for it.

Strolling on, strolling wet.

Every day face to face with the blank screen, thirsting for an immensity intimately her own, she sees herself at once painfully smaller and so very larger than She whom she yearns to project, embrace, or imagine through words, sentences, language events. The word machine names in zero-and-one binaries, but truth manifests itself in the between and lived reality appears in multi twilight shades. Sometimes a secret dies. For a while, writing is carried out with a specific passenger and reader in mind. The latter's absence remains very present on the blank page—as if the whole purpose of writing was to regain the attention of the one missing. Tell the world what only a lover's ear should hear, in all tenderness. The triumph at the end of the day is to have the printed words resonate beyond one's limits, exceeding all the while not losing what they once meant so intimately in the privacy of a loving body. Once published, it would feel like sharing one's bed, sheets, and pillow—the lovers' haven—with every passerby. Yet, never is it a mere question of unveiling or shedding light on a hidden subject. Sometimes the secret speaks not, not because time excels in effacing what no longer knows how to speak its way out, but because it remains utterly indifferent to speech's quest. Thus, a small secret dies not an imposed death but a natural one, yielding room to *the secret* that has no single content and no private or public existence outside its temporal utterance. Freed from the need to address a known receiver, the gift of writing moves on blindly.

As is well known, the earth walk is full of perils, and yet a path often finds its way through the Blind Person. The rain's soft pattering gives music back to life and sets her course for the night. Walk, walk gently for rain . . . *There is beauty above you. There is beauty below you. There is beauty all around you. May you always walk in beauty*, says a Navajo prayer. When it rains, if it pains, no need to weep, it's all the same. When it rains, black ink, red ink, let it run. At night, it's all the same. When it rains, it writes like it paints; it types, cuts, pastes, deletes, prints, and even sings in tune with the wind. So it goes while inside, a zither with no strings plays along her footsteps. Before she realizes it, she's back on the road, walking the dark in the tread of ancestral wayfarers and wanderesses. *Walk as if your feet are hugging the Earth*. The child in her cannot help noticing the smell and turns around to catch the fragrance of a passerby's flower of freedom. The air is still full of water, but the rain has now vanished like a dream. All of a sudden, it's over. Time to begin afresh with the call of a new birth, with darkness turning. Gracefully, the night withdraws as it greets the dawning *pink* light that bleeds through hues of black; lifting and restoring, veil after veil, the world to its ancient everyday life-forms.

the new rebels

The Blank Page

The Internet is changing both China and Tibet, and their connections to the world. Two days after the famed events of March 14, 2008, a dozen YouTube videos showing sporadically bloody confrontations in Lhasa were removed or blocked. Internauts trying to access these YouTube videos consistently met with a *blank web page* on the screen. Other local sites such as 56.com, youku.com, or tudou.com—some of the largest video-sharing platforms in China—bear no trace whatsoever of the scenes that happened in Tibet. Like the blank space in people's homes and temples that conspicuously replaces the Dalai Lama's removed (and hence all-the-more-treasured) image, the blank page as a manifestation of disappearance and censorship seems a fixture to the country's highly supervised netscape. China's Internet population may be the world's largest—604 million by the end of September 2013, including over 130 million rural members (figures from the China Internet Network Information Center)—but its Internet users' access to the web remains, proverbially, heavily controlled and their surfing physically monitored in cybercafes. However, with its long-standing policies of restricting its citizens' exposure to information, the country is facing ever-renewed challenges to its all-powerful Internet filtering system. When people dare to make their social and political views public, they may be at best temporarily silenced, but there's no turning back for them. Chinese netizens have their own workarounds, and information not available on the Chinese mainstream press does get through, *despite* China's "great firewall" and its closed system of surveillance.

A web search in China for reference to the Tiananmen events, for example, is said to yield no results, and yet such a silence and absence on cyberspace, like the blank page of censored sites, tells volumes about the government officials' fear and inability to account for what they want to forget. For over two decades now, every year, as with the March 10 date in Tibetan areas, on the day of June 4, severe precautionary measures are taken nationwide to prevent the possibility of any mishaps from "troublemakers." This seems to be the night fate of any government that slaughters its own citizens. (An example among many: more than forty journalists, scholars, activists, and lawyers—including the most celebrated human-rights lawyer Pu Zhiqiang—were recently [2014] held in detention ahead of the twenty-fifth anniversary of the Tiananmen Square crackdown.) Thus, *despite* the robust political repression in China, the spirit of Tiananmen thrives on. *Despite* the suppression of its memory and the numerous press reports affirming today's Chinese youth's indifference to the historical event of 1989, the prolific number of Chinese forums and blogs online attests to the contrary: "embers from the June Fourth movement still burn," as a poet and editor of *Tendency* (Bei Ling) puts it. And, *despite* the government's tight control and heavy censorship, the Internet has generated, among the younger generations of urban, educated Chinese, an online public with a fast-growing community of savvy netizens and cybernauts, eager to voice their grievances against local officials' corruptions and to call for social justice. They collectively know they are not alone. "The people paid for their protests in blood," as a Beijing-based journalist and former editor of *Bingdian* (Li Datong, who lost his job) remarks, "but it was the party and the army that were most deeply damaged. No longer could they claim to be the 'people's government' or the 'people's army.'"[1]

The speedy rise of social media continues to play a powerful role in growing civic awareness around the world. A government's lack of trust for its people is bound to nurture in reverse a deepening lack of trust from those it tries to govern. Mutual mistrust and distrust lie at the core of social volatility as manifested in the waves of protests rocking nations around the world and more particularly here, in the rising high-profile outbreaks of revolt that erupted in China in the last few years. Firewall censorship has gained ground in a dozen countries, and the Canada Center for Global Security Studies and the Citizen Lab has already warned some time ago that "the problem of Internet control is becoming an issue for more than human rights concerns." As previously seen in the United States with the National Security Agency's expanding surveillance powers, huge leaps have been taken in the last ten years in interception technology, and the Internet as a tool of emancipation has adversely also become the most effective shortcut to totalitarianism. Under the pretext of filtering for porn, or of protecting people from illegal information and harmful rumors, it is political filtering that governments put into force, and in China, this is particularly enforced around key events like anniversaries of the Tiananmen Square protest. The more pervasive the tightening of regulations aimed at monitoring internet usage, the more viral the people's need to vent their anger publicly and to spread graphic protest reports online—which continue unfailingly to be deleted, as official censors (or "Web Traitors," according to netizens) escalate their crackdown on Internet freedom.

In their quest for mass surveillance, it is striking how the two world giants come to meet in their practices, despite the divergences in appearance. The biggest hacker on the planet finds no qualms in blasting its potential rival for doing the same. While in the United States, the administration had been secretly implementing a massive spying program aimed not only at "foreign terrorists" but, more insidiously, at its own citizens and at citizens from around the world, as China continues its aggressive digital domestic surveillance. It has been steadily stepping up censorship of the microblogs (whose use has been increasing dramatically—for example, from 63 million to 195 million in a mere six-month period, January to July 2011) and gathering followers for its blocking technology from authoritarian regimes around the world. Launching an Internet "cleansing" campaign dubbed "spring breeze" in the spring of 2012, the Chinese authorities have, for example, reportedly arrested over a thousand users; deleted hundreds of thousands of "harmful" online messages; issued warnings to over three thousand websites; punished some seventy Internet companies; and barred users of two of the largest microblogging services, Sina Weibo and Tencent Weibo, from commenting for a few days so as to effect a "centralized clean-up."[2] Such blocking became in itself one of the most discussed topics, generating a huge wave of comments by netizens, some of which read: "A Weibo without 'comment' function is going to end 'rumours'? . . . . The more you stop people speaking, the more 'rumours' there'll be"; "Make the most of this opportunity! All those things you wanted to post but were afraid of being criticized harshly for, you can now post!" or, "Is stopping comments an April Fool's joke?"

New technologies have time and again proven to be double-edged swords, making it difficult to foretell whom the diversifying "winners" and "losers" turned out to be. If the Internet opens wide the venues of online expression and dissent, it also provides more comprehensive and sophisticated tools to the ruling authorities to hunt down, monitor, persecute, and arrest those ordinary citizens and activists who question the political orthodoxy in protecting human rights. *Despite* the Open Door Policy adopted since 1978 in China, the government's use of content-filtering technology to tighten its control over the flow of information continues to be part of a comprehensive effort at extending political censorship. *Despite* the enormity, if not futility, of the task of checking and *braking* people's thinking, the Communist Party has been spending an equivalent of ten billion US dollars on surveillance and employing an estimated thirty thousand cybercops to censor Internet traffic. And, *despite* the systematic repression, a leaked report also showed a conservatively estimated 127,000 antigovernment protests occurring in China in 2008 and 58,000 "mass incidents" breaking out in 2009 during only the first three months of the year.[3] Rather than slowing down, the pace has nearly redoubled in a year's time.

The recent shift from microblogs to instant messaging platform WeChat (or Weixin in Chinese), known mostly for private chatting and photo sharing over mobile devices, has gained huge popularity (over 800 million users, with 500 million monthly active users in March 2015) as an unofficial news channel for information that would usually be censored. In response, China hastened to launch what WeChat members called a "pre-emptive strike," "an invasion of individual privacy," using "antiterrorism" rationale for the extended clampdown as an excuse to purge government critics. Social media platforms have become an effective space of citizens' protest, giving citizens an opportunity to put to debate the system's failures, while allowing the authorities to take measure in assessing and controlling public sentiment. Ultimately, what matters is not so much who wins or who loses in these real and cyber conflicts but how, through winning and losing in public, the comprehensive censorship network has been forced out into the open. Abuse of power begets defiance of power—as with the case of the former National Security Agency contractor Edward Snowden, whose expertise in exploiting the blind spots of America's most secretive spying systems has shown hacking, leaking, and disclosing to be endemic to tightening and revamping computer security for massive electronic-surveillance purposes. Awareness of the public officials' egregious behavior in China continues to grow, while off-line citizen activism has been giving Chinese independent lawyers and human-rights defenders a crucial role in challenging, via the very "rule of law," the government's system of *secret* power and control.

"Sensitive Cases"

> The one whom I enclose with my name is weeping in that dungeon.
>
> Rabindranath Tagore

"China is a country ruled by law." The party's favorite mantra speaks of a goal sanctified in its constitution since 1999. With the gain in size and in visibility comes the scrutiny from both inside and outside. In developing a modern legal system, the "emerging great power" would want the cake and eat it all. But the assertive official promise for a rule-of-law society has also given rise to growing demands for constitutional rights, desperate searches for justice against abuses of power, and with these, the need to publicly put on trial the very power of the rule of law. The legal profession in the country has steadily grown to be an important social-service profession, as the lawyers' function shifts from merely serving in the domain of public authority to protecting rights and interests in the domain of private parties. Lawyers in China do not enjoy high political status, nor are they adequately protected by the system in their rights, so Chinese law scholars have assessed. Much has been said regarding the repressive environment of legal practice and the risks incurred in providing legal services to society's disenfranchised and most vulnerable citizens.

Often made a pawn of the powerful and the corrupt, the law has become a front line in the context of China's modernization under one-party rule. Of growing importance is the role lawyers are playing for promoting greater legal awareness in daily civil life—by defending victims of abuse, helping ordinary petitioners in pressing their grievances to the central government, providing them with legal advice in leading them to the courts where, to the authorities' distaste, their complaints could be resolved by rule of law. As the lawyers' level of education often turns out to be higher, and their knowledge of the field more extensive than those of the judicial officials in charge of managing them, fundamental issues of jurisprudence inevitably arise with regard to the party's role in China's struggle toward the rule of law. It is hardly surprising, for example, that the president of the Supreme People's Court of China (Wang Shengjun) is neither a lawyer nor a judge but an agent of the party apparatus and a former public security official. (Examples from around the world continue to tell how the problem of power between political administration and professional competence are likely to remain irresolvable in regimes where the function of the cadre in charge is above all to control the ideological aspect of the profession.) With the relentless work of human-rights lawyers, many miscarriages of justice have thus come to light, which raises questions as to whether the officials serve the law or the law serves the officials.

"The party covers the entire process of justice," wrote a blogger and former editorial head of *Xinhua* magazine (Zhang Wen). China's justice minister (Wu Aiying) had made it clear that lawyers should observe discipline and obey the party, whose liaisons, as she promised (in 2009), would be sent to all law firms to "guide" their work. Officials often apply the law selectively as an instrument against their critics, while readily exempting themselves from behaving lawfully. When lawyers take a stance against the whims of rulers to vigorously defend the rights of common people, including those of controversial clients and causes, they do so invoking the weight and purpose of the law as sole support. Their hope, as they have been insisting, is to contribute to changing a judicial system set up to protect not the rights of victims and suspects but the authority of the government. Such was also the aim of some 303 prominent Chinese citizens inside and outside the government (including not only lawyers, writers, artists, activists, and intellectual dissidents from diverse walks of life but also workers, peasants, mid-level officials, and rural leaders) who—on December 10, 2008, the sixtieth anniversary of the Universal Declaration of Human Rights—dared to risk their lives and livelihoods to petition the government for democratization. Modeled after the Czech Charter 77 led by Václav Havel, the petition, called Charter 08, asked where China is heading in the twenty-first century and proposed nineteen specific recommendations for restoring the rule of law in the governing of the country.[4] Despite the ban put on local and state media—forbidding them to report on Charter 08 and to interview anyone who signed it—shortly after it was issued, the petition garnered more than seven thousand signatures.

The year 2008 saw not only extensive unrest across the Tibetan plateau but also numerous signs of a broader public political reawakening in Chinese civil society. *Lawful* dissidence appeared through a range of events during this year, of which Charter 08 as well as the "Twelve Suggestions for Dealing with the Tibetan Situation" petition are examples well known to the international community. Daring to offer an unexpected, collective voice in the midst of aggressive Chinese nationalism, a group of twenty-nine leading Chinese intellectuals, writers, artists, and activists released the open letter on March 22, when disturbance was spreading wide across Tibet. Their hope was to eliminate "interethnic animosity" in the goal of achieving unity. Appealing "to the Chinese people to reflect deeply on what is happening," they emphatically demanded that the trials of those arrested "be carried out according to judicial procedures that are open, just, and transparent;" and among other propositions, they called on the government to guarantee human rights, to abide by the freedom of speech and religious belief, and to open a direct dialogue with the Dalai Lama.[5]

Charter 08 was a large-scale, civil-society movement, hailed as the most significant act of public dissent against the Chinese Communist Party (CCP) since the Tiananmen Square event in 1989. It circulated widely in China and many of its supporters were also prominent figures, including some former party officials. Proportionately, 2009 saw one of the fiercest crackdowns on human-rights writers and lawyers in the country. At least seventy of the initial signatories were summoned for police interrogation, while the main authors of the charter underwent dire harassment: the writer Wen Kejian was detained in Hangzhou; the scholar (and former member of the Communist Youth League) Zhang Zuhua's home in Beijing was ransacked, and his passport, computers, books, and notebooks confiscated; while the professor and human-rights activist Liu Xiaobo, who was first detained in December 2008, was formally arrested in June 2009, and later, in December 2009, sentenced to eleven years in prison as previously mentioned. The absent recipient both of the 2009 Homo Homini Award and 2010 Nobel Peace Prize, Liu was also the head of the International PEN center in China.

Liu's two-decade-long history of active dissent might have led many to speculate on his leadership role in the release of the Charter 08 manifesto, but of equal importance was the publication of an open letter written and signed by twenty-three retired elder members of the party on October 1, 2010, one week before the announcement of the Nobel Peace Prize. Unlike Charter 08, which was directed more generally toward Chinese citizens (both officials and common people), the letter, addressed to the Standing Committee of the National People's Congress, called specifically on China's highest state body to dismantle the system of censorship "in favor of a system of legal responsibility."[6] The letter further urged political reform, deploring the lack of freedom of speech and of the press due to the secret actions by the "invisible black hands" of the Central Propaganda Department that violates the Chinese Constitution and is placed above both the Central Committee of the Communist Party and the State Council. Thus, even Premier Wen Jiabao's public speeches were reportedly edited so that sections on the importance of "political system reforms" were all removed when transmitted on China's Central Television's *Xinwen Lianbo* and in official news release from Xinhua News Agency.

> Fear is a habit.
>
> Aung San Suu Kyi

Over and over again, the charges of "counterrevolution" and of "incitement" have been invariably used to silence all criticisms of the government, as threats to and detentions of signatories of Charter 08 continue relentlessly since its publication. Numerous illegal punishments, non-notified arrests, unofficial detentions, and unexplained disappearances mark China's current period of intense repression. Intent on crushing dissent, the crackdowns have further extended to citizens who persevere in denouncing other abuses. Aside from human-rights activists and online writers (including independent journalists and bloggers), those to whom increased restrictions also eagerly applied continue to be migrant workers and individuals who persevere in seeking to petition the central government on abuses by local authorities. Singular and solitary protests—many from the middle class—over local grievances have also recently surged in China. More well known to the foreign media are, for example, cases of owners rebelling against forced evictions and the demolitions of their homes; farmers fighting against the confiscation of their land with no adequate compensation; and villagers standing up against unfair treatment by corrupted officials. Although these protests have rather concrete demands that are narrower in scope, they are, together with the rise of high-profile mass protests, indicative of a civil society's awakening "local conscience" and powerful aspiration to justice.

In an apparently desperate case, for example, a seventy-seven-year-old retired doctor is said to have publicly unleashed her anger over the demolition of her property in a prospering Shanghai neighborhood by stripping naked on the step of a courthouse.[7] The symbolic power of such a gesture eloquently speaks to the condition of arbitrarily enforced dispossession in the land of officially claimed harmony. As succinctly summarized by a Chinese businessman, Wang Shixiang, in another case: "I know my life is in danger, but I just can't swallow this injustice." The man has made some ten trips to Beijing to petition for the prosecution of corrupt policemen, "each visit ending with no exception in detention."[8] More recently (on August 2, 2012), a woman from the southern province of Hunan, Tang Hui, was sentenced to eighteen months in a re-education through labor center in Yongzhou, with no formal trial, for her persistent efforts to seek justice for her daughter. Having spent the last seven years to indict the seven men convicted of having kidnapped, raped, and forced her then-eleven-year-old daughter into prostitution, she continued, after the verdicts were passed, to fight for harsher penalties and to protest against police support for one of the defendants' call for leniency. The detailing of her cause and punishment has outraged the public and rallied China's online community (an estimated 60.2 million daily active users on Sina Weibo until November 2013), prompting the authorities to cave in and to release her shortly after (August 10, 2012).[9] Tang Hui's case not only revives public critical debate over the government's controversial use of the *laojiao* or "re-education-through-labor" system, a controversial feature of China's legal system that allows for detention without trial, but also led to the publication (on August 14, 2012) in several Chinese newspapers of an open letter by ten lawyers from different cities. The letter was sent to the Ministry of Public Security and the Ministry of Justice, calling for reform of the *laojiao* system and warning that the punishment of the rape victim's mother could result in abuses of power and "violation of international human-rights treaties." Tang Hui subsequently (July 15, 2013) won the lawsuit at Hunan Provincial High People's Court, which ruled that she be compensated for infringement on personal freedom and for mental distress by the *laojiao* authorities in Yongshou.

This successful conclusion to a closely watched legal battle was said to be a rare indicative of the growing power of China's vast Internet and blogging classes. But analysts also saw the Tang case as all show, doubting that there has been any *change of heart* for, while the government and its state-run media champion the rule of law, those made "criminals" by the state continue most likely to be those made to disappear without due process, precisely for demanding legitimate justice. Thus, equally worth noting, for example, is the way Beijing has been working at removing the legal channels through which ordinary citizens can voice their grievances. Here, persistently targeted are homegrown adversaries such as the civil-rights lawyers who, working at enhancing China's legal system, were not afraid to take on politically tinged cases and to "lose all" by walking into grave taboo areas.

For having offered legal recourse to defendants of Tibetan detainees, the Falun Gong practitioners (a castigated spiritual group), or those whose relatives were victims of the Tiananmen bloodshed (all deemed by the government and, more specifically, by the judicial authorities' jargon to be politically "sensitive cases"), for example, these lawyers were effectively disbarred with trumped-up charges. The Chinese regime's weapon against those often considered to be "the new enemies of the state" was to cancel their licenses or to decline to renew their annual registrations, thereby turning what used to be a perfunctory matter into an effective instrument of pressuring not only the individual lawyers concerned but, more generally, law firms and the whole of the profession, as well as any citizen in need of legal representation. "If even a famous lawyer gets arrested, what can we ordinary little people do?" said Tong Zhongjun, a migrant worker whose son developed kidney stones from drinking tainted baby formula.[10] Indeed, when it comes to "little people"—those with no wealth and material power—the police, in China as elsewhere, tend to turn a blind eye on their cases, no matter how heinous the offense against the law. Under commonly employed false charges (such as that of "tax evasion"), threats of being accused of a serious crime, and physical intimidation, these rights lawyers have been denied their license to practice law and have been beaten, detained, or imprisoned for having dared to raise the justice authorities' ire through their actions.

Rising surveillance, intense harassment, interference, and retaliation against top human-rights lawyers continue relentlessly in recent years. Tightly controlled, intimidated, and harassed, these lawyers have been *walking on thin ice*, and as it has become known among those concerned in China, "the best lawyers are the ones who can't obtain a license." To mention just a few who were persecuted for taking on politically delicate cases: Tang Jitian and Liu Wei, two lawyers accused, in their defense of a Falun Gong member, of having "disobeyed court personnel and disrupted order in the courtroom" (actually, of having objected to being videotaped—which is illegal in Chinese courtrooms), have had their licenses revoked permanently. Gao Zhisheng, known for his vocal defense of religious minorities, as well as of victims of official corruption and police abuse, was repeatedly subjected to long periods of detention and of torture by security forces. Once a celebrated lawyer praised by the Communist Party, which he left in 2005 to denounce the government's treatment of Falun Gong, Gao also saw his legal license revoked and his practice shut down; he vanished into police custody in September 2009, his forced disappearance lasting over two years before his relatives could confirm he was alive in a prison in the remote part of Xinjian (March 24, 2012).

Other causes célèbres among human-rights advocates whose names have become "sensitive words" on the Chinese Internet: Chen Guangcheng, the blind, self-taught lawyer on whom the international spotlight was recently focused, and whose passage to the United States was the object of a week of frenetic negotiations when his escape from village house arrest in Shandong Province to the US Embassy collided with a visit to Beijing by Secretary of State Hillary Clinton. An advocate for women's rights, land rights, and the welfare of the poor, the rural, and the disfranchised, he was known for having exposed abuses in China's birth-control program. Fighting official corruption and advocating for fiscal transparency, "Xu Zhiyong," a legal scholar at Beijing University, a passionate rights activist, an elected legislator, and founder of Gongmeng, the Open Constitution Initiative (a legal aid and research organization fined and banned), who has been placed under house arrest without charge numerous times since 2009, was detained (July 2013), as were forty others involved in the campaign, and was sentenced to four years in prison (January 2014). Among his "crimes": calling for the release of activists and campaigning against government abuses; previously, publishing a blog post that called for a "new citizens' movement" in "a free China ruled by democracy and law, a just and happy civil society with 'freedom, righteousness, love' as the new national spirit" (May 29, 2012)[11]; helping organize citizens' raids on "black jails" used to detain petitioners coming to Beijing to present grievances; helping parents campaign against discriminatory barriers that prevent children from the countryside from enjoying the same educational privileges as urban residents; representing migrant workers, victims of the tainted milk scandal, people locked up in these secret undeclared jails, or else, a group working to ease discrimination against people with hepatitis B; writing and breaking the silence of Han Chinese on Tibetan self-immolations; in brief, constantly pushing for the rule of law and human rights because, as he fearlessly put it, "if the world is to become a better place, then someone has to pay a price."

More than five hundred attorneys in China have reportedly been detained in recent years in connection to sensitive criminal, political, religious, property, and environmental cases, and 80 percent of those detained between 1997 and 2002 were eventually found innocent of wrongdoing. "There aren't many left who tell the truth these days!" wrote netizens, who have not hesitated to comment sarcastically on life in China by referring to President Xi Jinping's signature slogan "the Chinese dream" (meant to emulate the "American dream") in these terms: "Prisons are dreaming the Chinese dream"; "Funeral homes will be holding a series of 'Chinese dream, the dream of cremation, my dream' events"; or else, "China = prison? So this is the truth! Prison comrades, you have been under the tender loving care of the party and the people!" While fully understanding that they are violating the law, especially in "sensitive cases," officials continue, by necessity, to legitimize their practices by reiterating the hollow claim that everything they do is "according to Chinese law." Certainly depending on it is China's public face as an emerging superpower thriving on a modern legal system. And ironically enough, it is this very contradiction that gives lawyers an edge in their struggle to elevate China's legal system.

Politically controversial cases are so many test cases for the officials' mantra claim. The more they lean publicly on the rule of law to justify their acts, the more they provide opportunities for these dedicated lawyers to embarrass them by exposing the Great Gap between pretense and practice. The reawakening in China's civil society may not look at all political on the surface, but the true breadth of the "little people's" problems is what makes officials "*that scared*" of the countryside and "terribly afraid of people organizing," as a legal activist puts it (Chen Guangcheng). Decisive pressure for change is at the grassroots level and often comes from ordinary people who "grasp the law and push." Indicative of the scope of the problems involved and the extent to which the government is marred by these embarrassments is precisely the fierceness with which it continues to crackdown on lawyers, journalists, writers, artists, cyber-activists, and all those who have been playing a role in "giving voice" to victims of human-rights abuses. The Internet effect has put into relief Beijing's great fear and intolerance of collective "rights consciousness" among China's citizenry. Promoting legal awareness "for the sake of social progress and fighting injustice" (Xu Zhiyong), prominent rights lawyers are often those made to lose their own rights for, as astutely remarked, one cannot be a rights defender in China without being a rights case oneself (Gao Zhisheng). China's rule of law has been paradoxically driven by the obsessive compulsion to "*Get Them Lawyers*."

displaced, dispossessed, disappeared

The Great Uprooting

> Being Indian is mainly in your heart. It's a way of walking with the earth instead of upon it. A lot of the history books talk about us Indians in the past tense, but we don't plan on going anywhere . . . . Mother Earth is not a resource, she is an heirloom.
>
> David Ipinia

With the twenty-first century being often referred to as the Chinese century, there is a general China-phobia developing in proportion with China's economic rise. In a special report on her quest for natural resources (March 15, 2008), the *Economist* did not hesitate to refer to China's leaders as "The New Colonialists." As it is well known, the Old colonialists are ever fond of having the blame switched so as to position themselves as the saviors. Like the famed, debated case of "white men saving brown women from brown men" (Gayatri Chakravorty Spivak) in postcolonial contexts where colonizers are represented as protectors (the case was particularly given a new lease on life in the recent war rhetoric of saving Iraqi and Afghan women), the China-Tibet conflict as a possible case of white men saving oppressed "red-faced" men from dominant Han-yellow men has also been the subject of acrimonious disputes. Here, however, the contention could be located not only between imperialist and nativist discourses but also between two discourses of imperialism. Furthermore, certain analysts readily condemn the Tibetans' cause célèbre, speaking with scorn about the involvement of rock stars, movie directors, and Hollywood actors, as well as the sentimental over-focus on the monk-warriors. By framing the conflict within the context of British colonialism and the lingering effect of its propaganda machine, such viewpoints not only patronize the cause as a mere result of British newspeak or of Western spiritual fantasies, thereby denying the people's agency (both Tibetan and Chinese) in the prolonged struggle, they also often end up endorsing the Chinese official narrative that seeks to divert attention from its internal policies' failures by blaming these on the "Dalai clique," "the foreign enemy," or all "Western supporters."

As the West becomes increasingly threatened by its achievements, "China" as a new object of interest in theories of globalization comes to dominate the media and the economic circles, as well as the academic milieus. In addition to indulging in "power grown out of the barrel of a gun" (Mao Zedong), Beijing is also intensively invested in large-scale ethnic and environmental-economic colonization—or in the power of authoritarian capitalism to undermine all ungovernable social relations of old. Set to become the world's largest economy by 2025, China is undergoing a Great Uprooting—promoting, with her mammoth urbanization drive, rapid shifts from production to consumption, and from countryside to city and megacity. Across the nation, some twenty cities are currently being built every year as bulldozers continue to level entire villages, replacing people's small rural homes with standardized high rises and obliterating the rich, labyrinthine architectural urban fabric of a traditional Chinese city. By 2025 China would have fifteen supercities with an average population of twenty-five million. The government is pushing ahead with the plan to create a consuming class of new urbanites and to *conquer the countryside* by turning remote corners of China's territories into giant construction sites, paving vast swaths of farmland, and moving some 250 to 400 million rural residents to newly built towns and cities over the next twelve years. The scale and the pace eloquently speak to the Orwellian effort deployed in this civilizing-the-poor modernization project, which officials have heralded as a "milestone in development."

> We like to believe in Brazil that we live in a peaceful, happy place, when the truth of our existence is far more complicated. It's like we're Narcissus gazing into a pool of sewage.
>
> Malu Fontes, on the lack of attention given to the rapes of poor women in Rio de Janeiro

In China, as in the United States, national policy often makes a global difference. Urbanization fast tracked as device both for raising consumption and for social control has been ushering in a new era of voracious development and city living that is changing both the notion of a

"city" and the face of the planet. Intensifying the *divide* between the urban and the rural, while claiming to *integrate* them, such an authoritarian citification contributes to the rise of a new system of domination and subjection. The more powerfully a city acts as a magnet for migrants, the sharper the divide between urban and rural, and the stronger the apartheid against this urban underclass (or "second-class citizens," as the official media sometimes called them). What exacerbates further the situation is the persistent legacy of Mao's *hukou* scheme—or household registration that has routinized discrimination against migrants from the countryside (as well as their urban-raised and city-born children). In this system of urban supremacy, better service means better control, "improvements" enable new structures for consolidating bureaucratic power, and with these, everyone is bound to gain a tractable locality—that is, rehoused in a zoned, permissible place—while close, continual, state surveillance becomes the norm. Today, disappearing the countryside and controlling the cities has become key for Beijing, as outrage over socioeconomic disparity has contributed to an upsurge of rural resistance to state dominance in recent years, while the advent of supercities as (highly complex and vulnerable) global hubs could also mean the undoing of the centralized empire-state.

It is in relation to this context of staggering forced migration of dislocated people and of compulsory urbanization for economic growth across the country that Beijing's unremitting efforts to "civilize" and assimilate Tibet could be first viewed. In official speak, "Tibet is now *marching* toward modernization in urban appearance," moving from "backwardness to progressiveness, from poverty to prosperity." However, particularly problematic in the snow lion country (although still at a rate considered 20 percent lower by Beijing's standard) is how the modernization drive monolithically equates the urban not only with standardization, development, linear progress, and profit, as convention has it, but also with "peaceful liberation," state management, rationalization (and repression) of religion, as well as commodification (and subjugation) of cultural traditions—which require, among others, the phasing out of Tibetan language in schooling, severe restrictions on Buddhist temples, and intensive re-education programs for the monks toward a "better life" or "brighter future." The patronizing ("returning pastures to grasslands") resettlement of nomadic herders to towns is yet another form of urbanization that, aside from reducing formerly self-sufficient families to impoverishment, further equates sedentarization, engagement in business, and acquisition of Chinese language (Mandarin) with modernization.

In the so-called ethnic minority regions where populations are relatively smaller, accelerated urbanization has further political implications, as its actual success remains bound to Han Chinese (the dominant ethnicity) in-migration, and its ideological importance, far more complex than in Han-populated development zones. Forced modernization and Sinicization go hand in hand, for example, in the preferential socioeconomic policies that underlie the increasing influx of ethnic Chinese settlers into Tibet and in what former president Hu Jintao called a "leapfrog development" program of mass rehousing and relocation of Tibetans, designed to strengthen political and military control over the region's rural population. On the one hand, to make the Tibetan countryside more accessible to the state, over two million Tibetan villagers have been moved to look-alike townships and roadside settlements since 2006. Aside from restrictions, suppressions, coercive control, and *enhanced* security presence, Beijing has also deployed comprehensive efforts to "*enhance* living standards" by: urbanizing the region rapidly; establishing an economic development zone in Lhasa, the heart of Tibet; and building *enhanced* transportation links such as the world's highest Qinghai-Tibet railway linking Lhasa to eastern China and the Tibet Autonomous Region to any other province. On the other hand, to attract the alleged millions of Han immigrants in Tibet, they were offered job opportunities, economic incentives, and preferential treatment (Han Chinese are said to own, manage, and profit from large companies that dominate the main industries and to occupy most government-related employment, with 95 percent of official Chinese immigrants employed in state-owned enterprises). Thus, "bringing profit to impoverished Tibet" seems to benefit first and foremost the Chinese, thereby raising constant questions as to whose interests the urbanization drive truly serves.

Accelerating a number of projects aimed at drawing the plateau's natural resources into eastern and central China, the railway project has been flooding the region with unprecedented numbers of Han migrants and visitors (estimated at twenty million a year by 2020, currently with 93 percent of the tourists being Chinese). It facilitates large-scale transfer of population as well as speedy transport of troops to control restive "minority areas," a.k.a. "sensitive areas." Although it is adamantly defended by the government as a successful attempt at linking the plateau's economy with inland economies, the extensive railway project is also a constant reminder of the classic mode of colonial consolidation and exploitation. It was through "railway imperialism" that empire-builders ensured the economic and political control of the hinterlands of ports they commanded. Memory recalls with irony how the first railroads were introduced into China over a century ago by the British in cooperation with the Japanese to strengthen their imperialist control over China—including control of foreign military and of the transfer of Chinese resources out of the country. Colonial railways have been an intrinsic part of the spread of empire, with its values and beliefs, its institutions and economic patterns—that is, production of new needs, new commodities, new populations of consumers and producers, newly adapted policies and security measures to make the conquered territory safe for exploitative investment.

Sea of Immigrants

China wants Tibet and not the Tibetans.

"Why Tibet Is Burning," The Kashag

Much has been written on the far-reaching impact of bringing the railway to Lhasa City and to the southern corridor of Tibet. Expansion of the railway network on the Tibetan plateau (six more lines to be in operation before 2020) is part of China's Great Western Development Strategy, but to quote former president Jiang Zemin, the rail line, which consolidates a strong Chinese presence in Tibet, is a political project meant to address "two major issues in Tibet—economic development and social stability." In the dominant's unifying rhetoric, the tendency to appropriate is skillfully couched in the language of progress and development. But, with policies created to facilitate Chinese immigrants' exploitation of opportunities in Tibet, the basic questions "for whom?" and "in whose interest?" inevitably arise anew with every claim to development and betterment. The primary industries being owned by the state, the exploitation of this resource-rich region, and more particularly of Tibet, would have little effect in aiding the local economy. Chinese scholars analyzing the situation have been pointing to a *"dual profit-loss"* that the western region suffers because of the cheap export of raw materials and the comparatively expensive import of processed products from eastern and central China. The existing economic gap between China and Tibet would thereby keep on widening.

Such a program of development and its discriminatory practices is also viewed by certain analysts as part of China's policies of "demographic aggression"—shifting the ethnic balance and engaging in accelerated cultural erasure (via imposition of Chinese cultural hegemony and forced commodification-cum-elimination of indigenous languages, customs, and beliefs) as a strategic solution to Tibetans' continuing resistance. The railway network would pervasively change Tibet's indigenous demography as well as its environment, as assessed by environmentalists (despite the authorities' promise to prevent ecological damage). Two-thirds (200,000 out of the 300,000) of the people now residing in Lhasa are reportedly ethnic Chinese, and an estimated ten million Chinese have been transferred to Tibet since 1949 while Tibet's own population stands at six million. To turn around an old racial stereotypical image—the alleged "Yellow Peril"—the concern now voiced focuses on how in its relentless course, the vast man-made sea of Han immigrants threatens to disappear a whole oppressed people, tacitly diluting and eroding their distinct cultural and spiritual heritage. Today, Tibetans are said to face the prospect of losing control not only over their lands and their economy but, more insidiously, over their culture and identity. Comprehensively dispossessed while becoming a minority within their own territory, they are made to function as "cultural relics" protected by Beijing, whose display in international events remains tightly monitored.

> What has happened to the Native Americans, to the native Australians, is happening in Tibet.
>
> Lhasang Tsering

Rising in parallel with the protests of discontent Han workers and peasants are thus the multifaceted struggles of the oppressed nationalities fighting as much for survival as for freedom. Strangely enough, and yet not surprisingly, Beijing is eager to endorse the West's global consumerism of Tibetan cultural authenticity, giving themselves the license to primitivize at will, all the while blasting any defense of such authenticity as product of external capitalist powers' meddling. Every disturbance in the region is impulsively attributed to "overseas forces" and their aptitude for distorting truth. But, it is in its unremitting efforts both to assimilate and to commodify Tibet that the Chinese government remains *in conformity* with Western colonialism—taking Western othering practices even *a step further*, especially when promoting Tibetan culture to its consumerist masses. Easily recognizable, for example, is the need to essentialize (the other's) identity and exoticize (the other's) culture: authenticity is conveniently defined in the dominant's terms, as well as strategically produced in their own interest. At stake is not merely the question of making "pseudo-events" and producing staged authenticity in tourist settings, whose function could be to help keep the outsider out of contact with the locals. In this relentless process of modernization-cum-Sinicization, what abound are instances of Chinese authorities making clever, damaging use of fakes and imposing the terms for how traditional Tibet should appear. Central to a political smear tactic, some of these fakes have contributed substantially to falsifying the image of the Tibetan struggle in China and abroad.

The need to uphold the official narrative of national *unity* and of "harmony" between Tibetans and Han has often been linked to the advent of strategic counterfeits made to cause *disunity* among Tibetans and undermine their struggles. Not only are Tibetans compelled to stick to the archaic image the dominant has of them and to act *more Tibetan than themselves*, but they also have to contend with fake Tibetans in their territories for survival. For example, Han Chinese employees of numerous travel agencies have been sent to popular tourist destinations, dressing up in Tibetan clothes to sell fake Tibetan goods, wearing robes in monasteries, thereby passing for genuine Tibetan monks and lamas to perform ceremonies and divinations at very high prices. A walk in a famous place of historical or religious interest is said to be quite similar to a walk in the marketplace with Buddhist culture becoming bait, monks turning into businessmen, and Buddhist accessories into merchandise. Mercantilism is deliberately pursued within the very framework of monasteries, and what may appear rather harmless in the realm of competitive commerce could prove to be highly destructive in its comprehensive political implications.

The scope and depth of strategic deception via masquerades and counterfeits in all things Tibetan include, among others, the move to "institutionalize the management of reincarnation" (an oxymoron or a malapropism that could otherwise induce laughter), alongside the making and legitimation of fake Tulkus, Geshes, and Lamas; fake violent Khampa fighters (used to alter the world's perception of Tibetan demonstrations as being mostly nonviolent); fake Tibetan villages (twenty-two model villages to be constructed, for example, in Nyingchi County to lure visitors to the troubled region); and even a fake Potala Palace facing the real one in Lhasa (a state-delivered project built across the Kyichu River to promote high-end tourism while serving as a tool to appropriate history by asserting, via the controversial mega-production of Princess Wencheng drama, China's civilizing and harmonizing role in Tibet). The authorities' plan is to attract fifteen million domestic tourists per year to the region by 2015. Thus, in the name of liberation and modernization, pervasive development, comprehensive commodification of the culture, and massive population influx via immigration and tourism go hand in hand with severe socioeconomic marginalization as well as extensive repression of Tibetan identity across the plateau. "Sinicization via the back door" is the term given by some analysts to this colonization by other means, whose magnitude has also prompted many involved to speak of nothing less than "cultural genocide"—the deliberate destruction of a people's cultural heritage (traditions, values, beliefs, language, and other constituent elements distinguishing one group from another) for political, ideological, ethnic, or racial reasons. Despite Beijing's attempts to refute the charge, "genocide" was a term already used, over fifty years ago, with a more limited emphasis in the 1960 International Commission of Jurists' Report on Tibet and China, which indicted the Chinese authorities for committing acts of genocide in an attempt to systematically destroy the Tibetans as a religious group.

Rising from Mud and Muck

> The whole world is medicine.
>
> Yunmen

China's tourist industry has boomed out of proportion even as the nation struggles to sustain the rapid rates of economic growth it has seen over the last decade. Its negative impact both at home and abroad has time and again made headlines in the international media, as many domestic and foreign societies find themselves unable to cope with the overwhelming inpouring of visitors. The surge of these imperious buyers and settlers has given rise to many tensions and public confrontations, such as those in Hong Kong around abusive birth tourism (an alarming wave of mainland Chinese mothers came to Hong Kong to give birth so as to gain the right of abode and education for their children) and controversial "Anti-Locusts" protest marches that call for restrictions on tourists from the mainland. These were accused of "limitless invasion" and of hogging the city's already congested resources. As bad got worse, the tension between Hong Kong and the mainland spread wide on the Internet, with netizens throughout China's major cities (Beijing, Guangzhou, Shenzhen, then, Tianjin, Chengdu, and Chongqing, among others) posting, one after the other, mimic-illustrations in response. What became Internet meme was the famed anti-mainlander advertisement, funded by some Hong Kong residents and published in the *Apple Daily* newspaper, with a giant locust overlooking the Hong Kong skyline and manifesto-like lines that began with "Hong Kong people, we have endured enough in silence." Among the many parodies the ad generated was, for example, the one from Shanghai, copycatted with only changes to the words that paraphrased in local dialect: "Shanghainese have had enough. Because you have come for the gold rush, we have to receive 17,566,700 outsiders. Because you want to settle down, we have to receive 380,000 of the outsider laborer's children."

Labeled as "the most resented tourists" in the *New York Times* (September 2013) and considered to be "the world's second-worst tourists, after Americans" (2012 poll by the US-based e-commerce site Living Social), China's millions of novice visitors have been causing dire embarrassments to their own fellow people, prompting China's vice premier to rail publicly against them for their poor "quality and breeding" likely to tarnish their homeland's reputation. Aside from the more usual xenophobic complaints around outsiders' insensitive habits and misbehaviors (some regarding mainland Chinese displayed on YouTube), the biggest gripes voiced concern these visitors' lack of respect for local cultures and ecological environment, their imposing number and purchasing power—in short, the disproportionate nature of their unnerving impact on local citizens' lives. Beijing has devised new tourism regulations for this rapidly growing class of traveling consumers, calling on them to "respect the norms of civilized tourist behaviors" and to mind the way they comport themselves abroad. However, their impact remains complex: the problem does not lie only in their "bad manners" on unfamiliar grounds, for ultimately, the solution does not lie merely in their grooming up for foreigners' or neighbors' sake. Troubles erupting abroad are often homegrown. As China's diverse national and internal struggles show, what happens at home, at the regional scale, is often carried on abroad at the global scale, albeit in differing or at times seemingly opposite manifestations.

The situation becomes all the more threatening, as in the case of Tibet, when such massive tourism proves, in its overbearing course, to be an intrinsic part of both a ruthless, resource-hungry drive to develop and a comprehensive Sinicization process. (In 2013, 12.91 million visitors came to the region, as Chinese authorities recorded.) Lately, however, amid all the negative accounts, Chinese tourism in the Tibetan region has gained another, unexpected repute. A report from an issue of *Index on Censorship*[1] tells how, in sharing holiday snaps and comments online with friends and relatives back home, Chinese tourists appeared to have inadvertently breached the Great Firewall of China. While Tibet has been closed to foreign media and often sealed off from foreign visitors, Chinese tourists were still allowed entry; and while Tibetans face severe restrictions (with Internet connections accordingly shut down en masse) and unrelenting punishment whenever they try to pass on information about their situation, Chinese sightseeing microbloggers have, comparatively, been afforded greater leeway by the government. Hundreds of social-media images and messages have thus leaked out, despite the extensive security apparatus and the new system installed for monitoring both Internet and phone traffic (which allow the authorities to systematically delete posts originating from Tibet). These tourist images and comments have been recovered from the microblogging website Sina Weibo and preciously documented by the International Campaign for Tibet.[2]

Whether read with or against the grain, the documents retrieved put Chinese tourists in a unique position: as witnesses of the Tibetans' current situation and providers of information forbidden to the outside world; but moreover, as unsolicited attestation of the governmental internal censorship that has kept them in the dark as to the endless war unfolding in their very backyard. On the one hand, they effortlessly evidence the systematic militarization in Tibet and the harsh repressive measures implemented, which the government has taken draconian measures to cover up. On the other, they reveal the Tibetans' living conditions from the eyes of *The Innocents Abroad* (Mark Twain's ironic take on tourism)—or from the perspectives of ordinary Chinese tourists who face a reality of Tibet sharply different from what they expect. Their visual and verbal postings unwittingly agree with the reporting by human-rights groups and other international bodies. Exclamatory and inquisitive remarks on the forces deployed to patrol Tibet abound: "Everywhere you can see People's Armed Police standing guard, the Police Association, Auxiliary Police, the People's Militia, plainclothes police . . . it feels like living through an era of war" (2012); "Every three steps there's a heavily armed People's Armed Police checkpoint, there are armoured vehicles and tanks which you wouldn't dare to photograph"; "The Jokhang [Temple] is surrounded by heavily armed, fire-extinguisher toting People's Armed Police"; "There are more People's Armed Police and regular police than other people combined. Is that really necessary?" (2012); "Tour guides [at the Jokhang] say, you can't wear revealing clothing, keep your eyes open when you visit, but keep your mouth shut! Has life here always been like this?!" (2012); "What kind of device is that sniper on the rooftop using?"; "Tawu county was like a war zone. People's Armed Police and Public Security standing along the street, heavily-armed Special Police at each door! We were told you can't stay overnight in the county town, and you can't stay on these streets!" (2011); "Tawu, in the square some people are doing a Tibetan dance, a bunch of Special Police came up to them, assault rifles and riot shields in hand, forming two rows in the square, silently watching them . . . . It looked like it could become a massacre" (2011); "Repression is in the air . . . . There's a pervasive feeling like the White Terror . . . . Could something happen? I'm really terrified" (Lithang County, 2013).

What is the blown hair sword?
Each branch of coral holds up the moon.

Zen koan, *Bìyán Lù* (*Blue Cliff Record*)

Has life here always been like this . . . Tibet behind the curtain, through Chinese eyes, remains profoundly unsettling. Most fearsome, as it has been witnessed, is the security apparatus at work. *It looked like it could become a massacre . . . I'm really terrified.* Governmental crackdowns in the region are certainly nothing new, but it is one thing to encounter these via professional news media venues and another altogether to see them unexpectedly exposed through the eyes of ordinary Chinese people seeking leisure on exotic land. Together with numerous photos showing the military occupation and inadvertently (?) serving as a back channel to the Tibetan struggle, the tourists' messages speak not only to the pervasive repression of Tibetans but also to their being kept uninformed or misinformed of Tibetans' dire conditions. *A war zone.* The postings offhandedly belie the official narrative of a "wealthy, civilized, and harmonious Tibet" thriving under the magnanimous leadership of the party. Yet, despite Beijing's escalating repression, Tibet behind the curtain is far from being subdued. The more coercive the system of *enhanced* control measures, the more inventive the Tibetan people prove to be in diversifying ways to manifest their discontentment. Always on the alert for new forms of protest, they continue to persist in cultural resistance through the arts (poetry and music being, among others, the most popular venues) and to carry out subtle acts of dissent, such as the weekly celebration of Tibetan traditions on their own terms known as *Lhakar* or "White Wednesday"—a nonviolent grassroots cultural movement that has been growing since 2008.

Driven by individual Tibetans rather than by their spiritual and political leaders, Lhakar was reportedly named in reference to the Dalai Lama's soul day (when prayers at the Jokhang Temple used to be secretly offered on Wednesdays for His Holiness's long life) and could be traced to several human rights–abuse incidences occurring in the region around that October Wednesday in 2007, when the Dalai

Lama was awarded the Congressional Gold Medal. Every Wednesday, a growing number of Tibetans both inside and outside Tibet observe simple cultural practices meant to assert their identity (as non-Chinese), as well as partake in the making of a political statement.[3] Think, talk, listen, eat, and buy Tibetan: Lhakar vigils have been rapidly gathering momentum and have spread to over sixteen cities around the world. Numerous initiatives to globalize the impact of this self-reliance movement (also known as the "Lhakar Revolution" to its participants) have led to a cultural revival that not only helps to preserve Tibetan language and culture under heavy restriction but is also changing the landscape of Tibetan activism. *Each branch of coral holds up the moon.* Says a posting: "Half a century after Gandhi died, his *satyagraha* is reborn in Tibet. This time its name is *Lhakar*."[4]

> In these days,
> in these days when a spring wind is rising under the clouded sky,
> shoots from the inner depths of the earth give vitality
> and confidence to someone's young sun of hope.
> Now, once more the gorgeous peach blossoms bring to the people's minds
> a certain compassionate and youthful face–
> that face from far far away is brought to mind,
> is brought to mind.
>
> Sakyi Tseta, "Longing for the Deities" (translated by Tenzin Dickyi and Dhondup Tashi Rekjong; originally published on *Tso Ngonpo* [*Blue Lake*] blog but subsequently taken down)[5]

With the severe crackdown on acts of protest in the public realm (where large demonstrations can no longer get off the ground), cultural rituals take on a political dimension and individuated acts of defiance and dissent spread in the domestic, digital, as well as virtual realms of daily activities (home, workplace, computer, and other personal space, both visible and invisible). Through Lhakar's emphasis on what may be called *tactic* mobility with a *strategic* scope,[6] activism is said to be decollectivized; culture becomes political strategy, if not an explicit weapon; and noncooperation, a Ghandian style of effective action.[7] Appealing to the simple basics of freedom—the way people make decisions while they go about their daily activities (where to buy their food, which restaurant to go to, what language to speak, or what music to listen to at home)—Lhakar is a response to Beijing's superstructure of repression that works at quelling all forms of public collective dissent, reinforcing Han hegemony via discriminatory practices while disempowering indigenous cultures through assimilation, appropriation, and commodification. *Each branch of coral holds up the moon.* Thus, while some other members of the Tibetan communities have chosen, in the most tragic of ways, to set themselves alight in protest of Chinese repressive policies, a growing number tacitly commit their individual spaces to the struggle through weekly singular acts of resistance. Lhakar could then be perceived as the undercurrent force of resistance that thrives in parallel with the conspicuous current of public self-immolation whose "earth-shattering" course continues to shake Tibet and shame the world.

Shaken and *shamed.* Tibet behind the curtain remains, as poet and political blogger Tsering Woeser remarks, a "giant prison crisscrossed with armed soldiers and armored vehicles."[8] Tibetan cultural and spiritual heritage is being made to disappear while the people are being dispossessed of their identities and traditions, forbidden to mourn publicly for their departed and to long for their "long-lost love" (or for the Dalai Lama in exile). *Despite* state censorship of any public yearning for that peach-blossom face of compassion "from far far away," *despite* the government's intensified security operations, the police's roving fire extinguishers, and the fire brigades' omnipresence at various monasteries, and *despite* the war on self-immolation, with harshest retributive actions against family, friends, "helpers," or any "suspects" allegedly associated with those who set themselves ablaze, the flames of resistance are far from being doused. Self-immolation continues to be a severe challenge to both Chinese authorities and the Tibetan leadership in exile. For years on end the problems kept on piling up with no possibility to vent, even constructively. Discontentment and resentment run deep, as the people have had to live under constant suspicion and mistrust. Locked in a state of siege, that is, heavily policed with nowhere to turn, violently suppressed, shut up, blinded, sealed off from the world while being exploited, discriminated against, and marginalized in their own land, the protesters literally "walked out of the flames" (Ai Weiwei), showing not necessarily acts of despair but, rather, acts of altruism—of will, determination, and sacrifice for the sake of free Tibet (as revealed through the last words left by the self-immolators)—in their *extra*-ordinary, symbolic power.

Every time a human torch burns down, Tibetans from all walks of life have reportedly gathered in the thousands to pray and pay their respects—notwithstanding the authorities' warnings and threats. Their response across Tibet to the self-immolations bespeaks both solidarity and resilience among those who continue, in bold steps, to defend the core values of their culture. Indeed, just as one thinks one no longer has any option left, healing appears from possibly anywhere, and another path unexpectedly opens up in one's intimate walk. *The udumbara flower blooms in fire*, so it is said in Buddhist praxis, and self-realization comes about *in* this very life, with*in* this very world. As a harbinger of spring, the Old Plum Tree may flower in late winter, and magnolias blossom singly on apparently withered branch tips. With every inconspicuous act of cultural remembrance and creative perseverance, somewhere someones walk on in silence, reaching *in* to the cure and *out*—from one's very nature. *With every step, the world comes to the walker*. After a long, probing, and heartrending search, the healer happens to be just right here, where one is. The impasse can turn out to be a passage. Every Wednesday and beyond, healing comes about through the external healer within, there where daily life manifests itself—effortlessly, wholeheartedly. Sometimes in unexpected turns of small and large events, a sickness of the system may help to chart new ground, bring out what lies dormant, and open one's sight to *what's already always flowering within*. From mud and muck, the lotus rises clean and pure.

When a flower blooms, here and now the world comes into being.

> Life ablaze in the lap of the night sky
> Each flaming offering fades into the vast space
> A life long lamp enters my mind
> Kinsmen, searching for ancestors of flesh and bones
> May you sleep peacefully.
>
> Tsering Kyi, in Gar Samdup Tsering,
> "Life Long Lamp" music video[9]

The Odor of Fear

Oda Nobunaga (1534–1582), one of the most controversial figures of Japanese history, was known to be both a brilliant innovator in politics and economics and a tyrant whose exercise of power was utterly unforgiving. His rule, considered one of the greatest in Japan, thrived on the use of terror as a weapon by which he planned to reach, at the end of the Warring States period, his ultimate goal of unifying Japan. Among the legendary recordings of his life as a leader of unequaled military clout, some noted in detail that when Nobunaga came back from a battle, what his servants often found upon cleaning his horse's mounting and his clothes was that their almighty lord and warrior shat in his pants while in full action. When reminded of such minutiae in the midst of the lord's many irrefutable feats and deeds, people in today's urban Japan usually laugh by saying that perhaps he didn't have the time or the place to do it elsewhere but right there, in his pants. The same, they said, was known of other omnipotent warlords, such as Tokugawa Ieyasu, for example, who was the founder of the Tokugawa shogunate. These deified, invincible conquerors all did it. Any one of us—all the soldiers—would have done it too, as circumstances might require. No time, no place, no shame for the most basic need: this is the reality of war. The smell of bodies at war with one another remains an unmistakable index of humanity. It was altogether a question of urgency, so says the diurnal voice of official humanism. But a voice arising from the blues nocturnally contests: not quite, not yet it. Urgency aside, there's also the question of uncontrollable excitement and fear: the fear underlying the use of brutal force, and that very fear of loss—of bodily control, or more privily yet, of inner dignity. For it is fear that seems to be banned from all recollections of the vanquisher's life. And it is fear that dominates the cry of retaliation characterizing the imperial all-time-winning mindset of our time. Nobunaga, the man who set out to unify Japan, did not hesitate to quell any opposition or to inflict vengeance through unusually brutal and ruthless means. Widely framed in complicity with the ruling power, history often lets itself be caught in the dazzling light and glory of the victor, forgetting the manifold dimensions that come with every account of I or of the eye. Forgetting that no matter how bright the sovereign may appear in his prowess, there is always a darker side to his grandeur. Imagine how Nobunaga's victorious return could be replayed. Amid the joy, tears of relief, and celebratory mood of his loyal officers, what betrayed the profound state of things and invisibly struck the nose of those closest to him who welcomed him home—mother, wife, children, servants—was the foul smell of his battle feces. Every conqueror's story has its hidden olfactory dimension. The body speaks volumes there where the mind forgets and the pen remains silent. It speaks of the naked face of his inside, of what the Nobunaga of every victorious I carries with it despite all attempts at suppressing it. Among the Dogon and the Bambara people of West Africa, it is said that what comes in, what is eaten as food is the sunlight; and what comes out, what is ejected as excrement is night. The night side of Nobunaga or what gets expelled out of control is a secret whose knowledge only the women and the lowest servants who cleaned his excrement could have divulged. Only they intimately recognize the human or the mortal, vulnerable, childlike side of the tyrant. The supreme Master's nocturnal face challenges everything we know of his identity as invincible warrior at the same time as it dispels the mystery surrounding his diurnal personality as a brutal military leader. Here again, the voice from the blues wonders: When catching oneself in abject fear, jelly-legged and yellow-bellied, with limbs shaking uncontrollably, unable to stand, walk, or run, why not enter this shaking and let the body of internal night quake through and through in its viscosity? Like genuine tears, the feces, a reminder of what is true, is the body letting go, the body manifesting itself and its owner. War exposes every Nobunaga to the recurrent annihilation of his sunlit proper self. He was utterly common, doing his thing like any other man alive, learning anew the art of sphincter control and failing miserably on the spur of the moment, as a child would in his first step to social education. In the end, there is no true loss when, following the course of fear and feces, one returns from it capable of fully living fear. Having radically undone his image, the night takes away his name, his power, and his rank in the hierarchy of men, leaving him again kin to all kin. Nobunaga: God of War or Refuse of War?

interval of resistance

The Empty Chair

> Love is the minimal form of communism . . . for love to last, one has to reinvent oneself.
>
> Alain Badiou

In Tibet, where it has been forbidden to display the image of the fourteenth Dalai Lama, whenever monasteries were ordered to remove his picture from sight, rather than simply removing it and filling the gap left on walls and altars, for example, people kept its space empty, leaving a lacuna in between the photos of other Tibetan spiritual leaders or ancestors. Or else they replaced the image with a blank sheet of paper, thereby marking his absence with a visible interval in appearances. To the Chinese authorities' great annoyance, no matter how severe the censorship, the lack of a figurative image of His Holiness has not really succeeded to prevent the people from continuing to love him. Constantly evoked via the indirect, that "face far, far away," that "long-lost love" continues to be "a life-long lamp." Whether materially or immaterially manifested, the blank space remains alive with indefinite possibilities. It could be indicative of a profound determination not to forget, a means to leave evidence of repression, a tacit gesture to honor an absent presence, and hence, could serve as a constant reminder of both the censoring and the censored at the site of worship.

Every day, well over a thousand Tibetans undertake a tour of the Potala Palace, also known among the people as the "Peak," *Tse Potala*—or what in Lhasa continues to be the symbol of Tibet and of the Dalai Lama's home. Every day, hundreds of *khadas* (traditional silk scarves) heap up as offering before the empty throne in the Dalai Lama's meeting room, once known as the Chamber of Golden Radiance. (A song popular among Tibetans revels in disclosing: "On the golden roof of the Potala, rises the golden sun / It is not the golden sun, but the precious face of the Lama.") With the campaign against loyalty to the Dalai Lama becoming all the more aggressive over time, nowhere in the thousand-room palace could, reportedly, a single picture of the fourteenth Dalai Lama be seen, and his conspicuous visual absence next to the picture of his predecessor, the thirteenth Dalai Lama, apparently served to enhance his nonvisual presence. The sight of pilgrims repeatedly falling to their knees and lying flat on their stomachs in full-body prostrations before the vacant seat never failed to bring up questions among tourists. But, when asked who they were praying to with no one there, Chinese tour guides uniformly hastened to reply: "They are praying to the previous Dalai Lamas." Again, in the vacated living quarters where the current Dalai Lama resided before he went into exile, pilgrims were said to whisper among themselves at their sight and to fall into fervent prayers, rubbing their beads and scarves over any surface they could reach for benediction. Spared from destruction for having served as a backdrop for the Cultural Revolution, turned into a state museum, and dispossessed of its historical documents, scriptures, precious art objects, and treasures, the magnificent Potala Palace has itself become an empty shell for "unlimited commercial opportunities," as described in today's Chinese advertisements.

In the history of stage symbolism, the empty chair may be a common way of handling grief: as a sign of absence or loss—of a murdered victim, a missing beloved, an invisible guest, or someone who never shows up—it may also be a symbol of absurdity, longing, and loneliness. Sit and Wait, wait in silence. (Among many examples are those of Samuel Beckett's *Waiting for Godot*, Eugène Ionesco's *The Chairs*, or even Van Gogh's personifying chair paintings that have inspired a wide range of artists and designers.) But in today's times of trouble, this empty chair emerges as a site and a "material evidence" of enforced absence. It has often taken on the political role of exposing, as well as defying in absentia, the abuses of power and its diverse mechanisms of subjection via censorship. In the context of China, it sits snugly within a chain of suppression and elimination devices aimed at "harmonizing away" (wiping clean) all "sensitive cases." Worth noting is the recurrence on the world stage of such features as: the lone chair and the unoccupied seat; the blank page, blank space, bland sign; the screen gone white, with no content; the empty frame or the frame with no art; and, last but not least, the interval of silence—all potentially endowed with a powerfully haunting effect.

Memory recalls, among other well-known cases, how the 2010 Nobel Peace Prize was given to an empty chair and the award statement also read to this iconic chair, highlighting the absence of imprisoned Chinese literary scholar and dissident Liu Xiaobo. Honored with diploma and medal, his vacant seat at the podium was said to resonate powerfully with the distinguished international audience attending the award ceremony, despite a campaign by the Chinese government urging representatives from diverse nations to boycott the event. Unable to attend and to designate a family member or a representative to receive the award in person, Liu did not apparently become "The Forgotten Nobel" (*Le Nobel Oublié*), as French journal *Le Figaro* feared. The Peace Prize winner is not only constantly evoked at every annual commemoration of the June Fourth massacre (in Hong Kong and elsewhere, through the publication of his "June Fourth Elegies" anthology, and especially his "June Fourth in My Body" poem); both he and legal scholar–activist Xu Zhiyong have also been recently honored, still in absentia, with the 2014 National Endowment for Democracy Award. As expected, shortly after Liu's Nobel Prize ceremony, the term "empty chair" itself became a *sensitive* word banned in Chinese cyberspace. It featured as Word of the Week in China Digital Space's Grass-Mud Horse Lexicon—a glossary created by Chinese netizens of terms often encountered in online resistance discourse and widely used to mock, mimic, or subvert the official language around censorship and political correctness.

Empty chairs have repeatedly haunted China lately. Worth noting among several other prominent cases, was the empty chair at the 2013 International Women of Courage Awards. This time, the vacant seat among occupied others stood for Tibetan writer and poet Tsering Woeser, who sat under house arrest in Beijing while the US State Department (via John Kerry and Michelle Obama) honored her in Washington, DC. A daughter of Communist Party members, whose father served as a senior officer in the People's Liberation Army, Woeser was not only considered to be the first Tibetan public intellectual in China, she was also widely known as one of China's most respected writers on Tibet. Already barred by Chinese authorities from leaving for Oslo to accept the Norwegian Authors Union 2007 Freedom of Expression Prize given at their annual meeting in 2008, she was again denied the opportunity to receive the 2010 Courage in Journalism Award from the International Women's Media Foundation as well as the 2011 Prince Claus Award. Much sought after for its outspoken, well-grounded voice against Beijing's repressive, discriminatory policies, her published work, including her volume of poetry, *Tibet's True Heart* (2008), or more recently the book *Immolations in Tibet: The Shame of the World* (2013), are banned in China and her blogs shut down by decree.

The list goes on for other well-known cases of empty chairs, such as the one of Uyghur economics professor Ilham Tohti who was prevented from leaving the Beijing airport for a visiting scholar seat at Indiana University in the United States in 2013. With tensions flaring up between Uyghurs and Chinese security forces in energy-rich Xinjiang, he was formally arrested in January 2014 for his moderately critical views on the rights of China's beleaguered Muslim minority. He was later honored, in absentia, with the 2014 PEN/Barbara Goldsmith Freedom to Write Award. Religious figures from every region of Tibet have been forced into exile, and for Tibetans, the number of empty chairs is particularly difficult to keep track of. As posted in the *Tibetan Political Review*, "The chairs kept empty by Beijing have their own diversity . . . . They include bloggers, poets, lecturers, artists, bookstore owners, devoted wives, and beloved lamas. One thread that ties them together is their willingness to speak the truth despite the steep price Beijing extracts from them."[1]

The Image under Erasure

> A small amount of kindness is like a spark. It can grow and make the world bright.
>
> Tae Heng Se Nim

On the fifty-second anniversary of the 1959 Tibetan uprising, human-rights activist and analyst Ngawang Sangdrol came to Berkeley, California, to give a talk. A former monastic and China's longest female political prisoner, she was, as previously mentioned, known for the musical protest work she carried on with her fellow inmates—or what has come to be known as the thirteen Singing Nuns—in Drapchi Prison. Jailed at age thirteen and later sentenced to a total of twenty-three years of imprisonment, she was also one of the youngest political prisoners. Among the stories she told her audience then was a memorable little anecdote. This rather banal and yet strikingly moving anecdote has been heard before from other prisoners, but her cohesive account could relevantly be shared again in this context.[2]

Sangdrol recounted how sometime long ago, Tibetan prisoners would be shown newspapers by Chinese guards that included articles exposing the West in its keen support for the Dalai Lama and Tibet. They would share these as evidence of what they saw as the West's "brainwashing" efforts to subvert the high-minded agenda of China's Communist Party. But as time passed, the guards realized how, rather than being merely convinced of the West's degeneracy and China's superiority, their Tibetan prisoners were utterly elated upon reading these articles. So they performed their own brand of censorship and started delivering newspapers with missing stories—any article mentioning Tibet favorably being now transformed into *a hole* cut out from the page. However disconcerting this might have been, it did not deter the Tibetan prisoners from rejoicing upon seeing those *glaring holes*, for they knew it represented something good someone was saying about Tibet. A *lack* thus loses its negative connotation to become an affirmation, and an *absence* is here received as a much-anticipated presence.

Fullness and *emptiness* both yield a similar result in their representative function, and whether granted to view or censored from view, the articles had a similar effect on the prisoners.

The same applies when, after Beijing dubbed the Dalai Lama a separatist, Chinese authorities ordered people to remove the photos of the popular red-robe-clad figure. The campaign to erase the exiled leader's image from public life—governmental offices, monasteries, institutions, hotels, restaurants, and cultural events—as well as from private life, has had its intense and shallow moments. (The governmental ban was imposed in 1996 not merely on the public display of His Holiness's image but, more pervasively, on its possession.) There have been several instances when what appeared to be a policy shift and a relaxation on the ban was immediately followed by a period of intensified reinforcement of the ban: while in certain towns, Chinese authorities used the carrot-and-stick policy to forcefully lure Tibetans into having their leader's pictures on display, in other parts of the region, Tibetans were given lengthy jail terms for possessing such pictures, with the authorities placing further restrictions in the private realm—for example, stopping and checking all vehicles owned by Tibetans in the Yulshul area and burning in Tongkhor some eighteen sacks of photos of the Dalai Lama.

Certain visitors in Tibet noted how, unlike the markets in Nepal and India where the Tibetan diaspora live, the bustling markets outside the temples in Lhasa were devoid of the Dalai Lama's photographs. However, other visitors have also remarked how his photos were displayed discreetly in countless places: in small provisions stores, in monks' quarters, on cellphone screens, sometimes even in large temples where Han Chinese tourists flocked. If, according to some, household shrines in the region were bereft of his pictures, according to others, accounts of symbolic resistance to the ban abound in Lhasa. For example, people hide His Holiness's picture—the love of their heart—inside the frame, behind Mao's and other Chinese leaders' faces; street traders often placed empty picture frames on their stalls alongside photographs of permitted lamas as a gesture in defiance of the decree. Whenever His Holiness's picture was ripped out, confiscated, or destroyed in ordinary people's houses, absence and censorship were also made visible by a blank space manifestly maintained in its place among other spiritual ancestors.

"Why are they so afraid of a picture?" asked a monk from Rongwu, referring to the Communist Party that supposedly doesn't believe in anything, and not in the least, in the power of a mere image. Such a campaign to obliterate by force the picture of a people's spiritual leader has given rise to numerous absurd censored stories such as the one concerning the very censor at a local TV station in Beijing who lost his job after a picture of the Dalai Lama inadvertently aired in a documentary on Tibet. The censor's defense, which would have inevitably induced laughter if it weren't so tragic, was that he didn't know what the Dalai Lama looked like. He had never seen his picture because it never appeared in the Chinese press.[3] The paranoia ceaselessly caused in the minds of the authorities by His Holiness's image bears witness to the creative way in which the Tibetan struggle, constantly in silent action, imperceptibly remakes itself with every new repressive situation that arises. The affective need to keep a picture of one's beloved leader may speak of a nostalgia for a "long-lost love," but in the context of a political struggle against oppression, such a picture may quickly become what could be called an *underground ID card*: a sign of solidarity, if not of defiance in the face of censorship, a way of identifying oneself as Tibetan and of affirming one's belonging to an endangered, disappearing civilization. Needless to say, harsh punishments, insults, and threats did not diminish people's quiet devotions; on the contrary, these elicit visceral responses end up intensifying their unflinching loyalty to their "life-long lamp." The more fanatical the campaign and the interdiction, the more fervent the trust and pining for the "long-lost love." As Tibetans of all walks of life similarly put it when asked about the subject, "ultimately, it doesn't matter whether Tibetans are allowed to display photos of the Dalai Lama . . . because *in our hearts*, we worship him and that's enough" (Pema Rinchen).

By demonizing and debasing the Tibetan spiritual leader while demeaning Tibetan beliefs, language, and culture, Chinese authorities have been contributing most actively to the making of a Tibet and a Dalai Lama *in their image*—as the Enemy (or primary political foe) to be destroyed and as the Devil to fear beyond any rational, material means. *Why are they* (we) so *afraid of their* (our) *own image*, one may ultimately ask? The more they use force to vilipend the Dalai Lama, the further they help to mystify his figure as a living deity and to fan the flame of reverence and longing among his people. More recently China's United Front department (the agency handling relations with "minorities nationalities") resorts to a far more heinous strategy by funding, across nations, the leaders of a cult (the Dorje Shugden spirit worshipers), of which they make use in the hope of driving a wedge between the Dalai Lama and his people and of portraying him to the world as a "dictator" in Buddhist matters. The aim, easily recognizable in colonial tactics, was to divide and conquer: to promote religious rivalries and internal dissension by covertly provoking the majority of Tibetans who love him to act harshly against those who attack him; and hence, to turn world opinion against the Peace Nobel laureate's long nonviolent truth-and-justice campaign.[4] It would be unfortunate if such a strategy were to gain ground to the detriment of the Tibetan cause, but the need to resort to it is in itself a testament to the authorities' failure to expunge the loving devotion to the Dalai Lama, whose people have had to jump through hoops of all kinds while learning, again and again, to *walk in the dark* and to hear, touch, and *see with the heart*.

In its 1960s-and-1970s rhetoric of vilification, the campaign led against loyalty to the Dalai Lama resonates with definite overtones of the Cultural Revolution (as also previously mentioned by Liu Xiaobo), whose proclaimed goal was to "Sweep Away All Monsters and Demons." History has not forgotten how, in the name of revolution, the excessive abuse of power and the systematic campaign of destruction of all things and beings narrowly deemed to be politically incorrect ended up turning on its own population, reversing into self-inflicted violence and wreckage of great depth and massive dimension. In the Central Committee's words, the Cultural Revolution (1966–1976) "was responsible for the most severe setback and the heaviest losses suffered by the Party, the state, and the people since the founding of the People's Republic."[5] Tyranny certainly comes with a steep price for both oppressed and oppressor. Today the battle to aggressively suppress the forces that drive and nurture Tibetan resistance is also inflicting untold psychological damage on Chinese armed police. As revealed in a leaked internal training document handed to members of the People's Armed Police charged with containing the Tibetan areas of Sichuan Province, the latter have been in apparently dire need of help in combatting depression and posttraumatic stress disorder, including dealing with "flashbacks of brutal episodes"—such as instances of self-immolation—that cause incessant nightmares and insomnia. Again, in asymmetrical relations of power, it suffices that the oppressed survive, persist, and remain united while persevering in their resistance, for the government and its almighty-armed troops to lose their aura of invincibility. And again, in asymmetrical situations of conflict, the question arising is *not so much whether or not the dominant occupying forces will win* but, more pertinently, *when they will break down*. Says a post in response to the campaign to erase the Dalai Lama's face: "They can physically make Tibet devoid of HHDL but HHDL resides in the heart of 99 percent of Tibetans in Tibet."

Lotus Bomb(ed)

> The mind creates the abyss and the heart crosses it.
>
> Sri Nisargadatta

In its obsession with totalitarian control, the power exerting terror ends up internalizing terror and inflicting it on itself under the banner of harmony and security. Haunted by fear and suspicion, it often rushes headlong into the net of its own trap. The zeal to wage "pre-emptive strikes" can reach dramatic heights, bypassing all rationalization as in the event of the green lotus told by Ama Adhe, a mother of two from Kanze and a survivor of the Chinese "liberation" of Tibet who spent twenty years in nine different Chinese camps and prisons. The story goes that one day in 1975, on the lake at the base of the sacred mountain Sha Jara in Minyag Rangakha, a black nomad tent suddenly appeared as if sitting on the surface of the lake. At the sight of it, the amazed and alarmed Chinese authorities eyed it with their binoculars so as to figure out what it really was. When the tent suddenly disappeared, in its place a huge green lotus could be seen floating. Rejoicing over what they viewed as a sign of the return of the Dalai Lama to the country, all Tibetans in the region came to pray and make special offerings at the lake. This so terrified the authorities that, unable to stop the flow of prayers and scarf offerings, they decided to *bomb the lotus*. The people then picked up the scattered bits of the lotus on the water and took them home to put on their altars.[6]

Why are they so afraid of a lotus? A small story becomes vast as it walks you on the spiritual path. What the eye can't see (even with the aid of binoculars), the heart can with great intensity. The breathtaking image evoked shows: a snow-capped mountain, a lake, a tent, and a lotus. On the water, black appears and disappears to yield sight to green. Bewilderment in the face of awe-inspiring beauty suddenly arouses suspicion in the mind, leading oh so sadly and risibly to overkill for a mere vegetal growth. What makes a man bomb a flower? By what road did a green plant come to the onlooker as the Enemy? War inside and out: the extreme violence of the reaction bears witness to a profound lack of self-security—the very lack within that breeds uncontrollable fear and turns suspicion into panic. The lack, therefore, of a justifiable cause that could win over the people's hearts. As a Chinese saying goes, "laughter is the source of tears." Had it not been so surreally dramatic and pathetic, such a gesture would have induced convulsive laughter among those under attack. And yet, the path of *bodhicitta* (the yearning for enlightenment and the practice of compassion for the world's beings) remains *wildly creative*. Among the wide range of symbols it carries, the lotus is known for its association with purity, rebirth, and the feminine principle and, when in bloom, with divine birth, spiritual awakening, or Buddha's heart. The encounter of two worlds, two approaches, two views as sketched in Adhe's story uncannily speaks to the impasse of the China-Tibet situation: on the one hand, the lotus threat, the foe-flower to be annihilated, on the other, the magic lotus that continues to survive the ordeal of lethal explosive violence. The bombed-out flower, reduced to pieces that "felt just like grass," had undergone a transformation of appearances, but it remained no less a lotus—the way a fragment of a shattered mirror continues to function as mirror no matter the shape it ends up with. *Each branch of coral holds up the moon*. Each fragment contains the whole, and the world remakes itself anew piece by piece, step by step.

The Chinese government generates the very forces it tries to eradicate. Never has it succeeded to uproot the exiled leader from Tibetan hearts. Nor has it succeeded to snuff out his Light (the golden sun or "the face of the Lama") from the Potala—named after India's Mount Potalaka, the mythical alpine abode of the bodhisattva of great compassion Avalokitesvara (a.k.a. Guanyin or Chenrezig). Having historically served as Tibet's political nerve center, the Potala has also been its *spiritual heart*. As sung by Rigzin Dolma and written in Dong Yonten Gyatso's "The Magnificent Potala," which is "the vital blood of millions of Tibetans," embodies both "the mirror of the *past*" and "the path for the *future*." Being the soul of a people and the "proof of [their] inerasable history," the Potala—even when stripped bare to become an empty shell—functions as the seat of an ongoing theater of the sublime, whose symbolic impact persists well beyond its historical glory years as political and religious center of Tibetan theocracy.

Visitors commented on how its breathtaking, awe-inspiring sight "sent shivers down their spines," how its high walls are still seeped in the Lamas' presence, and how deeply they themselves are made aware of its historical, cultural, and religious significance as they walk its halls. A Western visitor who always thought of Buddhism as a mental discipline wrote how struck he was in facing "a Buddhist faith that went down to the bone" and seeing simple people bowing to an empty throne, risking imprisonment for revering His Holiness. Watching

bent-over-at-the-waist elderly women climb the floors of the Potala, he further remarked: "It seemed a large risk to their health. Yet in their faces was blissful happiness. *Many were crying*."[7] To give another hint of the Potala's affective impact, it may be worth recalling what a Chinese poet from inland China recorded not long ago, on a summer day in 1994 when two giant *thangkas* (Buddhist paintings on cotton or silk) were displayed on its outer white wall (a traditional ritual apparently not held then for over forty years): "Every spot in Lhasa from where one could catch a glimpse of the Potala was crowded. I saw many country folk. From where they were standing there was no way they could see the thangkas, yet facing towards the direction of the thangkas they *silently shed their tears* . . . on that day thousands upon thousands of people moved clockwise, circumambulating the Potala Palace. Dust was everywhere. Yet Tibetans, Chinese, Westerners, monks, and everyday folk . . . carrying babies, helping the elderly, looked like a great migration in human history."[8]

At the Potala in Lhasa, the Dalai Lama himself is, as noted, an empty throne in the conference hall. In South Africa, where he canceled his visit because of Pretoria's failure to grant him a visa of entry in time, he was also an empty chair on the day of Archbishop Desmond Tutu's eightieth birthday celebration. With Pretoria buckling under pressure from China, the 1984 and 1989 Nobel Peace laureates were prevented from meeting each other in honor of Tutu's nonviolent activism against apartheid rule. To mark and symbolize the Dalai Lama's enforced absence, Tutu's Peace Center insisted on having a visible empty chair at the event at the University of Western Cape where His Holiness was scheduled to deliver an inaugural peace lecture. As China remains the only nation (as of this writing) to keep a Nobel laureate in prison and to put his wife under house arrest, the archbishop also spearheaded a widely signed petition calling for Liu Xiaobo's release, echoing anew (what has been previously referred to as) the *seeing tears*—listening with the heart—of the Tibetan struggle when he specified his "effort is not to embarrass China but rather to *implore* the government to take a different approach."[9]

When all is being said, aside from marking an absence, defying censorship, and exposing the abuses of power, the empty chair in its complex reality could very well present yet another face. *The mind creates the abyss and the heart crosses it*. In responding to his people's expectation of him as the embodiment of Avalokitesvara, the Dalai Lama may after all not mind being an empty chair. *Empty, to the point where dualistic perceptions dissolve.* For, whether it is actually occupied or vacated, his is a seat on the Middle Way—at the center of the world—on which the suffering can sit and wait, wait and wail. What feels true to the heart—sorrow, anger, isolation, shame, desire, fear, and frustration—all are taken in and let go of. In his own being, he is empty. Realizing vacuity in the nature of things and beings underlies his quest to free the mind of afflictive emotions. Whenever Tibetans are required to fill out surveys asking them to choose between answer A ("Dalai Lama is good") and answer B ("Dalai Lama is bad"), many would simply return these *blank*—not wanting to get into trouble with the Chinese government but also not wanting to choose B "because he's great." Heightening his existential function as the Bodhisattva of Compassion (a.k.a. "*Holder of the Lotus*") who "watches over the Cries of the World," the empty chair, the blank space, the white screen, the hole on the printed page, or the bombed-out lotus do not so much represent his absence as they de-represent it, pointing instead to an *elsewhere-within here* that lies at the threshold of the symbolic. Comings and goings, suffering and healing all come about in this life-giving emptiness. Such remains the *Power of the Unseen*. The interval is where sounds, words, and images *go blank*, where mourning for a "long-lost love" manifests itself in white, and where an intensified struggle writes itself in silence.

> Embodying the integrity of a nation,
> Even though you are hurt you lick your wounds
> And stand proud in all circumstances
> While the sharp fangs of a dark beast
> A tailless dog pretending to be a lion
> Utters empty threats from its cave . . . .

Potala Palace!
From the first time I welcomed the sun and the moon
Until when the circulation of my blood stops
My loyalty to you in body, speech, and mind
Shall remain eternal

Tashi, "Potala Palace"[10]

the screensaver's light

The Ultimate Protest

> The loving
> are the daring.
>
> Bayard Taylor

> What I would really like said about me is that I dared to love . . . . By love I mean that condition in the human spirit so profound, it encourages us to develop courage and build bridges, and then to trust those bridges and cross the bridges in attempts to reach other human beings.
>
> Maya Angelou[1]

"Tibet was a land whose spiritual heart had been ripped out," said Chinese writer and painter Ma Jian, who traveled widely across Tibet's remote desert regions and whose book, *Stick out Your Tongue*, is known for its controversial, nonidealized stories of the harsh, degrading realities of Tibetan life in poverty. Not a slogan, not a dream; not a mystical Shangri-la, nor "a barren outpost of the great Chinese Party's nationalist propaganda concerning China's 'liberation' of the country" (Ma Jian),[2] Tibet today is "a giant prison" on fire; "a war zone" behind the curtains; "a cauldron of tension"; a longstanding struggle for survival; and a deep-seated battlefield against an imperial, resource-hungry Chinese rule that "wants Tibet but not the Tibetan people."[3] In their desperate attempt to quell the fire of Tibetan revolt, the Chinese security bureau now calls self-immolation "a crime"—fiercely threatening to ruin monasteries and hotels incidentally involved, and charging, as previously mentioned, even those remotely related to such an event with "intentional murder." Such a violent response from the authorities bears witness to Power's fundamental instability—here, the system's inner faltering, the fissures running deep among the ruling party members, as well as the mutual distrust between government and people as specifically highlighted in numerous class-infused protest cases.

Rather than heeding the pleas Tibetan self-immolators have passionately voiced in their final messages to their fellow people, Chinese authorities have typically *enhanced* their infrastructure of repression further with the implementation of a new "grids" system of social management and street-level surveillance (launched in Lhasa in 2012) "to form a bastion of iron" with "nets in the sky and traps on the ground" (Yu Zhengsheng, a member of China's Politburo Standing Committee). The same spirit prevails when, rather than addressing the troubles raised by China's ethnic policy and the causes of self-immolations (deep alienation and frustration accompanied with disfranchisement, humiliation, indignity), they focus, literally, all their efforts on *cleaning technologies* (sweeping away immediately and as fast as possible all traces of the incidence) and on *fire fighting*, devising, for example, an eighteen-man fire team in Ngaba, which the official news agency Xinhua called, with no qualm, "Firemen in Monk's Robes." Their criminalization of Tibetan self-immolations speaks volume of the pervasive fear they harbor toward those "Springtimes of the People" occurring around the world and their historical catalysts figures. Among the haunting legendary examples, it may be relevant to recall that of the street fruit seller Mohamed Bouazizi who set himself and Tunisia on fire (December 17, 2010), and whose ordeal had caused so much public outrage that it started an inwardly directed "people's revolution," serving as a catalyst for the Tunisian revolution that brought down the country's ruler and giving rise to a wave of upheavals across several Arab and non-Arab nations.

In a rather common case of abuse by thick-skinned bureaucrats catering to an indifferent, autocratic system of governance, it was the *extra*-ordinary impact of an ordinary man's act that caught all the attention of the press. (Ironically, it turned out to be a case of both class and gender inequality—or of being victim of a victim: the making of a culprit out of the woman municipal inspector who confiscated Bouazizi's fruits was further a clever tactic from the authorities who used her as an easy scapegoat to turn the spotlight away from them. The press happily endorsed the gender blame.)[4] The "Bouazizi effect" led analysts to revisit the question of "How a Single Match Can Ignite a Revolution" and to hail Bouazizi as a symbol for peoples across cultures in pursuit of dignity. The rise of an everyman above the ordinary has not only "changed the course of Arab political history" but also brought back to memory the iconic image of the Chinese "tank man,"[5] a.k.a. the "Unknown Protester," whose act of utter courage in the face of overpowering aggression captured people's hearts all around the world. Those concerned often *broke down* and *wept* when they recalled how powerfully such an image has come to symbolize the struggle for freedom and democracy at Tiananmen Square. Caught in one of the most memorable photos of the events is the tiny silhouette of a brave, solitary man who, the day after the government cracked down on the Tiananmen protests, stood directly in the path of a column of humongous approaching tanks, bringing these to a halt in a show of nonviolent action. Tank Man's images remain barred in China and, despite efforts by foreign reporters to identify him, no one knows for sure who he is or what his fate was after the incident, when he was pulled away from the scene and disappeared into the crowd.

The other haunting example further back in time was the one remembered as "The Ultimate Protest" by the Associated Press. It was an iconic image of the Vietnam War showing the self-immolation of elder monk Thích Quảng Đức (June 11, 1963), who gave himself freely in public, lighting the flame of freedom, shocking the world and igniting both local and global outrage that precipitated the end of Ngô Đình Diệm's oppressive regime. The event reduced Diệm's reputation to ashes and prompted wailing witnesses as well as thousand of Saigoneses to claim that evening they had seen a vision of *Buddha weeping*. As President John F. Kennedy stated then, "No news picture in history has generated so much emotion around the world,"[6] and the monk's self-immolation has become since then a touchstone reference in many discussions of the Vietnam War and beyond. One of the event's most moving details recounted and shown in the media was how, even after the fire and later the (re)cremation of Thích Quảng Đức's body, the monk's *heart* did not burn down. The leaders of the Buddhist Struggle for Equality instructed the monk in charge at the crematory to continue the process for six hours more. They did as told and even tried for ten hours more, but *the heart remained intact*.

crossed feet joined hands
a man without words without cries
confesses his flame on the screen
behind the fire the witnesses watch
the flickering in a last tongue of flame
for a while still it burns
the living torch of an entire people
reduced to silence

today a man burns
in a dark fire on a scarlet sky
little by little he is consumed
illuminating mute
the crowd riveted to his side
falls prostrate as the last view
is extinguished
the faithful turn over the ashes
collecting one by one the carbonized remains
out of strong desire to preserve
replace in the fire
his heart remained intact

his heart remained intact.

Trinh T. Minh-ha, "For Love of Another"[7]

Vietnamese folklore always knew about the *extra*-ordinary power of love through which a heart consumed by the dauntless inner-strength fire turned into crystal,[8] but this time, the crystal of compassion, the "Indestructible Heart," appears not in the realm of legend and myth but in the mundane realm of history—as an ultimate gift, a grand message from Bodhisattva Thích Quảng Đức. In his last letter, the monk respectfully *pleaded* President Diệm for compassion and for religious equality. As absurd as it may sound, the administration (via Ngô Đình Nhu, Diệm's chief political advisor) was said to have originally *confiscated the heart* (a sign of a sorely deranged humanity locked in the tyranny of a victory mindset). Such was the desire to win over and control another man's heart that even when he was no longer, even as defeat showed up at might's door, the despot still futilely *grabbed the dead man's heart away from his loved ones* and appropriated what could not in any way be gained by force. Beijing's response to the event at the time was, ironically, also most memorable and would bear recalling in the context of a Tibet on fire: eager to circulate as widely as possible the photo of Thích Quảng Đức's self-immolation, the Chinese administration reportedly distributed millions of copies throughout Asia and Africa—as evidence of "US imperialism."

> —"The Zen patriarchs all leave relics, what are you going to leave us?"
> —"How about my heart?"
>
> Thích Quảng Đức in conversation with Thích Thanh Long, sometime prior to the day of his self-immolation

True Person of No Rank

> The more you are motivated by love, the more fearless and free your actions will be.
>
> The Dalai Lama

> For to be free is not merely to cast off one's chains, but to live in a way that respects and enhances the freedom of others.
>
> Nelson Mandela

In facing a systemic, state-induced "*terminal illness*," what Tibetans are denied is not so much the right to die by their own hand as the right to choose as they see fit, a specific way of dying—excruciatingly painful and tragic but also public and altruistic. Although meant to attract attention for a collective cause, and to take on a potentially powerful impact beyond borders, such a sacrificial political gesture is, above all, not intended to inflict harm on any other being and their material property or on the environment. Through this *extra*-ordinary act of taking one's own life in public, a radical gesture of sacrifice and deliverance is manifested, whose spectacle could often be said to feature (oneself as) nothing less than *raw human suffering, endurance, and agony*. In other words, what tends to be suppressed for over five decades is being harrowingly offered to view in the very bodies set ablaze. As a monk in Ngaba clandestinely shared: "because of the Chinese repression and the Dalai Lama's exile, [Tibetans] are as alive as a dead body waiting to be cremated. Thus, in setting their bodies on fire they are in reality cremating themselves—and also mocking their tormentors who, unable to establish supremacy over the hearts and minds of Tibetans, forever seek to control their bodies."[9] Said to "walk out of the flames" (Ai Weiwei), the *self-cremators* thus left behind the all-too-human body of desire, delusion, and suffering—yearning, through their one torch-body, for thousands of candles to be lit without bodies being sacrificed.

Lovecidal . . . love suicided.

When all the lethal might of those in power fail to snuff out the flame of freedom—here, the "Fire under Snow"—whole people find themselves empowered in the sheer force of saying No. A dramatic No, rising from a fundamentally non-armed struggle (not even armed with David's sling and stone while standing up to Goliath) that differentiates them from other fighters, all the while bonding them to oppressed communities of the world. The power of No lies in its core ability to unsettle (No, but, not quite), for what one refuses is not merely that other hated face of oneself or of (in)humanity but also that easily acceptable liberal face offering peace or "harmony," willingly or unwillingly on the dominant's terms. Whether manifested in their tyrannical or their benign states, complex forms of compliance in contexts of unequal power relations make it all the more necessary to keep the ground of refusal alive—as an embodied undercurrent, unexpected within the all-too-expected, unconforming within the very effort to conform (Yes, but, not quite). The power in the end to say No to Yes, but also *No to No*—canceling out the binary in both positive and negative reactions.

> To me, the response of the Tibetan people to the self-immolations tells us something significant. It tells us about a particular moment in Tibet, a moment when ordinary people are coming together to protect what is most precious to them. There may be unbearable oppression, but as one young Tibetan said to me, "Who can say with any certainly that there is no hope?"
>
> Namkho, from the Amdo area of Eastern Tibet, now in exile[10]

At the core of the testimonies and notes left behind by self-immolators is the call for *life-affirming actions*—that is, for the protection of Tibetan cultural identity and for solidarity among Tibetan people in determining their destiny.[11] Two of the wishes voiced almost unanimously were: the return of the Dalai Lama and the freedom of Tibet. What the people reportedly resented to the core of their being was Beijing's demonization of the Dalai Lama and its policy to force Tibetans to do likewise. As a Tibetan monk put it: "In my heart, the Dalai Lama is as precious as the stars and the moon in the sky. Without him, the world would be dark. I'd rather die then. I'm willing to give up my life for him. If I say anything bad about him, I won't return as a human being in my next life."[12] Another monk, Gartse Jigme, sentenced to five years in prison for having written the book *Tsenpoi Nyingtop* ("The King's Valor") on Tibet with political contents including self-immolation protests, affirmed: "By branding Dalai Lama as their enemy and neglecting the demands of self-immolators, they have shown that they consider more than 99 percent of the Tibetan population as their enemies." Ending the second volume on a chapter titled "My Heartfelt Appeal to the Chinese Government," he insisted that the book was not written to prove his scholarly credentials or his heroism, but to *shed tears*, to "[*cry*] once with the suffering of my fellow country men . . . amid the waves of *truth* and *justice*."[13] What the Dalai Lama represents resonates deep within people of all walks of life. Rather than dwindle with time and distance, the affective impact of the exiled leader on his people continues to grow and glow in scope and intensity. A Western visitor traveling in Tibet in 2009 noted with surprise: "There was a restless hunger to

be in the presence of the Dalai Lama, and touch him and hear his voice. I hadn't expected that."[14]

> Space has a name but no form
> You can't possess it and you can't lose it.
>
> Bodhidharma

Such an extraordinary bond and unblemished faith in the Dalai Lama could only raise the ire of Chinese authorities, who, for having internalized the terror they exert, continue to see in the people's unadulterated love for him an act of sedition. With their ever-renewed need to *enhance* security and their bastion-of-iron approach to problems of the heart, what seems again to escape attention is their own complicity in the "crime" they so strongly reprehend. In dire need for a face to point their finger at, they have been *enhancing*, via an intensified public relations campaign against the Dalai Lama, the individualist mystification of him by focusing disproportionately on his person, attributing every trouble related to Tibetans to his doing (thereby distorting the nature of Tibetan protests), and singling him out as the main threat to their power and legitimacy in Tibet, or as they would rather put it, to the "unity" of the Chinese nation. Whenever the Dalai Lama goes on an overseas tour, official receptions for his visit never fail to infuriate Beijing. The warmer the reception, the more virulent the reactions of the Chinese officials who vent their rage at the nation involved, issue warnings and threats, or take retaliatory steps. So imperious is the craving for totalitarian control that the reactions could at time degenerate into infantilism—such as the repeated attempts to deny His Holiness's global religious status so as to speak of official meetings with him in international contexts as "gross interference in China's internal affairs," or worse, the enactment of a law *prohibiting* the Dalai Lama *to be reborn* anywhere but on Chinese-controlled territory.

Angst over the Dalai Lama's aura seems like a perennial condition of Beijing. But as certain Tibet studies scholars affirm, the Dalai Lama's main appeal lies in his ability to be "*an empty space* that travels around in which we can place some of [our] fantasies."[15] In accounts across cultures, Tibet used to be the empty space on the map—one on which outsiders could not only put to work their imaginations but also *find peace in voiding it* (the blank no imagination can fill up). Such an empty space accounts for the fact that his broad-based constituency spans across several generations, from the very young to the very old, and "can range and change from Indian conservatives to American hippies."[16] It suffices to attend some of his public talks or to follow his many interviews and interactions with groups of people to note how genuinely and effortlessly he transmits the core truths of Buddhism by speaking in the Now, as a "nobody" (his own term)—*never on top* of his audiences, always on the same level, *with* them and *as one of them*, sharing mundane experiences accordingly and joking away as with old friends. Revealing the simple secret that makes this Dalai Lama the most beloved spiritual figure in the world, a novelist remarked: "It's almost impossible not to be inspired by him, to be warmed, to be clarified, to feel that you've come into a presence of rare goodness and uncanny, omnidirectional compassion."[17]

In his world journeys, the Dalai Lama has not only been visiting politicians, scientists, religious leaders, and media people but also mothers concerned about the youth of their country and students of all ages, some barely out of kindergarten—"giving himself to the schoolgirls as attentively and enthusiastically as if he were visiting the White House or the Vatican."[18] The future happens in the Now and, as is well known, His Holiness takes great joy in talking to children and teenagers in schools—those who, in adult speak, will be making the world of our future in the next few decades. Attending to their answers "as if they were his guides," ready to learn from every interlocutor, and listening with consummate attention to all questions raised, regardless of the speaker's status, age, or background, the "nobody"-Dalai Lama gives genuine practical advice and *discourages all myth making*. Accordingly, words when spoken directly from the heart and intently with one's whole being (as in his case) could hardly be received with the same ear as the one used routinely for conventional rationalizing. (The latter is the ear authorities often take for granted as the only right ear when they try to dismiss, control, or reason with matters of the heart—subjecting all manifestations of affect, creativity, and spirituality to the logic of dominant ratiocination and material conditioning.) As the exiled Tibetan leader often stresses, "when educating the minds of our youth, we must not forget to *educate their hearts.*" All the while assuming the role of the Dalai Lama, he seems to dwell in the wonder of the ordinary, embodying the "*true person of no rank*, constantly entering and exiting the openings of your face" (Zen koan, Linji Yixuan [d. 866]). Many among His Holiness's audiences commented on how his teachings come fully in tune with the way he walks through the world. A reincarnation of the multi-eyed, multi-armed Avalokitesvara, he often manifests an all-absorbing state where he is one with who, what, or how he meets. Through him, or *empty space*—one of the many names he has been given—the world comes alive.

Snake in the Can

On human condition, a sage sharing his lightness to a group of sentient listeners offered the image of a snake struggling inside a can, beating its head against the shell, turning restlessly topsy-turvy, biting its own tail in the process, knowing not how to get out from where it gets itself in.
The emphatic call to witness the doings of self-jailing and self-escaping in attempts both at dwelling in the can and getting out of it is immediately met with lively responses from the listeners:
—"But we need the can, if we are ever to realize that we are closed in. There's no freedom without that can!"
—"I have decided not to get out and have learned to like the can."
—"I want to affirm the beauty of that can."
—"The snake's tail is already out of the can, wiggling free . . ."
Falling and rising in its momentum and forever refined in its insider's language, the struggle of the snake inside the can continues. How else but relentlessly?
For the one who does find effortlessly a sudden way out, the words used in life may be the same, but the language—absurd, paradoxical,

illogical, incomprehensible, opaque to many ears from inside the can—is, no doubt, one free of the confinements of the canned-in condition: a double-edged, outside-the-can language. Yet, outside is not a livable place, and it does happen that those who've gotten out end up getting right back in, for the fear of vastness is, how else to say it?—vaaaast. Some, unable to squeeze back in, walk for some time the path of boundless solitude and then manage to return inside, out of consideration for their loved ones. But, the sage adds, beware, you don't know how cunning and skillful one can be when one decides to do so . . . and the room resounds unendingly with his laughter.

A Bridge, a Boat, a Spark of Plenty

> There was such natural beauty,
> the forest full of wildlife, and especially the meadows full of flowers
> when you walked in these mountains, when you came home,
> you would find flowers between your toes.
>
> Ama Adhe reminiscing on her native land, Lobasha in Kanze

Tibet seems so far and yet so near. She has found the way to the hearts of peace practitioners and seekers of freedom and justice around the world. Viewed under the light of everyday *bodhicitta* (the yearning for enlightenment and the practice of compassion for the world's beings) as evoked earlier by the Dalai Lama's focus on the flowering of humanity, modern control society, with its addiction to economics, proves to be strangely, if not downright, "underdeveloped," since it has forgotten on its way to the peak of science and technology how to cultivate the heart. As is well known, power and harmony cannot be obtained from the barrel of a gun, and development needs not be measured in terms of material gain and physical results. A farmer near Labrang summarized it all when, in response to a question concerning how progress might have changed his life, he typically responded: "Conditions have improved in the last five years. But no matter how developed Tibet becomes, our hearts will always be empty if the Dalai Lama does not return to Tibet." For over half a century, China and Tibet have been locked in a no-win situation. And yet, when asked whether he thought China was victorious over Tibet, the Dalai Lama was happy to oblige: "win-win position. Inside, outside . . . Not bad." It is by losing that he wins. In his own famous definition of the "true hero," he often proves to be one "who gains victory over hatred and anger" and exhorts his audiences to see for themselves—again, to rely on their *seeing tears* or on the heart's listening—so as to tell the world. Warning them to heed neither Tibetan nor Chinese propaganda when they investigate the reality of his people, he has also repeatedly specified that in committing himself to the Tibetan cause, he is actually not fighting for Tibet (per se) but for *justice.*

One of the memorable calls the Dalai Lama made in response to his people being subjected to beatings, humiliation, and detention for carrying his picture or refusing to condemn him, was to urge them to denounce him "without any hesitation" if the Chinese authorities force them to do so for "the act would be seen by any sensible man as having been committed under duress, under gunpoint." As he further reminds, "We are all on this planet, as it were, as tourists . . . . The world is presented to us as essentially competitive, divided into 'the winners' and 'the losers,' but that too is a false vision, deliberately false. It is a rapid scan on the surface, which eliminates any descent into the self, any meditation and reflection."[19] For the dominant, however, it is paramount that the binary opposition be kept intact, if winning were to mean anything at all. (To quote Gore Vidal, "It is not enough for me to win—the other must lose.") Thus, as Chinese legal scholar and activist Xu Zhiyong movingly deplored, after having visited the home of a Tibetan self-immolator, "We are victims ourselves, living in estrangement, infighting, hatred, and destruction. We share this land. It's our shared home, our shared responsibility, our shared dream—and it will be our *shared deliverance*."[20]

> What is life?
> It is the flash of a firefly in the night. It is the breath of a buffalo in the wintertime.
> It is the little shadow, which runs across the grass and loses itself in the sunset.
>
> Blackfoot proverb

As a spark in the blind night, a manifestation of the Buddha who resides within every being, always in the process of budding and flowering, the Dalai Lama does not see himself as a "semi-God" or "God-king," as he is often presented in the press. He jovially talks about the many names he is given, but his status is nothing like Mao's godlike status. (Common slogans to promote Mao idolatry and cult of personality read, for example: "Parents may love me, but not as much as Chairman Mao"; "Warriors love reading Chairman Mao's books most"; or else, "The sunlight of Mao Zedong thought illuminates the road of the Great proletarian Cultural Revolution.") With profound trust in the goodness of humanity, the Dalai Lama is quick at demystifying his status as a "living deity" and insists on being *thoroughly a human*. Such a (de)positioning underlies the lively earthly nature of his interactions with his audience and readership. Seeking to educate the heart across ideologies and religions rather than converting anyone to Tibetan Buddhism, he crosses the abyss of the mind and draws us closer to ourselves through hilarious stories of his being that always remind us he is no different from anyone else.

As a presence that often inspires awe and reverence despite his undoing, the Dalai Lama is full of mundane surprises. Referring to his falling sick with a liver infection, for example, he commented on how "some people used to say the Dalai Lama lives as a prisoner in a golden cage," and added, "on this occasion, I was golden-bodied too" (affected by hepatitis B).[21] During a visit in Fukuoka, Japan, he immediately broke the ice with his audience and drew laughter of delight from some six hundred young female students by telling them how his tutor used to keep two whips for him and his elder brother—one of which is yellow, a "'Holy Whip,' [whose] effect is the same as from the other one. 'Holy Pain.'"[22] Holiness is not immune to suffering, and one catches here and there a glimpse of his cheerful compassionate energy in the face of his people's tragic plight. Readers unfamiliar with his many Buddhist writings often comment on how inspired and struck they were by the tone of his autobiographical books—unassuming, down to earth, without the slightest hint of pretense—and by the sense he gave them of his being a fundamentally ordinary individual—an everyman, born from a small farmers family, before being severely disciplined (with Holy Whip) and monastically educated to assume the responsibilities (or Holy Pain) of the Dalai Lama.

> The tree that bears much fruit bows low.
>
> Hindi saying

Despite his most active globetrotting life, the Dalai Lama has time and again affirmed his being at heart "a simple Buddhist monk." Whenever he was introduced as "a living Buddha" during his visits across contexts and nations, he would repeatedly and vigorously rectify: "I am not a living Buddha, I am just a monk"; and for an audience of future CEOs, he would add: "a Marxist monk, but a true Marxist." Sometimes referring to the historical Buddha as his "boss," he would remind his listeners not to accept his words out of regard for him but only after due examination for themselves. As he noted, in his dreams as in his memories, he sees himself not as (the set of practices that define) the Dalai Lama but first and foremost as a monk—one who walks the path of the bodhisattva and has given himself over fully to the practice of the dharma. It is primarily through his monastic being that he maintains his three commitments to humanity, in which the Tibetan cause comes third: promotions of human values, inter-religious harmony, and peace. To all who have attended his talks in arenas filled to capacity, the sight from afar of the monk's small silhouette instinctively bowing and stooping in full humility to the thousands of people coming to listen to him remains a most moving and endearing sight. The Dalai Lama's dignity is not built on glorification and adulation but on his warmhearted simplicity.

When reduced to its bare bones, the world seems to be driven by two sources of strength. As Buddhist teacher Jack Kornfield puts it, "One is the force of hatred, of those who are *unafraid to kill*. The other and greater strength comes from those who are *unafraid to die*. This was the strength behind Gandhi's marches against the entire British Empire."[23] And one may add here, behind every wo/man's, mother's, grandmother's walk against global Patriarchal Empire, or else behind every nun's, monk's, and other Davidian dissident's nonviolent gesture against a Goliathian armed Empire. *Lovecidal, the suicide of love*. Such strength of heart has redeemed human life in every circumstance of harrowing difficulty, allowing the repressed and disfranchised to face tyranny and injustice with truth and compassion. For those who remain close to the roots of humanity's sorrows, a similar classification of the human could also be found, for example, in a novel by the influential Vietnamese novelist and essayist Phạm Thị Hoài. First published in Hanoi and subsequently banned by the Vietnamese government, *The Crystal Messenger* (*Thien Su*, 1988) denounces the totalitarian regime's corruptions and incompetence with dry humor and oblique imagery, while offering a scathing commentary on modern patriarchal society. Human nature is seen through the eyes of a woman physically trapped in her body (she stopped growing at the age of fourteen) and in her 16-square-meter (or 172-square-foot) room (literally, a woman's place), who spends her time filtering the world outside through the magic rectangle of her window—a world she radically divides between homo-A, *those who love*, and homo-Z, *those who love not*. Such a reduction of mankind, of place, and, as she affirms, of her own body is not fortuitous; it is the bittersweet fruit of many years of mental and physical exertion. Despite its unsparing sarcasm, what ultimately lies at the core of the novel's unsentimental, humoristic worldview is *love*.

Two lights, two paths, twofold, two-hold, many twos in the two kinds of people. The empty One comes in multiplicities. However, the conqueror's world remains, oblivious to the multiform of the between, as it thrives on straight binary oppositions that end up backfiring when reappropriated by the marginalized. In the radical reclassification of humanity by the woman protagonist of *The Crystal Messenger*, there's no midrange spanning from A to Z, in other words, nothing else between two apparent absolutes: the *fully living* and the *living dead*. What may at first sound like a joke or at best a utopia, may somewhere down the line hit ordinary consciousness as intimately as with statements made at the end of one's life, when delusions lose their grip and one looks back, ready to leave: "I love you," "Forgive me," "Did I live well?" "Mama." (The first one, "I love you," being, for example, the succinct and most recurrent phone message left to their loved ones by the September 11 victims in their final moments.) Indeed, what would it be like when love is at the base of every system of mundane evaluation? When the ability to love determines every person's identity? Or when attention is given to the invisible work of love (the way we touch with our hearts or are unexpectedly touched by the world) likely to shift ground in the spheres of law, politics, and economics, or of science and technology? Sharing his experience of compassion's night action, John Tarrant Roshi wrote, for example: "When all the stories about how to live fall away, what is left might be the real . . . . What to call it? . . . What if the word might be love? When there was *simple seeing*, that would be love."[24]

For many of us, the dilemma arises there where we think we are not: in the hatred so blind it crosses our fundamental fear to kill and in the compassion so capacious it crosses our fundamental fear to die. Somewhere between the two . . . perhaps there's a path for the song of those who *dare to love* (Maya Angelou) to find its way to those who, out of greater inner fear, act unafraid to kill. And perhaps, there's a nightly way for the song of Tibet's vast "oceanic heart" (meaning of the name "Dalai Lama") to find its way to China, more particularly to China's ruling ears, even as the authorities shut off and turn their back to its call. *"We share this land . . . and it will be our shared deliverance"* (Xu Zhiyong). The lure is irresistible and ungovernable. For positive change in Beijing's stance toward the Tibetan struggle would not just benefit the Tibetan people but transform China as a whole.

The strange power of the *Siren's song* (the voice of the abyss, one's true singular voice) lies in it being sung to men (trained to appear) fearless in their impulses, who nonetheless make a colossal effort to defame and discredit it—for fear of letting themselves be enticed to a place they did not want to fall into (the descent into the questioning self). *In the night of becoming* . . . Would they (we) *dare to love*? Would they (we) take the risk to listen carefully (to the mermaids of their [our] own dangerous making)? Or would they (we) hold on deadly to their (our) "iron bastion" security? The struggle is not that of giving voice to the voiceless (or of making them hear what they don't want to hear) but of letting the *unheard song* (the invisible, the not-quite-not-yet-seen) quietly work its way through, within the hearable (the visible, the all-too-visible). Ulysses's distinctive deafness is that of he "who is deaf because he *can* hear."[25]

Our own heart is our temple.

Dalai Lama

The blooming of the udumbara flowers is a rare event said to happen only once every three thousand years in Buddhist scriptures. Botanically, it takes place seasonally, but the flowers' perfect blossoming remains hidden to sight, enclosed inside the udumbara fruit. The question raised with the *unseen* flower is not whether the flowering happens or not but *whether one can see* the flowering happening *within*—one's own lantern. In the Lotus Sutra, the udumbara flower appears in reference to both the rarity of seeing a Buddha (a fully awakened person) and the always-present potential for enlightenment in each and all beings. No duality set up between the sacred and the secular, or between awareness and existence. Everyone is an udumbara flower blooming in *fire*, as Buddhahood is realized not *away from* but *within* this very world.

Today, "to literally become a follower of the Dalai Lama . . . one need only click a button."[26] Access to his daily teachings could be gained by thousands of people on Twitter and Facebook. To download *for free* an image of His Holiness, it suffices to Google "Dalai Lama image" or "HHDL pictures," for example, to find many designed as a tribute to him and as posted online, "to bring some peace to your desktop . . . to practice [peace of mind and kindness] in our daily lives, not just in a church or a temple." No wonder that with people in Tibet carrying his portrait much like an underground ID—keeping him close to their hearts and available to their call at their (surreptitious) finger swipes on cell phones—the Dalai Lama seems most happy to offer round-the-clock digital company and haptic visuality to those in need: once when asked by the press how he identifies himself, he instinctively responded, "I am a *screensaver*."

If, in global economics, the man of our millennium is widely said to be Chinese, among those learning from Tibet he is said to be no longer the man who *conquers* but rather the man who *absorbs*. Deeply moving but sadly strange to hear was how, in their grievances, certain Tibetan monks cried while invoking the Dalai Lama as a wanderer, erring homelessly for over fifty years, separated from his people and deprived of his land and nation. For many of us, it is easy to forget that the Dalai Lama is politically a "homeless" person and a refugee of our time, who was compelled through displacement to remake himself as he walks the path of uncertainty and instability with his people (both inside and outside Tibet). But *empty space* is where man, country, and the world merge as one. It is by *losing* that he *wins* the world's freedom, heart and mind. It is through exile that Tibet and he have come to be, as he put it, "the most successful refugee in the world." For, remaking himself entails radically remaking an unrepresented nation and culture in exile, as well as readapting and setting a progressive course for Tibetan Buddhism in relation to other religions and systems of knowledge, such as science (neurobiology, physics, psychology, cosmology), technology, and environment. For him, homelessness has become, in fact, a way of living intimately *the world's homelessness*. Being at home in the world, he would not hesitate to evoke his refugee status as a blessing or as an opportunity to fully practice his humanity; with the freedom, via resilience and wise flexibility, not only of blooming in the fire of the Chinese rulers but also of voiding and emerging moment by moment—released from his own past and from the future of the institution of the Dalai Lama.

Their names I know not,
But every weed has
Its tender flower.

Sampu

No one calls the Dalai Lama by his name, Jetsun Jamphel Ngawang Lobsang Yeshe Tenzin Gyatso, or by his birth name, Lhamo Dondrub (or Thondup). In our age of ever-bigger powers and of bit-size information, "love is key to human life," the Dalai Lama reminds us while offering himself to be shared. Far more concerned about "filling the human heart with compassion" than merely "filling the human brain with knowledge," he has no definite shape, rank, or identity in his being and is, so to speak, much larger than his own self. *The one whom I enclose with my name is weeping in that dungeon* (Rabindranath Tagore). What the Dalai Lama ultimately represents is bound to resonate deeply within people of all walks of life. Responding to a widest range of appellations, he is through these pages at once: a light (the sun's "Golden Face," "the stars and the moon in the sky"); a lamp ("long-life lamp"); a space and a place, a material and spiritual environment ("an empty space," "the Peak," or the Potala, the Norbulingka, Tibet); an affect ("the long-lost love," "a rare goodness and omnidirectional compassion"); an empty chair, a vacant throne; an interval (the hole in the news, the blank frame, blank page, blank in-between); an image ("the forbidden picture"), a poster, a pass, an ID card, a screensaver (all kept underground in Tibet); a sign (of solidarity), a song, a prayer, a spark (of kindness); and, last but not least, a flower (the Green Lotus, the udumbara blossom): *the heart of his people*.

In the night of becoming, love, abiding nowhere and coming forth from just about anywhere, draws one back into the nitty-gritty of worldly life. The "Dalai Lama effect" is usually known in the world of politics and economics for the negative impact on exports due to China's retaliatory measures against a host country's official meetings with His Holiness. But in the world of spirituality and creativity, such an *effect of emptiness* has often evolved into a life-transforming experience, the way, for example, a woman attending numerous public audiences and living near His Holiness for a year remarked: "I had long ago observed that wherever he goes, the Dalai Lama inevitably leaves behind a wake of beaming faces, folks of every age, race, and creed smiling as tenderly as if they've all just fallen in love."[27] Is it at all surprising that he who is said to reside in the hearts of 99 percent of his people, and through whom Tibet comes alive, be a consummate heart opener? When people prostrate themselves before the Dalai Lama, are they merely prostrating before a powerful individual or a religious celebrity (what in Zen is called "the stink of Zen")? Are they revering the man, the famous leader, and his supreme title, as the Chinese authorities so fear? Or,

Are they simply bowing in all humility to a loving heart—*their own heart*?

Their own good medicine.

Love is a state of creative being. The "long-life lamp" constantly evoked among Tibetans is a light nurtured in the seat of love, through which every being shines with its own light. *Our own heart is our temple.* This is the very light that sustains life in the dark and makes an opening for tenderness and laughter in the midst of immense suffering. Tears in the instance of boundless joy. This is also the very light that turns every ending into an infinite opening within the finite. Every day is a good day, noted Yun Men (864–949). Every day above ground, said an AIDS patient, is a great day. Every day: on earth, under the sky, before the divinities, among mortals, with flora and fauna, etc. "Every day, think as you wake up, today I am fortunate to be alive, I have a precious human life, I am not going to waste it," suggests the Dalai Lama, whose commitment to the flowering of humanity begins every morning with the performance of an eighth-century Buddhist prayer (Shantideva's), whose shortened popularized version translates as follows:

> May I be a guard for those who need protection
> A guide for those on the path
> A boat, a raft, a bridge for those who wish to cross the flood
> May I be a lamp in the darkness
> A resting place for the weary
> A healing medicine for all who are sick
> A vase of plenty, a tree of miracles
> And for the boundless multitudes of living beings
> May I bring sustenance and awakening
> Enduring like the earth and sky . . . .[28]

this sky which is not blue

> What would a sane Martian observer make of our dedicated march towards destruction?
>
> Noam Chomsky on the twin threats of environmental disaster and nuclear war

In response to the endings and beginnings apocalyptically evoked for decades ahead, when the Y2K crisis was pending, the colors of the sky during the last years of the millennium took on a strange grayish hue. The Argentinian town of Perugorria dyed itself sporadically during a month of September with blue rains—caused by ashes, they said, from walloping forest fires. On the diary page of the planet, a lightning bolt was reported to have killed eleven members of a Congolese soccer team and burned thirty others, miraculously leaving the adversary team unharmed. Lava spewing from the Nyamuragira Volcano in eastern Congo was said to have lit up the nighttime skies of Goma, the very headquarters of dissidents who had fomented a revolt against the country's president earlier in August. Elsewhere, three thousand people met with death when a tidal wave, set off by an offshore earthquake, struck the northwestern coast of Papua New Guinea. Further up on the world map, weekend storms caused disastrous flooding in southwestern England, and eleven rivers busted their banks in Wales, sending hundreds of its inhabitants away from their homes. Following the Way of mountains and water, powerful surges of water racing down the Yangzi River in China and spreading north to Inner Mongolia continued to pose new threats to the lives of the 240 million inhabitants already profoundly affected by their recent past flooding, including the one of an unsettling September that had killed over two thousand people. While sustained rainfalls causing mudslides in South Korea had made 260 dead and 140,000 homeless, the many-month-long drizzle in the small town of Salalah in southern Oman was attracting an influx of sixty thousand Gulf tourists—who, weary of the daily temperatures elsewhere in the area, eagerly drove for days across the desert to spend their holiday in the luxury and watery delights of the town's temperate climate. During the same month, landslides in the Himalayas also caught people by surprise, killing three hundred, including sixty Hindu pilgrims crossing from India to a holy lake in Tibet. Of the floods and blazes that have occurred in several parts of southeast Asia from record punishing weather not directly associated with any tropical events, it is reported that the worst flooding in fifteen years for Vietnam has devastated seven provinces in the south, wrecking half a million homes and affecting the lives of nearly three million people. The worst also to strike the Chanthaburi River in Thailand in eighty years affected nearly sixty thousand area residents, a figure coinciding strangely with the amount of Philippine residents forced, during the same period, to evacuate around the inundated city of Manila. Numbers, to which numberless zeros can be added when it comes to sum up human lives affected, have grown so insignificantly large on the global scale, and the line distinguishing natural from man-made disasters so conveniently blurred on occasion, as to lose all pertinence. Memory recalls the recurring times when the fires blamed on plantation owners in Indonesia enshrouded for weeks the islands of Sumatra and Borneo with a haze of smoke that caused extensive harm to inhabitants' health and lives and to the ecologies and economies of the region. The sun blotted out by the poisonous smog—which for months spread east to west covering six countries of Southeast Asia and an estimated seventy million people—intermittently re-emerged when the wind and rain brought about a respite from the smoldering flames. The fickle clearing of the smoke-laden skies was then a fresh dawn whose effect poignantly drew attention to the irreversible damage the disaster would inflict upon the planet. Among the Hot news gathered a month before another more recent September, worth mentioning was the heat wave that had swept many parts of the world, killing scores of people from India and France. The extreme heat ignited numerous wildfires across Europe, producing sick air quality in major cities and scorching Italy's land with thousand-acre blazes. The continent reached record temperatures despite the eager call of the pope, who urged all believers to pray for rain for the sake of the world. The same shift that has turned Europe into an oven is also responsible for freak floods along the edges of the Sahara Desert. Algeria and Sudan are said to have undergone the worst storms in living memory, and severe inundation has brought about death and destruction all across parts of Africa, from Senegal to Eritrea. Meanwhile along Florida's Atlantic beaches, unusually strong onshore winds caused the upwelling of chilling deep ocean waters and a thousand cold-shocked baby turtles were compelled to undergo treatment for hypothermia with a mixture of electrolytes and sugar water. The sunny state has, most recently, become known for its repeated hurricane disasters: Charley, Frances, Ivan, and Jeanne took turns to visit, killing and tearing across the land, and leaving 42,000 homeless. Urged to flee by the millions, residents and tourists streamed inland in bumper-to-bumper traffic on Labor Day, during the month of September. As the year struggled to its close and as the Western world awoke from its Christmas Eve's sweet celebrations, giant waves of destruction caused by an undersea quake of 9.0 magnitude off the coast of Sumatra swept across the Indian Ocean from Thailand to Somalia, hitting at least eleven countries of southern Asia and eastern Africa, killing an inadequately estimated 181,000 people and leaving five million homeless, injured, and destitute. All islands of the shattered region were affected, and while more than fifty aftershocks centered on Andaman and Nicobar Islands, for a moment, the entire Maldives was said to disappear from the planet Earth. The news of the devastating, hour-by-hour rise of the tsunami death toll irrupted into the homes of web surfers and television watchers, and while over here, certain merrymakers fretted over their dinner preparations for New Year's Eve, over there, countless dazed and grief-stricken people desperately searched for clean water and for food, picking through rubble on streets littered with decomposing bodies. In the gray apocalyptic landscape of death and destruction, utterly distraught survivors checked corpse after corpse, combed the beaches, turned every car, every boat, every piece of wood, metal, and rock to look for their missing loved ones, leaving literally no stone unturned. Striking on exactly the same date a year after the Bam calamity in Iran, the December 26 tsunami tragedy was then said to be history's worst natural disasters ever, a global catastrophe of unprecedented scale, and the fourth strongest quake on Earth since recordings of magnitude began in 1899. The Earth has shifted, and the waters washing across the lands have changed the topographical map of the region's coastal areas. Witnesses recalled the terrifying experience of being caught in thundering walls of water that swallowed up everything on its way, blasted away buildings, razed entire towns and villages, and destroyed almost all of the capital of Banda Aceh. Tourists on vacation described, in utter disbelief, the shock of being on a paradise island one moment and swimming in a living hell the next. As the ranks of the displaced kept swelling, so did those of the dead in locals quickly transformed into open-sky makeshift morgues across cities and villages of the afflicted countries. For the exhausted inhabitants of the islands, dwarfed by the scale of the suffering, the task of pulling out the dead bodies never seemed to end. In the multitude of dying, to keep tally of the dead, one would have to go on counting for weeks and months, for the numbers gathered differed from one institution to another. Nordic countries, also unexpectedly hard hit by the tsunami's impact, were taken by surprise and traumatized by the death toll of their citizens, as well as by the absence of information on the whereabouts of the large number of their "disappeared." Among the many Western vacationers who traveled south to escape the harsh winter of northern Europe, some twenty thousand Swedes seeking bluer sky and sea were reported to have flown to Thailand during the holiday season. Casting a shroud over the world precisely at a time when people were joyously breaking into end-of-the year festivities, the devastating wrath of nature expresses itself acutely and mercilessly. The New Year opened sadly with heavy, tragic mourning and with sinister hues of contaminated air and water. The living grieves for the living, saying the dead, at least, is spared of the sorrow of witnessing. Shortly after, what happened over there found its equivalence over here (albeit in a different scale). Closer to home, in the heart of the secure homeland, a cataclysmic-storm-turned-catastrophic-flood devastated seventy miles of Mississippi's coast and shattered the homes and lives of hundreds of thousands. A major city crumbled overnight. That very crescent city some have compared to ancient Pompeii, while others have invoked as a third world within the first world. For a while, the stink of decay was all over New Orleans. Residents were spared the full brunt of Katrina's hurricane force, but breaches in the levees created catastrophic flooding that left some 80 percent of the city flooded. With the rising tide, over a million people turned overnight into refugees. They came not from elsewhere—neither from South and Southeast Asia nor from Latin America or the Caribbean—but from the heart of the homeland, with no houses, no jobs, their career, family, and property being all abolished in vertigo. Bloated bodies were seen floating on foul water. No dignity in death, exclaimed a journalist in New Orleans who reported, for example, the decease of Vera Smith, 65, killed in the chaotic aftermath of Hurricane Katrina. Her body lay in the street, at the junction of Magazine Street and Jackson Avenue, under a tarpaulin, for five full days. Significantly, hurricane floodwaters were said to bring out all the snakes . . . and Katrina certainly did fulfill her role of snake releaser. Terms repeatedly featured on the news in relation to Katrina's aftermath spoke volumes about this effect: some called it "a national disgrace," "a United States of Shame," or "the larger hurricane of poverty that shames our land," and others deplored the lethal ineptitude, personal inadequacy, and failure of leadership. With the watery nightmare, New Orleans became the "damp grave" overnight. Graves in this city are not underground and marked by discreet headstones; to avoid previous mistakes of burial resulting in bodies floating through the streets with recurring floods, these graves are built aboveground in spacious, gleaming white "cities of the dead." New Orleanians were thus conveniently said to have long had a close relationship with death. With Katrina, New Orleans was plunged into agony, hell and high water, and again, with "a chilling lack of empathy" and "stunning lack of efficiency" from the administration, the dead lay on the streets—"Killed by Contempt," as the press saw it. Day after day of media visuals showed displaced citizens' lives on the brink, revealing, more covertly, the fate of white America's Other. Distraught families pleading for help, begging for water, asking news reporters and cameramen "Where's the bus?" "Where's the Red Cross?" The tap of images, first closed, was wide opened, as Katrina exposed to the world the full color of the disaster, with its raw class and racial divisions. In the 9/11 (2005) issue of Newsweek on "The Lost City," the photo of a white man looting was captioned: "Desperate needs: a man hunts for supplies in a ruined Wal-Mart," while the photos of Blacks and Chicanos caught in the same act got comments such as: "Out of control: some locals decided to take advantage of the chaos in the city and loot the stores." The Associated Press called "refugees" the million Katrina survivors, raising anger among critics from the Black community, since the term could imply the storm victims—with African Americans being among the most affected—were not US citizens. Here again, the refugee appears as a central figure in political history whose existence challenges the very foundation of the modern nation-state. The disasters related to Hurricane Katrina are, in the end, not the hurricanes themselves. In New Orleans, rumors of Katrina being "Hurricane Bush" surreptitiously spread, as the case was said to provide a startling confirmation of the axiom "There's no such thing as a natural disaster."

> It is early, early morning. It's that time when it's still dark but you know the day is coming. Blue is bleeding through black. Stars are dying.
>
> Markus Zusak, *Underdogs*

Ancient readers of the colors of the sky and the signs of the earth affirm that catastrophes and calamities are indicative of the times. Often a prelude to civil unrest, they invite one to cast off the masks of cynicism and indifference in order to make a difference and to take one's destiny in hand or else be the cause of one's own destruction. With the ongoing battle of red versus blue on a global scale, the forecast promises further devastation on an evermore-massive scale. Skeptics laugh hard at the slightest mention of chaos being just round the corner, for oracular visions abound in evangelical preaching, and alarming predictions on climate change being an existential threat or leading to "Global Warring," "Climate Conflict," and "Planetary Suicide" have become commonplace in recent publications. However, in the transmutation of positive and negative energies, when sky and earth, above and below are polarized, water, wind, and fire do bring relentless damage. Nature shows its fiercest face, and what is known as "acts of God" intricately wedded to acts of Man in the course of global warming—droughts, floods, tornadoes, hurricanes, quakes, fires, crop failures through the alternating chills and sweats of record-breaking highs and lows—continue their steady courses, reaching apocalyptic dimensions in their destruction around the world. "Normal" weather patterns are not holding and "unusual" ones followed by recurrent disasters are more and more spoken of in strings of bor-

rowed superlatives ("the worst in history," "the most deadly catastrophe," "the driest in the last hundred years," "the most violent in living memory," "the most powerful on Earth in forty years"). Despite the abundance of theories put forth, specialists seem at a loss with adequate words to describe what may be building up in the weather cycles that they have never quite experienced before. Climate change is what many scientists see as the biggest threat to humanity's existence on the planet. The debate over global warming remains rancorous, and although no single weather event can be merely attributed to climate change, its long-term impact on our de-natured environment raises endless deliberations about the nature of "natural" events and their "natural" cycles of devastation. The change, whose magnitude calls for action both top-down and bottom-up, has alarmed the world in a way it never has before, to the unequivocal and incalculable ripple effect of warming. Meanwhile, negative energies activated through feelings of fear as triggered by anger, betrayal, loss, grief, hostility, insecurity, loneliness, and helplessness keep on multiplying with little heed to the warnings issued. Everywhere on the world map, signs of nature's pure, immediate violence on the "vibration fields" seem to rise in proportional largesse with signs of global man-made crises, in which human relations have savagely deteriorated among the civilized, and the focus is competitively on actions of ever-grander-scale destruction. Since the world needs a culprit and it is easier to blame nature than to shield a nation, catastrophes—both man-made and nature-caused—receive such generic names as "major tragedy of modern times," "planetary damage," "earth on alert," "climate-related apocalypses to come," and are repeatedly attributed to monster "weather makers" of other kinds. (And since Natural and Man-made can hardly be separated, creating and fighting the multi-head monster always seems to go hand in hand. For example, in the aftermath of the 2011 Tucson shooting that left six people dead and Representative Gabrielle Giffords clinging to life, the blame went not only to Arizona's permissive gun laws but also its "toxic political environment" [Sheriff Clarence W. Dupnik]—or more generally, to the toxic us-versus-them environment that permeates the spectrum of US political discourse.) On the weather page, it is remembered that for a while the blame consistently went, for example, to the same kid, La Niña, then to her male counterpart, El Niño, whose periodic patterns of exceptional cooling or warming were found to be singularly disruptive to the southern hemisphere. Since then, many token names of culprits have come and gone in attempts to fill in this no-one-to-be-blamed vacuum, and when all is said, it is also admitted somberly that never from its century-long documentation have the consequences associated with these culprits been so devastatingly far and wide in intensity and in scope. "It took generations to foul the planet as badly as we have," reckons a report on global warming that also affirms "the verdict is in." The blame inevitably falls on the biggest corporate players and energy wasters, shifting strategically among misusers, from industry to politicians to voters, and reciprocally. But in the end, does it matter who exactly caused the worst problem and who continues to be the key culprits in squandering earth's resources? The blame can hardly be pinned on individual dealmakers—whether these are local or multinational. In a world of global trouble, the problem (once considered by conservative politicians as "the greatest hoax ever perpetrated on the American people") cannot be reduced to any single cause. Nor can it be stopped in any short time frame; the treatment and the cure would have to be collective and comprehensive if they were to be effective in the long term. Home is where the *health* is. Thus, what many voters in the United States see, for example, as most important in the current state of emergency are not so much taxes, immigration, and terrorism (in their discriminatory colorings) as the official networks have it but the immense needs of the physically, mentally, and emotionally wounded. In other words, *health care*—that is, *heart care*.

North and South writings on the one sky never run out of contrast in displaying their differing blues and reds. But as they reach their peak in brightness and darkness, the two hues inevitably join forces on the killing field, triggering both tears and laughter in gray terror. Optical illusions upheld in normal perceptions tend to define the sky as primarily blue, but sky readers seeing through the appearances of colors have long warned that with a divisive mind, what the eye perceives are only dead colors. There's no evidence "the sky is blue," for it is only via scattering (of the blue component of visible light) and only because of the limitations of human eyes that the sky looks blue. Although the sky is found to contain fifty times more violet than blue, we see blue instead of purple. So much delusion is taken as substance and the lure of blue remains one of the most persistent. Not only do different color appeal to different people, but in each appears, differently, *all colors*.

"In the end," says a Buddha-like quote circulating on Facebook, "only three things matter: how much you loved, how gently you lived, and how graceful you let go of things not meant for you." Perhaps blue never appears as celestially blue as when the sun is streaming, the earth feels round, and one is about to savor a juicy, terrestrial orange. "*La terre est bleue comme une orange*" (attested Paul Éluard in his love poetry). No doubt, the earth is then blue blue blue like an orange. Normal sight claims what it perceives to be all there is to perceive. It goes blind at noon with the innumerable colors called sunlight. But there where the radiance is at its brightest and where the mud explodes with colors, only there does one's lotus eye realize how infinitely more to a blue there is to the blue one sees. Now again *strangely*, the sky is *blue*.

> Such azure blue heavens . . . Are they really blue,
> or is it that they stretch away without end?
>
> Chuang Tzu, *The Inner Chapters* (trans. D. Hinton)

Notes

how to write an ending?

1. Brian Montopoli, "Obama: I Won't Release bin Laden Death Photos," CBS News, May 5, 2011, http://www.cbsnews.com/8301-503544_162-20059739-503544.html?tag=contentMain;contentBody#ixzz1LQIYriCf. Italics added.

2. Brian Montopoli and Nancy Cordes, "Three Senators May Have Been Fooled by Fake bin Laden Pictures," CBS News, May 4, 2011, http://www.cbsnews.com/8301-503544_162-20059844-503544.html.

3. Who's the headsman, indeed? The Navy SEALs who carried out the night raid, Obama and Bush, the warmonger, the Photoshop artist, the steel company office manager, the direct consumers (steelworkers), or their indirect accomplices (the onlookers-clients)?

4. *Economist*, May 7, 2011, 22.

5. David Sirota, "'USA! USA!' Is the Wrong Response," *Salon*, May 2, 2011, http://www.salon.com/news/politics/war_room/2011/05/02/osama_and_chants_of_usa.

6. Massimo Calabresi and Michael Crowley, "Homeland Insecurity: Do We Need to Sacrifice Privacy to Be Safer?," *Time*, May 13, 2013.

7. James Bamford, "The NSA Is Building the Country's Biggest Spy Center (Watch What You Say)," *Wired*, March 15, 2012.

8. Michael Scherer, "The Geeks Who Leak," *Time*, June 13, 2013, http://www.time.com/time/magazine/article/0,9171,2145506,00.html.

9. In "Sense, Sensibilities and Spying," *Economist*, July 6, 2013, 55.

10. Marjorie Cohn, "Former CIA Employee, Snowden, Blows Whistle on NSA's Dragnet Surveillance," Truthout, June 10, 2013, http://truth-out.org/news/item/16866-former-cia-employee-blows-whistle-on-dragnet-surveillance-of-americans.

11. Dave Lindorff, "Where's the Bullshit Repellent When We Need It?" NationofChange, June 10, 2013, http://www.nationofchange.org/where-s-bullshit-repellent-when-we-need-it-1370872269.

12. Tom Engelhardt, "How to Be a Rogue Superpower," NationofChange, July 16, 2013, http://www.nationofchange.org/how-be-rogue-superpower-1374033286.

13. Bruce Schneier, "What We Don't Know about Spying on Citizens: Scarier than What We Know," *Atlantic*, June 6, 2013, http://www.theatlantic.com/politics/archive/2013/06/what-we-dont-know-about-spying-on-citizens-scarier-than-what-we-know/276607/.

14. Simon Jenkins, "NSA Surveillance Revelations: Osama bin Laden Would Love This," *Guardian*, June 7, 2013, http://www.guardian.co.uk/commentisfree/2013/jun/07/nsa-surveillance-osama-bin-laden.

15. Reed Williams, "RIC Airport Protester, Federal Officials Present Arguments in Lawsuit," *Richmond Times-Dispatch*, August 11, 2011, http://www2.timesdispatch.com/news/2011/aug/11/tdmet01-ric-airport-protester-federal-officials-pr-ar-1231274/.

16. Ibid.

17. Among the many reports on the subject, see Ron Myer and Michael Billy, "Gropes of Wrath—Fed-up Flier 'Molests' TSA Screener," *New York Post*, July 17, 2011, and myfoxphoenix, http://www.myfoxphoenix.com/dpp/news/crime/some-support-woman-who-assaulted-tsa-agent-7-17-2011.

18. Jennifer Abel, "The TSA's State-Mandated Molestation," *Guardian*, December 29, 2010.

19. Shaun Rein, "Airport Security: Bin Laden's Victory," Forbes.com, March 3, 2010, http://www.forbes.com/2010/03/03/airport-security-osama-leadership-managing-rein.html.

20. fliegeroh, comment on "TSA's Airport Security Body Scans Spur US 'airport rage,'" YouTube video, 1:16, posted by "Taiwanese Animators," November 16, 2010, http://www.youtube.com/watch?v=TBL3ux1o0tM.

21. John Leland and Colin Moynihan, "Thousands March Silently to Protest Stop-and-Frisk Policies, *New York Times*, June 17, 2012.

22. Quoted in Alex Altman, "Ferguson Protesters," *Time*, December 22, 2014, 112.

23. "The Story of Millions March NYC," Synead Nichols and Umaara Elliot in an interview with Gina Sartori, SocialistWorker.org, January 15, 2015, http://socialistworker.org/2015/01/15/the-story-of-millions-march-nyc.

24. Dave Lindorff, "Like Hale's Philip Nolan, Snowden Has Become a 'Man without a Country,'" NationofChange, July 15, 2013, http://www.nationofchange.org/hale-s-philip-nolan-snowden-has-become-man-without-country-1373889427.

25. Radley Balko, "He Won," *Agitator*, May 2, 2011, http://www.theagitator.com/2011/05/02/he-won/.

26. Harry Waizer, as quoted in Elizabeth A. Harris, "Amid Cheers, a Message: 'They Will Be Caught,'" *New York Times*, May 2, 2011.

27. Robert Klitzman, "My Sister, My Grief," *New York Times*, The Opinion Pages, May 3, 2011.

28. President Obama at a public meeting in Istanbul, April 7, 2009, quoted in *Economist*, April 25–August 1, 2009, 40.

29. Michael Schwartz, "Colonialism in the 21st Century," SocialistWorker.org, July 13, 2009, http://socialistworker.org/2009/07/13/colonialism-in-the-21st-century.

30. Charles Q. Choi, "Military Developing Half-Robot, Half-Insect 'Cybug' Spies," Fox News, July 16, 2009.

31. James Denselow, "The US Departure from Iraq Is an Illusion," *Guardian*, October 25, 2011.

32. Janet Weil, "Moving of Chess Pieces: The Illusion of Withdrawal in Iraq," June 30, 2009, CODEPINK.

33. Quoted in Gareth Porter, "Politics: Despite Obama's Vow, Combat Brigades Will Stay in Iraq," Inter Press Service, July 16, 2009, http://ipsnews.net/news.asp ?idnews=46264.

34. Michael Schwartz, "Colonialism in the 21st Century," *Socialist Worker*, July 13, 2009, http://socialistworker.org/2009/07/13/colonialism-in-the-21st-century.

35. Anthony Arnove, "Moved On from the Struggle," SocialistWorker.org, Issue 692, March 13, 2009, http://socialistworker.org/2009/03/13/moved-on-from-the-struggle.

specter of vietnam

1. Zainab Salbi, quoted in Jodie Evans, "Iraq: What We Leave as We Withdraw," CommonDreams.org, June 30, 2009, http://www.commondreams.org/views/2009/06/30/iraq-what-we-leave-we-withdraw.

2. Layla Anwar, *An Arab Woman Blues: Reflections in a Sealed Bottle*, May 6, 2011, http://arabwomanblues.blogspot.com/.

3. Marvin Kalb, "The Other War Haunting Obama," *New York Times*, October 8, 2011.

4. In *Mother Jones*, December 2007, 38–51; *Newsweek*, April 23, 2007, 36–39.

5. Michael Duffy, "How to Walk Away," *Time*, July 30, 2007, 24–31.

6. Warren, June 23, 2005, comment on Helena Cobban, "US/Iraq: Dimensions of the Pullback to Come," *Just World News*, June 22, 2005, http://justworldnews.org/archives/001307.html.

7. Toni Morrison, "Cette Guerre a une odeur d'argent," interview in *Le Nouvel Observateur*, November 15–21, 2001, 140. My translation.

8. Michael Hastings, "The Runaway General," *Rolling Stone*, 1108/1109, July 8–22, 2010. The first quote is from Major General Bill Mayville.

9. Chris Hedges, "It's Obama's War, Now," TruthDig.com, March 2, 2009; CommonDreams.org, March 15, 2009.

10. Alexandra Grey, quoted in *Time*, August 6, 2012, 6.

the matter of war

1. Released online in Jonny Lieberman, "Lessons of Darkness," *Ruthless Reviews*, March 15, 2006, http://www.ruthlessreviews.com/reviews.cfm/id/885/page/lessons_of_darkness.html.

2. Gore Vidal, *Perpetual War for Perpetual Peace: How We Got to Be So Hated* (New York: Thunder Mouth's Press/Nation Books, 2002), 18.

3. *Economist*, June 30, 2007, 32.

4. Robert Fisk, "The Only Lesson We Ever Learn Is that We Never Learn," *Independent* (U.K.), March 19, 2008.

5. Christopher Doyle, "New Oil Law Means Victory in Iraq for Bush," Truthout, January 8, 2007.

6. Michael Duffy, "How to Walk Away," *Time*, July 30, 2007, 31. Emphasis added.

7. Nancy Gibbs, Briefing, *Time*, May 7, 2007, 19.

8. Roger Cohen, "Iraq's Biggest Failing: There Is No Iraq," *New York Times*, December 10, 2006.

9. Ibid.

10. Michael Schwartz, "Myth and Reality of Iraq's 'Fragile Peace,'" SocialistWorker.org, October 9, 2008, http://socialistworker.org/2008/10/09/myth-and-reality-iraqs-fragile.

11. David Stout, *New York Times*, November 10, 2006.

12. Anna Mulrine, "Taking Stock of Iraq," *U.S. News and World Report*, December 24, 2007.

13. Abigail Hauslohner, "When Will They Be Ready?" *Time*, May 12, 2008, 38–39.

14. Timothy R. Reese, quoted in Michael R. Gordon, "U.S. Adviser's Blunt Memo on Iraq: Time 'to Go Home,'" *New York Times*, July 31, 2009.

15. Compiled by Robert Dreyfus and Dave Gilson, "Sunni, Shiite? . . . Anyone? Anyone?" *Mother Jones*, March–April 2007, 64. See also, Christopher Dickey and John Barry, "The Perils of Pulling Out," *Newsweek*, April 23, 2007, 38.

16. *Time*, July 30, 2007, 28–29.

17. Peter Beinart, "Cut Your Losses, Save Your Legacy," *Time*, February 12, 2007, 6.

18. Quoted in Robert Parry and Norman Solomon, "Behind Colin Powell's Legend: Part Four," consortiumnews.com, December 26, 2000, http://www.consortiumnews.com/2000/122600b.html.

19. Stephen Lee Myers, "Bush Defends Iraq War in Speech," *New York Times*, March 20, 2008.

20. Abraham Sadegh, quoted in *Time*, December 22, 2008, 8.

21. Gregory S. McCoy, *Time*, December 22, 2008, 10.

22. "The unique merit of colonialism lies in the fact that it has to show itself to be intransigent in order to last, and by its very intransigence, it prepares its death." Jean-Paul Sartre, *Situations V* (Paris: Editions Gallimard, 1964), 47 (my translation).

23. Stephen Biddle, "Victory Misunderstood: What the Gulf War Tells Us about the Future of Conflict," *International Security* 21, no. 2 (Fall 1996).

24. Robert Byrd, "Reckless Administration May Reap Disastrous Consequences," commondreams.org, February 12, 2003, http://www.commondreams.org/views/2003/02/12/reckless-administration-may-reap-disastrous-consequences.

between victor and victor

1. Sun Tzu, *The Art of War*, trans. Thomas Cleary (Boston: Shambala Pocket Classics, 1991), 27.

2. Ibid., 17, 11. Emphasis added.

3. Sun Tzu, *The Art of War*, trans. Yuan Shibing (Hertfordshire, UK: Wordsworth Editions, 1993), 106.

4. Adrian Wooldridge, "After Bush: A Special Report on America and the World," *Economist*, March 29, 2008, 10.

5. Tom Engelhardt, *The End of Victory Culture: Cold War America and the Disillusioning of a Generation* (New York: Basic Books, 1995), 298.

she, the wayfarer

1. Samuel Beckett, *Worstward Ho* (New York: Grove Press, 1983), 7, 21. Emphasis added.

2. As quoted in Steven T. Jones, "Resistance Is Futile—Or Is It?" *San Francisco Bay Guardian*, March 19–25, 2008, 14–19.

thriving on a D-stroll

1. For a more detailed account of the event, see George Black and Robin Munro, *Black Hands of Beijing: Lives of Defiance in China's Democracy Movement* (New York: John Wiley & Sons, 1993), 234–46.

2. See the eyewitness accounts given in "The Counterrevolutionary" and "The Tiananmen Father" in Liao Yiwu, *The Corpse Walker: Real-Life Stories, China from the Bottom Up*, trans. Wen Huang (New York: Anchor Books, 2009).

3. Nicholas D. Kristof, "A Reassessment of How Many Died in the Military Crackdown in Beijing," *New York Times*, June 21, 1989.

4. Murong Xuecun, "I, Too, Will Stand Up for Tiananmen," (trans. from the Chinese), *New York Times*, May 23, 2014.

5. Didi Kirsten Tatlow, "Tragedy of Tiananmen Still Unfolds," *New York Times*, June 13, 2012.

6. "A Mother's Hope Endures 15 Years of Disappointment," *Asian News*, June 3, 2004.

7. Interviewed by CNN Beijing Bureau Chief Rebecca MacKinnon, "Ding Zilin: An Advocate for the Dead," June 1999, http://www.cnn.com/WORLD/asiapcf/9906/02/tiananmen/MacKinnon/ding.zilin.html.

8. The Dalai Lama, "Le Besoin de compassion dans la société: le cas du Tibet," in *Paix des âmes, paix des coeurs*, ed. Jeffrey Hopkins (Paris: Presses du Châtelet, 2001), 233. My translation.

9. According to Jim Hightower, "Go Granny, Go," *Utne Reader*, August 2000, 80.

10. Italo Calvino, *Invisible Cities*, trans. W. Weaver (New York: Harcourt Brace Jovanovich, 1974), 5.

the mole's empire

1. "McChrystal in the Bull Ring," *Economist*, September 5, 2009, 45.

2. "From Insurgency to Insurrection," *Economist*, August 22, 2009, 21.

3. Aryn Baker and Kajaki Olya, "A War That's Still Not Won," *Time*, July 7, 2008, 39.

4. Anton La Guardia, "Winning or Losing? A Special Report on al-Qaeda," *Economist*, July 19, 2008, 3–12.

5. Jerome Starkey, "Taleban Betrays Commander to Pakistan over His MI6 Contacts," *Scotsman*, February 12, 2008.

6. Bernard Newman, *Background to Viet-nam* (New York: Roy Publishers, 1965), 107. For a detailed account of the battle, see also Bernard Fall, *Hell in a Very Small Place: The Siege of Dien Bien Phu* (Cambridge, MA: Da Capo, 1985).

7. Bernard Fall, "Dien Bien Phu: A Battle To Remember," in *Vietnam: History, Documents and Opinions on A Major World Crisis* (New York: Fawcett, 1965), 114.

feeling the way out

1. According to David Halberstam, "Letter to My Daughter," in *Vietnam Voices: Perspectives on the War Years, 1941–1975*, ed. John Clark Pratt (New York: Viking Penguin, 1984), 663.

2. Ibid., 664.

3. Ibid., 665.

the world is watching

1. Jacques Derrida, *Memoirs of the Blind: The Self-Portrait and Other Ruins*, trans. Pascale-Anne Brault and Michael Naas (Chicago: University of Chicago Press, 1993), 126. Emphasis added.

2. Ibid., 127. Emphasis added.

3. "Tibet" is used here mostly to refer to the three original provinces of U-Tsang, Kham, and Amdo (sometimes called Greater Tibet), whereas the Chinese authorities mean the Tibet Autonomous Region (TAR), which includes only one province, U-Tsang. The TAR was formally inaugurated in 1965.

4. Dalai-Lama, *Cent éléphants sur un brin d'herbe*, trans. Lise Medini (Paris: Seuil, 1990), 80. My own retranslation into English.

5. "March 10th Statement of H. H. the Dalai Lama," March 9, 2009, http://www.dalailama.com/page.8.htm.

6. "Symbol of Tibetan Resistance Addresses Council," interview with Takna Jigme Sangpo by Pamela Taylor, *Human Rights Tribune*, June 5, 2008, http://www.humanrights-geneva.info/Symbol-of-Tibetan-resistance,3173.

7. Ibid.

8. Roland Barthes, *A Lover's Discourse: Fragments*, trans. R. Howard (New York: Hill and Wang, 1978), 180.

9. Quoted in Jim Yardley, "Chinese Nationalism Fuels Tibet Crackdown," *New York Times*, March 31, 2008. Liu Xiaobo was also one of the first signers of a pro-democracy manifesto, Charter 08 (December 10, 2008), that calls for fundamental political change in China and has attracted more than ten thousand signatures from Chinese supporters.

10. Claude Arpi, *The Fate of Tibet: When Big Insects Eat Small Insects* (New Delhi: Har Anand, 1999).

11. See, for example, Senthil Ram, "The Tibetan Nonviolent Resistance: Empowerment in an Extraordinary Situation," War Resisters' International, January 1, 2001, http://www.wri-irg.org/nonviolence/nvse22-en.htm.

12. Information given from Dharamsala by Litia Perta, March 15, 2008.

13. "Chinese Immigrant Influx in Tibet Is a Serious Threat: British MP," reported by the Office of Tibet, London, March 10, 2008, http://www.tibet.com/NewsRoom/londontibetday1.htm.

the new rebels

1. Li Datong, "Tiananmen: The Legacy of 1989," Open Democracy, June 4, 2009, http://www.opendemocracy.net/article/tiananmen-the-legacy-of-1989.

2. Kathrin Hille, "China Censors Microblogs Websites," *Financial Times*,

April 1, 2012, http://www.ft.com/intl/cms/s/0/cc7a802c-7b21-11e1-af45-00144feab49a.html#axzz22ubGbAjm.

3. Information given by Yang Jianli, President of Initiatives for China, in "China's New Rebels," *New York Times*, June 2, 2009, and by David Whitehouse, "The Changing Shape of Struggle in China," SocialistWorker.org, July 9, 2009.

4. Among many others, see translated documents on the sites of Human Rights in China and Open Democracy: http://www.hrichina.org/public/contents/press?revision_id=89851&item_id=85717 and http://www.opendemocracy.net/article/chinas-charter-08.

5. Among many others, see the following site: http://www.englishpen.org/usr/translation_of_petition_by_chinese_writers_on_tibet_2.pdf.

6. David Bandurski, "Open Letter from Party Elders Calls for Free Speech," *China Media Project*, October 13, 2010.

7. Barbara Demick, "Protests in China over Local Grievances Surge, and Get a Hearing," *Los Angeles Times*, October 8, 2011.

8. According to Andrew Jacobs, *New York Times*, March 9, 2009.

9. Among others, see "Demanding Justice," *Economist*, September 1, 2012; Associate Press in Beijing, "Chinese Mother Released after Protesting against Rapists' Sentences," *Guardian*, August 10, 2012, http://www.guardian.co.uk/world/2012/aug/10/chinese-mother-released-protesting-rapists; "Mother of Underage Rape Victim Released from Chinese Labor Camp," *Xinhua*, August 10, 2012, http://news.xinhuanet.com/english/china/2012-08/10/c_131775435.htm; Dan Levin, "Woman Sent to Labor Camp in China's Latest Abuse Outrage," *Daily Beast*, August 9, 2012, http://www.thedailybeast.com/articles/2012/08/09/woman-sent-to-labor-camp-in-china-s-latest-abuse-outrage.html.

10. Barbara Demick, "China Lawyer Who Fought Unfair Arrest Is Arrested," *Los Angeles Times*, August 7, 2009.

11. Mengyu Dong, "Xu Zhiyong: New Citizen's Movement," *China Digital Times*, July 13, 2012, http://chinadigitaltimes.net/2012/07/xu-zhiyong-new-citizens-movement/.

displaced, dispossessed, disappeared

1. Alastair Sloan, "Chinese Tourists are Inadvertently Reporting on the Tibetan Struggle," *Index on Censorship*, March 25, 2014, http://www.indexoncensorship.org/2014/03/tibet-china-tourist/.

2. "Has Life Here Always Been Like This?" International Campaign for Tibet, 2013, http://www.savetibet.org/newsroom/has-life-here-always-been-like-this/.

3. See articles posted on Lhakar: The Tibetan People's Grassroots Revolution, http://lhakar.org/. Fiona McConnell and Tenzin Tsering, "Lhakar: Proud to Be Tibetan," *Open Democracy*, January 7, 2013, http://www.opendemocracy.net/fiona-mcconnell-tenzin-tsering/lhakar-proud-to-be-tibetan.

4. "Tibet's Own Satyagraha," Lhakar.org, September 23, 2010, http://lhakar.org/satyagraha/#comments.

5. Sakyi Tseta, "Longing for the Deities," trans. Tenzin Dickyi and Dhondup Tashi Rekjong, http://tibetwebdigest.com/longing-for-the-deities/#more-1089.

6. While I am putting to use here the distinction Michel de Certeau made between tactic and strategy, I am also bringing the two concepts together in a nonbinary relation so as to address more specifically the complex nature of Tibetan activism. For de Certeau, see *The Practice of Everyday Life*, trans. Steven Rendall (Berkeley: University of California Press), 1984, 34–39.

7. Tenzin Dorjee, "Why Lhakar Matters: The Elements of Tibetan Freedom," *Tibetan Political Review*, January 10, 2013, http://www.tibetanpoliticalreview.org/articles/whylhakarmatterstheelementsoftibetanfreedom.

8. Quoted in Jonathan Kaiman, "Tibet Self-Immolations: Tsering Woeser and Ai Weiwei Collaborate on Book," *Guardian*, October 17, 2013, http://www.theguardian.com/world/2013/oct/17/tibet-self-immolation-book-woeser-ai-weiwei.

9. Tsering Kyi, in Gar Samdup Tsering, "Life Long Lamp" music video, trans. High Peaks Pure Earth, April 9, 2014, http://highpeakspureearth.com/2014/music-video-life-long-lamp-by-gar-samdup-tsering/.

interval of resistance

1. John N., "Another Empty Chair," March 13, 2013, *Tibetan Political Review*, March 26, 2013, http://www.tibetanpoliticalreview.com/articles/anotheremptychair.

2. Special thanks to Tenzin Mingyur Paldron who passed on this anecdote and shared much information related to the Tibetan struggle.

3. As related by Danny Schechter in *Censored 1998: The News that Didn't Make the News*, ed. Peter Phillips and Project Censored (New York: Seven Stories Press, 1998).

4. See, among many other articles written on the subject, Robert Thurman, "The Dalai Lama and the Cult of Dolgyal Shugden," *Huffington Post*, July 5, 2014, http://www.huffingtonpost.com/robert-thurman/the-dalai-lama-cult-of-dolgyal-shugden_b_4903441.html.

5. "Resolution on Certain Questions in the History of Our Party Since the Founding of the People's Republic of China," adopted by the Sixth Plenary Session of the Eleventh Central Committee of the Communist Party of China on June 27, 1981, *Resolution on CPC History (1949–81)*(Beijing: Foreign Languages Press, 1981), 32.

6. Related in David Patt, *A Strange Liberation: Tibetan Lives in Chinese Hands* (Ithaca, NY: Snow Lion, 1992). Special thanks to Tenzin Mingyur Paldron who gave me the book to read.

7. Stephan Talty, "The Dalai Lama: The Making of a Spiritual Hero," *Shambhala Sun*, May 2011, http://www.shambhalasun.com/index.php?option=com_content&task=view&id=3694&Itemid=243. Emphasis added.

8. Quoted in Tsering Woeser, "Decline of the Potala Palace," *Tibet Writes*, December 26, 2007, http://www.tibetwrites.org/?Decline-of-the-Potala-Palace. Emphasis added.

9. "Desmond Tutu Starts Liu Xiaobo Change.org Petition Calling for Release of Nobel Peace Prize Winner," *Huffington Post*, December 10, 2012, http://www.huffingtonpost.com/2012/12/10/desmond-tutu-changeorg-petition-for-liu-xiaobo_n_2271779.html.

10. In Alec Ash, "Out of Tibet," *Danwei*, November 12, 2012, http://www.danwei.com/out-of-tibet/.

the screensaver's light

1. Quoted in Lev Grossman, "Maya Angelou: Legendary Voice," *Time*, June 9, 2014.

2. Quoted in "Why Tibet Is Burning?" Gangchen Kyishong, Dharamshala, Tibetan Policy Institute, 2013, http://solidaritywithtibet.org/wpcontent/uploads/2012/11/Why_Tibet_is_Burning_Whitepaper-Final-PDF.pdf.

3. Ibid.

4. Such a manipulation was made clear in an interview with the woman concerned, Faida Hamdy, in the film *Controlling and Punishment*, codirected Ayten Multu Saray and Ridha Tlili, 2014.

5. Larbi Sadiki, "The Bouazizi 'Big Bang,'" *Al Jazeera*, December 29, 2011, http://www.aljazeera.com/indepth/opinion/2011/12/2011121713215670692.html.

6. Quoted in Seth Jacobs, *Cold War Mandarin: Ngo Dinh Diem and the Origins of America's War in Vietnam, 1950–1963* (Lanham, MD: Rowman and Littlefield, 2006), 149.

7. First published in *Aperture*, issue 112, Storyteller, 1988.

8. See my analysis of the tale of "The Love Crystal" in Trinh T. Minh-ha, *Elsewhere within Here: Immigration, Refugeeism and the Boundary Event* (New York: Routledge, 2011), 13–24. For more details around the Indestructible Heart, see also Vien Minh, "Why the Heart of Thich Quang Duc Did Not Burn in Self-immolation and Cremation?" Buddhist Translation Group, June 10, 2012, http://www.nhomphiendich.org/index.php.

9. "Storm in the Grasslands: Self-immolations in Tibet and Chinese Policy," International Campaign for Tibet, December 10, 2012, https://www.savetibet.org/storm-in-the-grasslands-self-immolations-in-tibet-and-chinese-policy/.

10. Ibid.

11. Ibid.

12. Quoted in Lindsey Hilsum, "Why China Is Frightened of Horses," *New Statesman*, August 7, 2008, http://www.newstatesman.com/asia/2008/08/dalai-lama-china-chinese.

13. "Tibetan Writer Sentenced to 5 Years in Prison for Writing Book on Self-Immolation" and "My Words Are Not Tainted by Lies and Deception: Gartse Jigme," Tibetan Center for Human Rights and Democracy, May 21 and 30, 2013, http://www.tchrd.org/2013/05/tibetan-writer-sentenced-to-5-yrs-in-prison-for-writing-book-on-self-immolation/, http://www.tchrd.org/2013/05/my-words-are-not-tainted-by-lies-and-deception-gartse-jigme-2/. Emphasis added.

14. Stephan Talty, "The Dalai Lama: The Making of a Spiritual Hero."

15. Robert Barnett in "Happy Birthday, Dalai Lama," *On the Media*, July 9, 2010, http://www.onthemedia.org/story/132840-happy-birthday-dalai-lama/transcript/. Emphasis added.

16. Brooke Gladstone in "Happy Birthday, Dalai Lama."

17. Pico Iyer, "Heart of the Dalai Lama," *Shambhala Sun*, May 2010, http://www.shambhalasun.com/index.php?option=content&task=view&id=3523&Itemid=0&limit=1&limitstart=0.

18. Iyer, "Heart of the Dalai Lama."

19. The Dalai Lama, *The Path to Tranquility*, ed. Renuka Singh (New York: Viking Arkana, 1988), 209, 358.

20. Xu Zhiyong, "Tibet Is Burning," trans. Yasue Cao, *New York Times*, December 12, 2012, http://www.nytimes.com/2012/12/13/opinion/tibet-is-burning.html?_r=3&.

21. The Dalai Lama, *Freedom in Exile: The Autobiography of the Dalai Lama* (New York: Harper Perennial, 2008), 184.

22. Quoted in Iyer, "Heart of the Dalai Lama."

23. Jack Kornfield, *A Path with Heart* (New York: Bantam Book, 1993), 295. Emphasis added.

24. John Tarrant, *Bring Me the Rhinoceros: And Other Zen Koans to Bring You Joy* (New York: Harmony Books, 2004), 136. Emphasis added.

25. Maurice Blanchot, *The Gaze of Orpheus*, trans. Lydia Davis (Barrytown, NY: Station Hill Press, 1981), 107. Emphasis added.

26. Talty, "The Dalai Lama."

27. Yolanda O'Bannon, "His Holiness the Dalai Lama Interview: On His Own Reincarnation," November 1, 2011, http://www.yowangdu.com/tibetan-buddhism/dalai-lama-interview.html#sthash.4d02R3ue.dpuf.

28. For a full version, see the Dalai Lama, *A Flash of Lightning in the Dark of Night: A Guide to the Bodhisattva's Way of Life* (Boston: Shambala Dragon Editions, 1994), 32.

Index